A PLACE
AT THE
TABLE

JUSTICE FOR THE POOR
IN A LAND OF PLENTY

JUDITH ANN BRADY, O.P.

A Place
at the
Table

JUSTICE FOR THE POOR
IN A LAND OF PLENTY

TWENTY
THIRD 23rd
PUBLICATIONS

In memory of
my parents,
George A. Willemse and
Margaret Willemse Brady

Some material in this book originally appeared in a different form in the journal of *Religious Education* (Summer 2006) 347-367 as "Justice for the Poor in the Land of Plenty: A Place at the Table" and is used here with permission.

Cover photo: ©Istockphoto.com/Michael Allebach

Twenty-Third Publications
A Division of Bayard
One Montauk Avenue, Suite 200
New London, CT 06320
(860) 437-3012 or (800) 321-0411
www.23rdpublications.com

ISBN 978-1-58595-609-8
Library of Congress Catalog Card Number: 2008921774
Printed in the U.S.A.

CONTENTS

Acknowledgments

Writing a book is like giving birth. Inspiration followed by gestation, the struggle to give life to ideas that swarm, all of which takes time and a huge effort to refine and create something worthwhile. An image sears itself into one's imagination, but how to capture it in words and communicate its beauty? Throughout this process my conviction that social justice is the right of all people, especially those who are poor, urged me to persevere. It is my humble hope that this book will inspire and assist others who will enlarge the circle of care and show how to achieve solidarity in our journey toward a more just and peaceful society.

Many people have inspired me in my quest for justice. First and foremost is my congregation, the Dominican Sisters of Sparkill, who have been my companions and provided loving support. The sisters with whom I worked, prayed, and lived were models of charity and justice. Together we have sought to make justice a habit of heart and mind.

I am grateful for the work of the Rev. Dr. Letty M. Russell whose example of liberating Christian education in East Harlem touched my heart, and whose writings gave me renewed enthusiasm for pursuing justice. It was an honor to meet her and to audit her class at Yale Divinity School in the spring of 2006. Letty Russell widened the circle of concern for those on the margins of society as she reached out to welcome and share wisdom with women from third world countries in their pursuit of higher learning.

David K. Shipler is both an excellent writer and a man of great empathy. His book, *The Working Poor*, captures the spirit of hardworking people as well as the realities of the social, economic, and political situations that limit their lives. His words gave me hope when I felt overwhelmed by the enormity of poverty in the United States and how deeply poverty limits people's lives.

I wish to thank those who graciously read and commented on the chapters of this book. Sr. Barbara Paul, O.P., former president of our congregation, offered insights from her many years as an educator and as a missionary among the poor of Peru. Rev. Mark Hallinan, S.J., Assistant for Social Ministries for the New York Province of the Society of Jesus, was an able advisor and encouraged my efforts. Sr. Barbara Lenniger, O.P., Executive Director of Thorpe Family Residence and Park Avenue Thorpe in the Bronx, has been an inspiration in terms of her work with formerly homeless women and children and for her efforts to enable the poor to have decent housing. Martin Fergus, recently retired Associate Professor of Political Science at Fordham University, devoted many years to guiding students to understand the reality of poverty, its causes, and the means for seeking social justice. Professor Fergus's comments added immensely to my understanding of poverty and urged me to write so students would grasp both the complexity of the issues and the humanity of those who are poor. James Nickolof, Associate Professor of Religious Studies at the College of the Holy Cross, refined and refreshed my understanding of liberation theologies, thanks to his scholarship and especially his experience in Peru working with Gustavo Gutiérrez. My friends and colleagues, Ruth Boser, Valerie Torres, and Tom Moroney provided insight from educational and catechetical perspectives, as well as examples of dedicated service to the poor. Finally, I am most grateful to Harold Horell, Assistant Professor of Religious Education at Fordham University, who consistently encouraged my quest for justice. His buoyant spirit and absolute dedication to truth inspired me to think globally. I am deeply grateful to Dr. Horell for challenging me to write with depth and clarity. Truly, there could be no better guide.

I am grateful to Twenty-Third Publications for the opportunity to publish this book. Special thanks to Dan Connors, Editorial Director, who guided this venture and valued its success and to John van Bemmel who encouraged my writing in the initial and final stages of the book's development. With their support, the message of justice for all will have a larger audience.

Thanks also to those who assisted my research at the Walsh Library on the Rose Hill campus of Fordham University, especially Helena Cuniffe and Bob Hinkel; and José De Leon and Rick Raguso who provided expert technological assistance.

It is my ardent hope that many will share my enthusiasm and commitment to making a place at the table of life for all people, especially the poor and oppressed.

CHAPTER 1

Justice for All

From childhood on, Americans recite the Pledge of Allegiance, which ends with the words, "liberty and justice for all." These words resonate as an ideal and a fervent dream of how life should be for everyone. People in the United States of America believe that justice is their birthright. United States citizens have a deep, abiding belief in justice. They are concerned with justice, most often envisioned as a basic sense of fairness that is expected in the workplace and at home, in the organizations they have joined, as well as in society at large. They also expect conformity to law and a reasonable interpretation of law with attention to honesty and impartiality. Justice is not just a fervent expectation, but also a deep-seated hope, even when circumstances short-circuit people's lives. Despite obstacles to achieving it, hope for justice is the basis for people's outlook on life and shapes their view for the future.

An understanding of justice of many, if not most, United States citizens includes a sense of social justice, the conviction that in a land of plenty all should have their basic human needs met: food, shelter, safety, health care, and education. Beyond that, they hope that all are provided with opportunities to develop their talents and pursue their life dreams. The reality, however, is that social justice in the United States is often shattered by the realities of poverty.

POVERTY: A JUSTICE ISSUE

In recent times the media has carried stories of celebrities and politicians who have focused attention on poverty. On February 3, 2005, former South African President Nelson Mandela, at the invitation of The Campaign to Make Poverty History, came out of retirement and traveled to Britain to speak to over 20,000 people gathered in London's Trafalgar Square. His speech compared poverty to slavery, because poverty is a prison that has entrapped millions of people. Poverty, Mandela stated, "is not natural. It is man-made and it can be overcome and eradicated by the actions of human beings." Overcoming poverty is more than an act of charity. Rather, it is "an act of justice," for it protects "a fundamental human right, the right to dignity and a decent life." Mandela directed his message to all people, especially world leaders who would meet that summer for the G-8 summit, an economic conference of the industrialized nations that included Britain, Canada, France, Germany, Italy, Japan, Russia, and the United States; he spoke as well to the United Nations delegates who would meet in September to continue work on the Millennium Goals that were first proposed in 2000. In effect, Mandela addressed not only his immediate audience but also everyone of good will so they would be motivated to work to overcome poverty. In his words, "Sometimes it falls upon a generation to be great. You can be that great generation. Let your greatness blossom."[1]

Bono, lead singer of the Irish rock group U2, had direct experience of how famine affects children. In 1986 he and his wife, Alison Stewart, traveled to Wello, Ethiopia, where they worked in an orphanage for six weeks. It was the height of a severe famine that ravaged the country and claimed the lives of young and old alike. Bono's involvement as a spokesman extended to his founding a Washington-based humanitarian organization, DATA, dedicated to addressing Debt, AIDS, Trade, and Africa. His vision is to alleviate the suffering and provide help and relief for the millions of people in Africa with programs similar to the Marshall Plan that addressed the problems of post-World War II Europe. DATA advocates for a combination of foreign aid, debt cancellation, and trade incentives.

When Bono addressed the National Prayer Breakfast in Washington, D.C., on February 2, 2006, he spoke about his involvement in Jubilee 2000, a movement that lobbied leaders of wealthy nations to forgive the debt of over fifty of the world's poorest nations. The idea was simple, as proposed in Leviticus 25:35–38, that those who had loaned money would forgive, or cancel, debts so poor nations once freed of debts owed to foreign nations would have funds to dedicate to health care and education. He went on to speak of Jesus' first public proclamation from the book of Isaiah: "The Spirit of the Lord is upon me, because he has anointed me to bring good news to the poor…to proclaim the year of the Lord's favor" (Lk 4:18–19). Bono is convinced that God is with the vulnerable and poor. In his words, "God is in the slums, in the cardboard boxes where the poor play house…God is in the cries heard under the rubble of war…God is in the debris of wasted opportunity and lives, and God is with us if we are with them." Bono pointed out that God is calling us to do what God is doing: to be with the poor. He urged the United States of America to increase foreign aid by an extra one percent in an effort "to change the world, to transform millions of lives." He made the connection with the Millennium Development Goals: "clean water for all; school for every child; medicine for the afflicted, an end to extreme and senseless poverty," goals that he called "the Beatitudes for a Globalized World."[2]

While world poverty attracts the attention of and raises the compassion of many people, poverty in the United States is a far less popular topic. One notable exception is former North Carolina Senator John Edwards's address to the Democratic National Convention in July 2004. He spoke of poverty as a threat to the lives of many Americans. In his words, there are "two different Americas: one for those people who have lived the American Dream and don't have to worry, and another for most Americans, everyone else, who struggle to make ends meet every single day."[3] His sense of the basic unfairness of poverty led to his serving as the first director of the newly formed Center on Poverty, Work and Opportunity at the University of North Carolina. He has traveled throughout the United States, meeting with people living on the margins and listening to their stories. In addition, he has talked with young people at colleges and universities to raise their awareness of poverty. In December 2006, Edwards announced his candidacy for the presidency of the United States in the Ninth Ward of New Orleans, an area known for the poverty of its residents that captured national and world attention after the devastation of Hurricane Katrina in September 2005. As one of his major campaign issues, John Edwards was committed to speaking about poverty. In an interview with Bob Herbert of *The New York Times*, Edwards explained why Americans need to be concerned about the issue of poverty: First, poverty confronts us as a moral issue that we cannot ignore, and we must devote time and energy to working to solve the many problems that are related to poverty if we are to be true to our national ideals; second, poverty is a threat to the middle class, many of whom are struggling and on the brink of falling into poverty, all of which weakens the American economy; third, poverty is a complex problem that demands a multi-pronged approach, including efforts to address low wages, to expand the earned income tax credit (EITC), to provide the opportunity for workers to organize, and to address the lack of access to good education, affordable housing, and health care.[4] In a book he co-edited, *Ending Poverty in America* (2007), Edwards's concern for the millions of people living in poverty is evident when he wrote that, "The real story is not the number but the people behind the number. The men, women, and children—one in eight of us—do not have enough money for the food, shelter, and clothing they need. One in eight. That is not a problem. That is a challenge. That is a plague. And it is our national shame."[5]

Poverty: A Threat to Society. Poverty is a topic that most people in the United States avoid discussing. Poverty, like a cloud blocking the sun, can effectively prevent the realization of the American Dream. Rather than become depressed or disheartened, most people choose not to think about or discuss poverty. But poverty is a reality not just for those who are at or below the official poverty threshold. It is a specter that haunts many persons who optimistically self-identify as middle class. As hard as some people work and as much as they want to prosper, many people are on the verge of slipping into poverty. Most Americans avoid discussing poverty, for to be poor carries a stigma and many consider being in poverty a disgrace.

According to Elizabeth Warren,[6] in the 1970s most families were able to live on one salary; in recent years families have to rely on two salaries. The standard of living in the United States has improved as is evident from the increase in home ownership, as well as access to a greater number of appliances, electronic gadgets, and other conveniences. But families now need two salaries to pay the higher mortgage rates, the cost of child care and transportation, which is a necessary consequence of both parents working. They also have to purchase medical insurance, pay for higher education, and pay higher taxes on their combined earnings. The advantages that American workers had come to expect—health care benefits and a company pension—are disappearing at a rapid rate as businesses and corporations are dedicated to providing ever higher profits for their owners and stockholders. The middle class is at risk and often faces economic crises: mortgages whose high interest rates are such a burden that some lose their home when they are unable to make timely payments; escalating credit card debt; and the high price of health care.

Credit card debt is insidious, for when one is late in making or misses a payment, there is the added burden of late penalties and higher finance charges. Soon this information is shared with other companies that in turn increase the interest rates on other credit cards. Even college students can get caught in the web of credit card debt when credit card companies send out credit card offers that appear irresistibly attractive. Yet many card holders do not realize that the credit card contracts often contain provisions that may drag them deeper into debt. Adults suffer the ill effects of credit card debt when they charge extraordinary expenses, such as when a family member requires expensive medical treatments, or when they need to cover ordinary living expenses when income is limited by job loss. When an adult is sick and unable to work, the family misses the wage earner's income, and extraordinary expenses not covered by insurance are often charged on a credit card. Families in the past often had savings to bridge the gap, but today many Americans are living from paycheck to paycheck. One extraordinary expense—such as when a parent cannot work, when a child becomes seriously ill, or when the family loses its home due to debt, storm damage, or fire—can plunge the family into poverty.

Of particular concern for college students is the crisis in student debts. In recent years as college tuition has risen steadily, the limited funds available from federal loans and the difficulty of completing the required loan forms have caused students to turn to private loans. Unlike federal loans whose interest rates are capped by law, private loans have variable rates that can reach twenty percent, similar to what credit cards charge. Students are often unaware that interest rates are compounding even while they are still in college. In effect, this is a problem affecting millions of students, one that will follow them through life. College students who use private loans are like indentured servants who will have to work for years to pay back the principal and all the interest. Declaring bankruptcy is no relief, because the bankruptcy law passed in 2005 holds students liable for repayment of federal and private college loans.[7] Entering adult life burdened by huge debt narrows the options a college graduate has regarding employment, a desire to volunteer in the United States or overseas, and the choice of a way of life; it may even delay a person's decision to marry and start a family.

Poverty is like a wolf lurking at the door, threatening to devour those within. Politicians speak of safety nets, but these are almost non-existent. In former times one parent was available to help if a relative got sick or injured; today a parent has to take unpaid leave or be unemployed for the time he or she is needed, and may even lose his or her job as a result of attending to family duties. Since families need two incomes to pay their monthly bills, having only one income is truly a hardship. Those who are single parents with the responsibility of raising children face this challenge all the time. A single parent, most often the mother, is severely handicapped by having only one income, lacking other financial resources, and earning a lower salary than her male counterparts. The choice is between working or caring for a feeble parent, a sick or disabled child, or recovering from one's own illness. As bills accumulate, the economic crisis is compounded by the physical, social, and emotional toll brought on by uncertainty and insufficient income. Families are also often separated from extended family support systems. Siblings, aunts, uncles, and other relatives are facing the same economic challenges, so offering help is not possible in many situations.

Making Poverty Count. Poverty in the United States is a pervasive problem. Statistics from the U.S. Census Bureau reveal that 37 million Americans, about 12.6 percent of the population, were living at or below the official poverty threshold in 2005. For a family of four, composed of two adults and two children under the age of 18, the poverty threshold was $19,806. It is obvious that families with such limited income could not afford to pay for housing, food, clothing, transportation, and utilities. Studies have shown that families need at least twice the dollar value of the official poverty threshold to cover family expenses. On a practical level, there are many more people living in poverty who are not counted in the official government statistics because the measure of poverty is set at such a low level. Despite these limitations, it is worth noting that the number of people living at the poverty threshold increased by 5.3 million from 2000 to 2004. In addition, poverty rates are higher in the inner city and in the rural areas of the United States. Most of those who are poor are working, but as is well known, those who work full time at a minimum wage job as their sole means of support are living in poverty.

Poverty is a greater burden for certain groups of people. Single women with children as well as children living with only one parent or guardian have a higher incidence of poverty. Racial minorities, namely, blacks and Hispanics, and recent arrivals—immigrants who left their home country to find work to support their families—are also more likely to be living in poverty.[8]

Poverty threatens millions of lives. Individuals and families need help beyond minimum wage jobs and government assistance. It might appear hopeless, but there are groups that are working to reduce poverty. One such group is Catholic Charities USA, which has dedicated itself to halving poverty by the year 2020. As an organization that responds daily to the many needs of the poor, Catholic Charities also works to counter the many misconceptions about poverty. First and foremost, they state the fact that poverty affects many Americans over their lifetime. "Almost half of all Americans will have experienced poverty for a year or more at some point in their lives by the time they reach age 60." Of those who have experienced poverty, about half will have lived in poverty for a total of four or more years. The second point stressed by Catholic Charities is that most poor people are workers. The majority of poor families, about two out of three families, have one or more workers. Since the federal minimum wage is low and not adjusted for inflation, a person can work full time for the entire year and not be able to earn enough money to support himself or herself, let alone children and other dependents. Third, to correct misperceptions, Catholic Charities points out that most poor Americans are white. Almost half of all Americans, about 47 percent, who are living in poverty are white.[9]

It is important to note that the United States is one of the richest and most powerful nations in the world. For our country to have such a high number of people living in poverty is a disgrace. While it is easy to blame the persons who are poor for their misfortune, it is more truthful to say that people are poor due to a combination of personal, social, and economic causes. Individuals can only work so many hours, and juggle so many debts. Society plays a major role in terms of its institutions and the policies that have allowed corporations and businesses to have so much power and influence that they often ride roughshod over the rights of workers. When profits go to highly paid CEOs and stockholders and not to those working to ensure the success of the company, especially at a time when worker productivity has soared, there is reason to question priorities. Workers are not the only ones who suffer; so too do their families. While some individuals profit, this comes at the expense of women and children who will suffer the ill effects of poverty. Those living in poverty cannot flourish—their health, education, and family life will be seriously affected. Poor mental and physical health, lower educational achievements, and a fast track for more years of living in poverty are the result of not paying workers a just wage for their labor.

The Ecology of Poverty. One can come to understand the difficult situation of American workers by reading David K. Shipler's accounts of the working poor. The working poor are entangled in a complex social network created by conditions of material poverty and it is difficult for them to free themselves from this social and economic whirlpool. In other words, they are part of "an ecological system of relationships among individuals, families and the environment of schools, neighborhoods, jobs and government services" that separates them from the broader society. The dynamics of this ecological system often work against the poor and thwart the efforts they make to escape from poverty. While charity and government programs have been somewhat effective, Shipler is convinced that "the full force of the nation's power can be mobilized only by the federal government. Only then can we alter the ecology of poverty."[10]

JUSTICE FOR THE POOR: A PLACE AT THE TABLE

A guiding metaphor for achieving justice for the poor is that of a place at the table. Is it possible in this land of plenty to make a place at the table for the poor, especially impoverished women and children? The table from a Christian perspective is first and foremost the sacred table, the table of God's love. Moreover, the image of the sacred table is captured splendidly in Andrei Rublev's icon, "The Holy Trinity." Based on the story in Genesis 18 when Abraham offered hospitality to three visitors, this icon is seen in the Orthodox tradition as a manifestation of the Trinity. The icon depicts three divine persons seated around a table. The figures are "equally sized," a sign of their equality and the fact that "no one dominates." Each figure is depicted "in full face," since "face to face eye contact" engages the viewer and encourages him or her to interact and, by means of the encounter, enter into communion.[11] "The Holy Trinity" invites the viewer to enter the peaceful, loving, active presence of God the Creator, God the Redeemer, and God the Comforter. This is a holy place with room for the viewer to listen and share in intimate conversation. This sacred table makes all people feel welcome. Once God's love is experienced, people realize the equality of all persons before God. Persons are then more likely to work in solidarity so that justice for the poor can truly be realized.

The table is also a place for decision making. This image of the table is presented in the United States Conference of Catholic Bishops pastoral letter, *A Place at the Table: A Catholic Recommitment to Overcome Poverty and to Respect the Dignity of All God's Children* (2002). The bishops claim that respect for persons who are created in the image and likeness of God requires us to make a place at the table of social decision making for all members of our community, especially women and children, since they have frequently been absent from the table of social decision making. Justice for the poor requires that all people learn to share power and responsibilities.

Letty M. Russell, theologian and educator, provides a clear understanding of how a place at the table empowers people. In her writings,

Russell refers to the table as an image of partnership, a central theme throughout her writings. God is the model for partnership. The communication of love among the persons of the Trinity allows humanity to marvel at the "Trinitarian image of reciprocity, joint sharing in the work of salvation and the mission of the world." God's activity of "being partner in God's self and being partner with us" is the model for partnership among women and men. Russell defines partnership as "a new focus of relationship in which there is continuing commitment and common struggle in interaction with a wider community context."[12] The paradigm of partnership is envisioned as a *circle of interdependence*. Diversity is valued and participation welcomed. "Authority is exercised *in* community and not *over* community."[13]

Letty Russell employs three images in her effort to work toward a global table. The first is a *round table* as "a sign of the coming unity of humanity." The round table allows each person to be seen and to have equal access to speak and be heard even as it becomes a welcoming center for people's lives and for resolution of their concerns. The round table is a metaphor for achieving the "*already* of welcome, sharing, talk, and partnership" as opposed to the "*not yet* of our divided and dominated world." The second image is the *kitchen table*. People carry out the myriad tasks of daily living around the kitchen table. Around this table people share their lives with family and friends. Like the early followers of Jesus, Christians share the bread of their lives. The kitchen table is the scene for solidarity as people reach out to include the oppressed and recognize them as neighbor and friend. The third image is a *welcome table*, a place where the community welcomes those who are often made to feel that they are not welcome. The welcome table, part of the black church tradition, "symbolizes the communion table and every other gathering at table. At God's welcome table those who have been denied access to the table of the rich white masters are welcomed and may welcome others as a foretaste of the final partnership with God."[14] The welcome table makes clear that women and men of all races, nationalities, and socio-economic status experience God's acceptance and love. In turn, all are called to appreciate the giftedness of each individual and to work together in partnership with God.

The table reminds us of our calling by God to seek justice for the poor. It can recall meals where good food and drink, and lively conversation among family and friends, nourished the mind and heart. It can challenge us to be more inclusive, to make a place for the poor at our table among family and friends. It can relate to the table of fellowship where a community of believers shares the word of God and the Body of Christ and then reaches out to others, especially those living on the underside of life. In its very simplicity it can bring home how all are welcome and how individuals are called to shoulder responsibility for one another and for the world. The table can be a symbol of love between God and humans, as well as a symbol of partnership with God. As God calls each to life and love, so too rich and poor are called to be with and for one another. Gifts of self and wealth shine more brightly in the brilliance of God's love for each of us.

HOW POVERTY BECAME A CONCERN

An interest in justice for the poor is the result of this writer's family background, religious congregation, and ministry commitments. As a white, middle-class, multi-national American woman born and raised as a Roman Catholic in the Bronx, New York, I learned from infancy the importance of family. When our father died at an early age, a maternal aunt volunteered to live with our family and became a second mother to all three children. Our mother worked outside the home at a time when most mothers could stay home and raise their children. A monthly Social Security check for each child was used to provide clothing, shelter, and food. Government assistance helped sustain the family in its time of need.

Years later when I entered the convent, the Dominican Sisters of Sparkill had a home for boys who were separated from their parents by death, divorce, or various social ills. Experience as an assistant group mother and later as a teacher introduced me to the limited options of the poor. An institution with dedicated sisters was no substitute for a child's own parents. In the course of time, the congregation assigned me to various teaching positions. Higher education and opportunities to travel to Spain, Mexico, Guatemala, and El Salvador provided the training to teach Spanish. Learning to speak Spanish was a way to think in another language and to experience other cultures. This opened the door to other people's minds and hearts, and to many more situations in which I saw firsthand the realities of poverty in the world.

Over the years I worked as campus minister, assistant principal, and then principal in three Catholic high schools in the Bronx. As Director of Campus Ministry, I coordinated a Christian Service program. An elective course for seniors, Christian Service was a religion course that offered young men the opportunity to volunteer in hospitals, nursing homes, or educational facilities, such as day-care programs and elementary schools. Direct service was combined with opportunities for reflection. The students were also required to do a study of a specific injustice, using a social analysis process. As an administrator, I interacted with parents as well as their children. Requests for financial aid increased as more parents found it difficult to pay tuition and meet their other expenses. One avenue for obtaining tuition assistance was the Inner-City Scholarship Fund. As part of the process I conducted interviews with parents and guardians. These revealed the strains on family life: illness, death of a parent, disability, dependencies, and limited income. Poverty was in the eyes of the single parent or grandparent, the newly arrived immigrant, the student living virtually alone. Questions arose, the most basic of which was: How do these women and children survive on such limited income in this urban setting?

Since their founding in 1876 the Dominican Sisters of Sparkill have worked with women and children in need. Like other religious congregations, the sisters responded to the Second Vatican Council's call for renewal. We met for many months to discuss governance and lifestyle. We elected delegates who met during a series of chapters, the result of which was the revision of our constitutions. On May 6, 1985, over one hundred years since its founding, the Dominican Sisters of Our Lady of the Rosary celebrated the official approval of their revised constitutions. First approved by the sister delegates at the Chapter of 1976, the goal that was subsequently approved by a majority of all the sisters, was a recommitment to the "proclamation of the kingdom of God through a ministry for justice wherein we focus on enablement of the poor, of the powerless, of the oppressed, and of the spiritually deprived people of our times."[15] In embracing the revised constitutions I recognized that I had already experienced firsthand the primacy of justice for the poor in my ministries with people. I am firmly convinced that only when justice takes root, especially among the poor, will we as a people experience the reign of God in this world.

THE PURPOSE OF THIS STUDY

The primary purpose of this study is to demonstrate that concern for the poor is an issue of social justice, and that concern about justice for the poor needs to be incorporated more fully into contemporary Christian religious education if we are to bridge the gap between Christian ideals of social justice and Christian efforts to link faith and everyday life in meaningful and responsible ways. To achieve this primary purpose the study draws upon economic data and contemporary sociological studies to deepen an awareness of the realities of poverty in the United States of America. It also provides a Christian perspective for understanding the realities of poverty by exploring biblical senses of justice for the poor, reviewing Catholic social teaching to uncover insights regarding poverty and justice, and working with the perspectives of liberation theology to demonstrate how we can move beyond the oppression of poverty to a renewed and enriched sense of justice in society today.

Christians can become more intentional advocates for the poor through education, prayerful discernment, and disciplined action. For instance, education about Catholic social teaching can focus attention on preferential love for the poor and seeking justice for them as constitutive elements of Christian faith. It can demonstrate how Christians can examine the U.S. welfare system and proposed legislation in the light of Catholic social teaching as they strive to discern how they might seek greater social justice for the poor. It can also review how the Catholic Church has had a powerful, yet limited, effect in embodying the message of justice and love for the poor, and how the church's role as an advocate for the poor can be developed more fully through the greater involvement of all Catholics responding willingly and creatively to their neighbor in need. In light of the guiding metaphor, *a place at the table*, the study demonstrates how Christians can intentionally include the poor by inviting them to the table to explore ways of sharing stories, experience, and power.

THE SIGNIFICANCE OF THIS STUDY

This study helps to bridge the gap between the senses of justice found among Christians and United States citizens and their failure to seek social justice for the poor in their midst.

Concern for justice, especially justice for the poor, has always been central to Jewish and Christian faith traditions. The Bible provides a rich interpretive context for helping one to develop a sense of what it means to seek justice for the poor. In the Hebrew Scriptures God enters history as a protagonist for the poor. In the Christian Scriptures Jesus of Nazareth brings a message of hope, reveals a loving, forgiving God, and stands firmly with outcasts and the oppressed. Catholic social teaching enlarges and informs our understanding of how justice should be understood and how it affects people. It draws deeply from the well of Sacred Scripture and relates it to the lives of all people. Once again, the poor appear center stage and are special both to God and people of good will. Moreover, one sees how Catholics strive to embrace the senses of justice found in Christian Scripture and often do acts of charity. For instance, students especially are encouraged to donate food, volunteer locally and in distant places like the Gulf Coast and Mexico, and contribute to charitable causes. What is needed, in addition to charitable acts, is to develop the skills to analyze injustice in society and seek ways to work together as a community to address it and change it to justice.

Christian concern for justice has a special significance and importance in the United States because of our deep, abiding belief in justice. We feel the sting of injustice when immediate needs for food, clothing, and shelter are not met, and when a willing, able person is unable to find meaningful employment at a living wage. We have a sense that something is terribly wrong in our society when people do not have opportunities to escape the grasp of poverty.

Unfortunately, as Christians and citizens of the United States we have tended to overlook the growing numbers of poor people, especially women and children, in our midst. While we have a basic sense of social justice, we have too often failed to reflect on how our actions contribute to poverty. Moreover, we have often neglected to devote creative energy to addressing and overcoming the realities of poverty. Thus, despite our Christian and national senses of justice, poverty grows.

As a society, we fail to act justly toward the poor when we do not ensure that they have the resources and opportunities needed to survive. Just as we have ignored the growing numbers of poor people in our midst, we have neglected to raise questions about social justice for the poor. As poverty grows in the United States, justice seems to wither.

It is my intention to broaden our understanding of poverty as an issue of social justice by connecting the empirical analysis of social science and our Christian belief that we are to value and respect each person as our neighbor. This study provides a resource that can enable students and religious educators, namely, parents, teachers, the church community, ordained and lay leadership, to integrate more fully the best from the public plaza with the wisdom of our Christian traditions. Principles of social justice based on a genuine love for one's neighbor are presented as a guide for informing, reforming, and enlarging the American Dream of justice for all. Overall, this book is an attempt to provide a framework for creating a table of Christian fellowship, a table of social decision making, and a table of partnership where we are all welcome guests, equal before God and enriched by each person's presence.

METHODOLOGY

"Research begins in wonder and curiosity but ends in teaching."[16] Curiosity leads to questions, a natural way to begin research. Gathering information and examining theories can whet our appetite to know more, so that eventually we weave a web. People and events, ideas and theories are woven together in delicate but resilient relationships. Since a web is transparent, it may also lead us to look beyond present concerns to an even broader, expansive landscape. This allows us to see how we are related in a world of intricate beauty and complex problems.

The overarching methodology for this study is a "circle of praxis," defined as a circular process of social analysis.[17] Joe Holland and Peter Henriot credit Paulo Freire with developing the concept of praxis, namely, action informed by reflection.[18] The elements of this circle of praxis are insertion, social analysis, theological reflection, and pastoral/educational planning. The primary data of social analysis are the experiences of persons and their communities, what is happening in their lives, their feelings and how they respond; these are the moment of insertion. Social analysis makes sense of experiences, examining both cause and effect, how events are linked, and identifying who the major actors are. This process sets these elements against a broader background and makes connections among events and people. Theological reflection searches and applies Scripture, tradition, and church social teaching to the experiences; it effectively allows the Word of God to raise questions, suggest new insights and new responses. Pastoral/educational planning emerges from the analysis and reflection upon experiences in the light of faith to arrive at appropriate responses on the part of individuals and communities. The response considers both short-term and long-term effectiveness. The action response evokes new situations that call for evaluation and a return to the process of insertion, analysis, reflection, and planning. The circle of praxis is more properly identified as a "spiral"[19] because there is an expectation that the process will continue and result in change. It is, in effect, an open, ongoing process that continues to analyze experiences and events to ensure that justice is available to all, especially those who are of little concern to the world, but of great concern to a loving God and community.

First, analyzing and comparing empirical and historical data provide an understanding of poverty in the United States. This analysis is the means for exploring the various aspects of the ecology of poverty in the lives of women and children. A review of responses to poverty in the United States reveals how individuals, organizations, and the government have reacted to those who are poor by showing what they are willing and able to do to assist the poor.

The exploration and analysis of the empirical and historical data generate meaningful understanding.[20] As noted, the poor, including the working poor, are increasingly separated from the broader society, which is socially shielded from understanding what it means to be entangled in the complex network created by the conditions of poverty. Consequently, this study uses empirical and historical analysis to help us understand more fully the multifaceted realities of poverty, including the suffering and hardship it inflicts, especially on women and children.

As Stephen Schmidt has written, there is always a need to approach history with "a hermeneutic of suspicion as well as a homiletic of hope" if we are to discover the "human values worth preserving."[21] Criticism and objectivity provide clarity, while openness to the future reveals hope. In this study there is a reliance on data to provide objective clarity, a critical analysis of policies and their impact on poor women and children to break open the meaning of the data, and a suggestion of hope for the future based on a discussion of the benefits of being more socially inclusive of those who are rendered powerless because of poverty.

Second, the heart of this study is theological reflection. Theological reflection is a disciplined attempt to gain some understanding of God's activity and presence in our lives and in the world, and to discern what God has enabled and required, and is enabling and requiring of people of faith. The theological analysis in this study focuses on Scripture and tradition, Catholic social teaching, and contemporary liberation and feminist theologies. Scripture reveals how God and people have interacted, and how a believing community welcomes all people, providing a table of fellowship as well as food, shelter, and comfort in times of distress. Catholic social teaching provides principles based on natural law and Scripture, as well as interpretations of issues of justice and poverty. Contemporary liberation and feminist theological critiques clear the way to welcome all to the table and to insure partnership in service based upon fundamental Christian beliefs about God.

In this study, theological reflection is coupled with and unfolds into social analysis. For instance, a review of Scripture and Christian traditions enlarges our understanding of justice for the poor. Scripture and tradition reveal a God who sides with the poor. Jesus' words of hope and compassionate actions for the poor challenged the early Christians as they formed a worshiping community whose members came from disparate economic situations. Faith communities today continue to address the realities of people from vastly different socio-economic conditions, and their confrontations with poverty can be understood in the light of Scripture and church tradition. Similarly, after reviewing Catholic social teaching in the light of social analysis it is evident that the church has directed attention to people's inherent worth and dignity, and that there is a compelling need for the church to continue to be an advocate for the poor today.

Third, as the study proceeds, a concern for what Christians can and should do will emerge. Stated differently, the study strives to inspire Christians to recognize what they can and should do to make a place or a better place at the table of life for the poor. In this part of the study I rely heavily on the work of Letty M. Russell, Thomas H. Groome, and Gabriel Moran. Letty Russell's discussion of educating for justice is based on God's mission to reconcile the world through Jesus Christ (2 Cor 5:18–20). It is a call to partnership with God and people in community as reflected in service, journeying with God to actualize the reign of God's justice and peace in our time, and welcoming others and working in solidarity with them to transform society and effect justice. Thomas H. Groome's writings enlarge the discussion with his emphasis on the responsibility of all educators—teachers and parents—to educate for justice, a justice that flows from spirituality, is modeled in relationships, and is truly a passion. Groome also provides suggestions regarding curriculum and pedagogies of social consciousness. Gabriel Moran's educational approach is explored as a way of engaging people in a method that builds on affirmation, acknowledges limitations, moves to prophetic resistance, and reorders life at a deeper level. Moran also argues that issues of justice are "at the center of the process" of religious education, and that this process requires taking "immediate steps to reduce the world's sufferings in a small but tangible way."[22]

The last chapter brings the study full circle. In the beginning the reader entered into the reality of poverty in the United States. At the end the researcher invites all Christians to be educated for justice so that they can deal "critically and creatively" with the realities of poverty and begin to discover how they can participate in efforts to seek greater social justice.[23] Ultimately, the researcher strives to reveal opportunities for welcoming to the table all those who had been excluded by poverty.

ORGANIZATION OF THIS STUDY

Chapter 1: Justice for All. The introduction examines the challenge of "justice for all" in the United States where poverty affects millions of people. Prominent people from politics and the arts are presented as persons intent on bringing justice to an unjust world. This chapter provides the background, purpose, and significance of the study, and its methodology is described. The guiding metaphor, *a place at the table*, is introduced as an image that can be used to encourage people to work for a future where all share in decisions and power.

Chapter 2: Poverty in the United States of America. This chapter explores the reality of poverty in the United States, beginning with portraits of the working poor: a family at risk of losing their home, women who moved from welfare to work, and the experience of a "random family" in the South Bronx. The U.S. Census Report is examined because it provides data to determine the extent of poverty. In addition, the reality of poverty for the working poor and the effects of poverty on women and children are explored. Finally, the chapter reviews the response to poverty in the United States from a historical perspective, as well as providing models for responding to poverty. The image of a tilted table is presented to reveal the injustice of the current government approach to poverty.

Chapter 3: Poverty: A Concern of Christian Faith and Social Justice. This chapter provides an analysis of poverty in the United States from a Christian faith perspective. It presents the biblical basis for justice, laying a foundation for this study in terms of how Scripture reveals a God of justice who invites all to respond with compassion for the poor. It also explores the early Christian community's response to disparities of wealth and poverty in their midst as a model that offers insights applicable in addressing the realities of poverty today. There is a focus on women and poverty in the early church, and an active overview of concern for the poor from the early Christian era through modern times. In documenting the suffering of the poor and revealing principles for addressing poverty and justice, Catholic social teaching serves as a foundational resource to understand poverty more fully and make us better advocates for making a place for the poor at our social table. Of special interest is the role of the Catholic Church in welfare reform, how the institutional church influenced American perspectives on justice for the poor, and an analysis of the church's effectiveness in working for justice for the poor. Finally, the U.S. bishops' document, *A Place at the Table* (2002), provides a model for addressing the needs of the poor and working together to provide a place for all at the table of decision making.

Chapter 4: Liberation Theology and Justice for the Poor. This chapter turns to the work of a number of carefully selected liberation theologians to enlarge the discussion of justice for the poor. It explores the road to liberation theology, using the documents of the Latin American Bishops Conferences at Medellín (1968) and Puebla (1979). Key principles for understanding justice and poverty from a liberation theology perspective are drawn from Gustavo Gutiérrez. Insights from Roger Haight, S.J., situates liberation theology in a North American context. Contemporary theologian Letty M. Russell is the primary guide for exploring a liberationist and feminist analysis of poverty and justice. Their writings enlarge the conversation and provide guidance for discussing how both rich and poor can better understand and respond actively and compassionately to the poor in social, economic, and pastoral situations.

Chapter 5: Educating for Justice. I propose fundamental principles for educating for justice from a Christian faith perspective in the United States today against the backdrop of understanding poverty and the problems it presents. Christian Scripture, history, and tradition provide depth and scope for examining poverty and seeking ways to relate with the poor, allowing rich and poor to interact as children of a loving God. The Rev. Letty M. Russell, Thomas H. Groome, and Gabriel Moran serve as guides for educating for justice. Letty M. Russell's writings, based on her experience as a Christian educator, provide a panorama for educating for justice by emphasizing the themes of God's mission, partnership, and hospitality. Thomas H. Groome's writings offer educators an understanding of justice as a mandate of faith, as a way of living, a justice curriculum, and pedagogies for fostering social consciousness. Gabriel Moran's four-step approach to educating for justice—as discussed in his book, *Interplay: A Theory of Religious Education* (1981)—provides a broad canvas for pastoral and educational planning. This chapter draws from these authors proposals for how Christians can be partners with a loving God in God's work for justice. These proposals present ways in which Christians, as coworkers with God, can learn to welcome the poor as those whom God prefers and as persons who deserve a place at the table. Methods for transforming an unjust society are explored in order to achieve a reign of justice. The theory of social justice as a continuum considers the value of each person's involvement and dedication to justice. Finally, case studies provide living examples of people who have made and are making a place at the table where all are welcome and where justice becomes a reality for all people.

QUESTIONS FOR REFLECTION AND DISCUSSION

1. What is your understanding of the words, "liberty and justice for all"?

2. Do you agree that most Americans have a sense of social justice? Explain why you agree or why not.

3. How and when did you become aware of poverty as an issue of justice?

4. How is poverty a threat to society?

5. Describe what is meant by the "ecology of poverty."

6. Discuss the meanings of "a place at the table" in terms of Andrei Rublev's icon and the U.S. Catholic bishops' pastoral letter. How do these compare with the thoughts of Letty M. Russell?

7. Based on your experience, explain how charity for the poor expanded your views about them and the challenges they face.

8. Discuss the steps involved in a "circle of praxis." What is needed for each step of the process? How could this process broaden your understanding of poverty and social justice?

SUGGESTED READINGS

Edwards, Senator John, Marion Crain, and Arne L. Kalleberg (eds.). *Ending Poverty in America: How to Restore the American Dream*. New York: New Press, 2007.

Herbert, Bob. *Promises Betrayed: Waking Up from the American Dream*. New York: Times Books, 2005.

Holland, Joe, and Peter Henriot, S.J. *Social Analysis: Linking Faith and Justice*. Revised Edition. Maryknoll, NY: Orbis Books, 1995.

Lardner, James, and David A. Smith (eds.), *Inequality Matters: The Growing Economic Divide in America and Its Poisonous Consequences*. New York: New Press, 2005.

Seymour, Jack L. "Power and History: History as 'Critical' Analysis," *Religious Education* 82, no. 3 (Summer 1987): 350.

Vrame, Anton C. *The Educating Icon*. Brookline, MA: Holy Cross Orthodox Press, 1999.

Wallis, Jim. *God's Politics: Why the Right Gets It Wrong and the Left Doesn't Get It*. New York: HarperCollins Publishers, 2005.

Warren, Elizabeth, and Amelia Warren Tyagi. *The Two-Income Trap: Why Middle-Class Mothers and Fathers Are Going Broke*. New York: Basic Books, 2003.

NOTES

[1] BBC News: In Full: Mandela's Poverty Speech. http://newsvote.bbc.co.uk/mpapps/pagetools/print/news.bbc.co.ul/1/hi/uk_politics/423260

[2] Transcript: Bono Remarks at the National Prayer Breakfast, February 2, 2006. http://usatoday.printhis.clickability.com

[3] "Senator John Edwards's Remarks to the Democratic National Convention," *The New York Times*, July 27, 2004. <http://www.nytimes.com/2004/07/27/politics/campaign/28TEXT-EDWARDS.html>

[4] Bob Herbert, "More Than Just Talk," *The New York Times*, May 8, 2007. http://select.nytimes.com/2007/05/08/opinion/08herbert.html

[5] Senator John Edwards, Marion Crain, and Arne L. Kalleberg (eds.), *Ending Poverty in America: How to Restore the American Dream* (New York: New Press, 2007), 256.

[6] Ibid., Elizabeth Warren, "The Vanishing Middle Class," 38-54.

[7] Diana Jean Schemo, "Private Loans Deepen a Crisis in Student Debt," *The New York Times*, June 10, 2007. www.nytimes.com/2007/06/10/us/10loans.

[8] Carmen DeNavas-Walt, Bernadette D. Proctor, and Cheryl Hill Lee, U.S. Census Bureau, Current Population Reports. P60-231, *Income, Poverty, Health Insurance Coverage in the United States: 2005* (Washington, DC: U.S. Government Printing Office, 2006), 13-19, 45.

[9] *Poverty in America: A Threat to the Common Good* (Alexandria, VA: Catholic Charities USA, 2006), 12.

[10] David K. Shipler, "Total Poverty Awareness," *The New York Times*, February 21, 2004, A15.

[11] Anton C. Vrame, *The Educating Icon* (Brookline, MA: Holy Cross Orthodox Press), 122-24.

[12] Letty M. Russell, *The Future of Partnership* (Philadelphia: Westminster Press, 1979), 18, 28-30, 31.

[13] Letty M. Russell, "Partnership in Models of Renewed Community," *Ecumenical Review* 40 (January 1988): 18.

[14] Letty M. Russell, *Church in the Round: Feminist Interpretation of the Church* (Louisville: Westminster/John Knox Press, 1993), 17.

[15] *Call and Response: Constitutions and Directory*, Dominican Congregation of Our Lady of the Rosary (Sparkill, NY, May 6, 1985), #19. Revised May 2007.

[16] Lee S. Shulman, "Disciplines of Inquiry in Education: A New Overview," Richard M. Jaeger (ed.), *Complementary Methods for Research in Education*, 2nd ed. (Washington, DC: American Educational Research, 1997), 6.

[17] Joe Holland and Peter Henriot, S.J., *Social Analysis: Linking Faith and Justice*. Revised Edition (Maryknoll, NY: Orbis Books, 1983), 8.

[18] Paulo Freire, *The Pedagogy of the Oppressed* (New York: Seabury Press, 1970).

[19] Holland and Henriot, 9.

[20] Jack L. Seymour, "Power and History: History as 'Critical' Analysis," *Religious Education* 82, no. 3 (Summer 1987): 350.

[21] Stephen A. Schmidt, "The Uses of History and Religious Education," *Religious Education* 80, no. 3 (Summer 1985): 349.

[22] Gabriel Moran, *Interplay: A Theory of Religion and Education* (Winona, MN: Saint Mary's Press, 1981), 143.

[23] Gabriel Moran, "Of a Kind and to a Degree," Marlene Mayr (ed.), *Does the Church Really Want Religious Education?: An Ecumenical Inquiry* (Birmingham, AL: Religious Education Press, 1988), 21.

Poverty in the United States of America

Poverty seems far removed from the lives of most people living in the United States of America. Ordinary people go about their daily routines of work and play, study and exercise, associating with people of their own class and, mostly, their own race. They devote time to work, family, and social activities such as church, politics, sports, and clubs. They assume that other people are doing as well as they are. They are unaware of the millions of Americans for whom poverty is a constant or near-constant companion. If they do reflect on those in poverty, they often think that welfare or social and governmental agencies address the needs of the poor. In fact, the poor are largely unknown and are invisible to the majority of Americans. When people are invisible, they are not only out of sight, they are also out of mind. As a result, the invisible poor struggle on without notice.

Sometimes those who are poor come to people's attention in dramatic ways. When Hurricane Katrina hit the Gulf Coast in August 2005, surging water breached the canals in New Orleans and the city was inundated. The media were eager to show the storm's effects. They encountered the people who had not evacuated, those who did not own cars or have a place to go to, who were without family or friends in places far from the storm's path who could welcome them. They did not have the means to obey the mayor's order to evacuate the city before the storm hit and it was evident that the government made no effort to provide buses for them to do so. Almost immediately the world was viewing images ✗ of men, women, and children carrying their few belongings and moving on foot to the sports arena which soon became an unsafe environ when it lost power. Without electricity, temperatures rose dangerously, and the wind damaged the roof so rain poured down on those inside. Without electricity, air conditioning came to a halt, as did the pumps that supplied water for sanitation and drinking water. Then viewers saw pictures of parents and children struggling to reach high ground, trying to get clean water as they fought for a breath of air in the extreme heat and humidity, with no place to rest. People who thought they could safely ride out the storm and protect their meager possessions were seen trying to reach the highest point of their houses; viewers saw them as they climbed out on rooftops, holding messages calling for help. They waited a long time for local emergency responders, and later the National Guard, to reach them and take them to safety.

Who were these poor who had not evacuated? The media used language that identified the people struggling for life as "refugees," as if they were from a foreign land. Perhaps they were, this mixture of humanity that included people of many races, though they were predominantly African Americans. There were infants and children whose parents tried to protect them from the late summer heat as they struggled to find food and liquids to sustain them. There were also handicapped and older people in wheelchairs relying on others to transport and care for them; some of these died from heat exhaustion and dehydration. Most people assumed that the government would supply help in a timely fashion. After all, FEMA, the Federal Emergency Management Agency, formerly an independent agency but since March 2003 part of the Department of Homeland Security, had provided help in previous disasters, as when Florida was devastated by three hurricanes in 2004 (Charley, Ivan, and Frances). In September 2005, however, FEMA was mired in red tape and lacked the leadership to supply the basic necessities: food, water, and shelter. The American Red Cross was present as it always is in disasters, and the American people, moved by the plight of families, responded to appeals for help. Church groups supplied meals, water, and a safe place to rest. So too did the cities and towns that welcomed the evacuees when the government finally provided buses for the people to move away from their storm-ravaged homes and the damaged arena. The response to Hurricane Katrina showed the best and the worst of American response to hardship and deprivation caused by a natural disaster.

This chapter examines poverty in the United States of America. Data will provide objective information about the extent and depth of poverty since 1959 when the U.S. Census Bureau began to keep detailed information on poverty. Stories of people who are poor will open our eyes to the complexity of poverty. Research will reveal how poverty affects people, especially women and children, as well as the factors that are common when poverty overtakes a family. Poverty has a history, and an overview of how the United States has responded to poverty will provide a broader perspective for considering current problems concerning poverty. Legislation that addressed poverty in recent history will be reviewed, especially the 1996 revision of U.S. welfare laws. What is most evident is an increasing reliance on a business model as the way to approach government and specifically welfare. An analysis of this reliance shows how a market approach to poverty is inadequate for addressing the multifaceted problems of the poor. Such an approach, while well intended, shows a lack of justice for the poor because it fails to address basic human concerns. This chapter examines the concept of the "ecology of poverty," that is, the complex network of social relationships that separates the poor from society at large and adversely affects the poor person's hope of realizing the American Dream of a rich and fulfilling life. The image of a tilted table will serve to illustrate how the system works against the poor.

Poverty has many guises. For some people it is pervasive, a way of life that some people experience on a daily basis, a persistent state and a thoroughly consuming reality that has marked their lives for many years. For others it is an occasional partner; despite their best efforts they fall behind in paying bills; debt sucks them down like quicksand, or serious illness consumes valuable resources, and before long they are facing bankruptcy. Poverty causes fear—one works frantically to pay this bill and buy time to pay that one, borrowing from one area to pay another, until the house of cards falls in on itself.

Though essentially an economic problem, poverty is also a sociological and political problem. Not having enough money to pay for shelter, food, clothing, transportation, child care, and health care diminishes a person, destroying his or her sense of self to such a degree that little pleasures appear to be luxuries available for most people, but out of reach for a poor person or family. Paying rent or the mortgage is essential, but when these payments are in arrears, the family can be evicted and forcibly removed from the premises. How does one carry all one's possessions and go to a shelter where safety is problematic and, due to limited space, privacy is a luxury? Such conditions break a person's spirit and further limit opportunities to live a normal life, a life in which children can attend a neighborhood school on a regular basis, adults can work at a job that pays a living wage, and the ordinary cares of life are addressed: health care, safety, the ability to function as an individual in society with a permanent mailing address, and a place to call home.

A PORTRAIT OF THE POOR
IN THE UNITED STATES

Poverty can be viewed objectively and subjectively. The objective view includes data from the U.S. Census Bureau. The subjective view is the experiences of those who are poor. Both of these views inform and enlighten our understanding of what it means to be poor. One could rightly say that people in the United States are not poor compared to people in countries where they live on a dollar a day. Yet there are poor people in the United States, our highly industrialized nation that boasts some of the highest earnings and wealth in the world, who lack the basic necessities of life, and who, because of this lack, suffer and are denied opportunities for full human growth and development.

Several authors have spent years studying groups and individuals who live their lives coping with poverty. Their writings show a depth of spirit and reveal an empathic concern for the persons whom they interviewed and with whom they spent much of their lives. In a very real sense the writers were embedded with people over several years so their observations and insights are valuable for revealing the real world of poverty.

Poverty can be called many things. When the limitations it imposes on people become apparent, it is like living in a gated community, not one with security guards who limit access to all but the residents and their invited guests. No, this is more like an invisible barrier limiting those who live within its confines, a community where people are imprisoned by lack of opportunity. Another image is the reality of pain. Persistent, deeply felt pain blocks out other concerns; its presence is all-consuming. A person in pain cries aloud and seeks relief. Any respite, however brief, is welcome. So too poverty can take over a person's life and hold that person hostage. How can these bills be paid? Where can my children go for medical and dental care? Why does working full time and in some cases, overtime, not pay all the bills? How can our family survive in this economy and in this neighborhood? Why are violence and crime so prevalent and fear a gnawing reality?

Broke on Two Incomes. Who are the poor in American society? Before studying data from the Census Bureau, it helps to meet some persons who live with poverty. Sad to say, poverty can visit even families that work hard and play by the rules. One such example is the book *Broke on Two Incomes* by Elizabeth Warren. A professor at Harvard Law School, she has for over thirty years studied families with financial troubles. Warren and her daughter, Amelia Warren Tyagi, who was trained in economics, have written about such families. Their research was based on the 2001 Consumer Bankruptcy Project that had studied families that had to file for bankruptcy. In their book, *The Two-Income Trap*, they share the story of a middle-class family, Ruth Ann and James Wilson, who did all the right things, but who were reduced to poverty in spite of their best efforts.

Ruth Ann was a college graduate who had majored in accounting. After graduation she returned to her hometown of Wylie, Texas, where she lived near her family, worked, and built up savings. When she met James Wilson, a friend from high school, she realized that he was the man of her dreams, someone who inspired confidence because he was dependable and hardworking. They married and a year later had a son, Dexter. In 1997 they invested in a home that they could afford at a cost of $84,000. There were drawbacks: the roof needed to be replaced and the kitchen needed updating. But there were also three bedrooms and a big yard, perfect for a growing family. Shortly after the birth of their daughter, Ellie, James learned that his boss had to close his store. With a national megastore opening a short distance away, their carpet and flooring store would no longer be profitable. One day shortly after Christmas in 1999, James lost his job as manager and entered the world of the unemployed. Unable to find a job that paid a comparable salary, James did odd jobs because, in his words, "I figured any work is better than no work." Ruth Ann, who had worked all these years, asked for extra hours at her job, but the company could not accommodate her request.

Economizing is what people do when there is less income, but the truth was that the Wilsons were not living extravagantly. Their money went for basics: paying the mortgage, day care expenses, food, and car payments. Within three months they missed a mortgage payment. In an effort to raise cash, they had two garage sales. Their families helped with a gift of $4000 from James's parents and a loan of $1500 from Ruth Ann's brother. They would soon have to acknowledge that these were only temporary fixes.

As Ruth Ann and James struggled to pay their debts, they used credit cards to charge their day-to-day expenses. Over time this increased their indebtedness, since credit card companies impose late fees and then charge higher interest rates on subsequent bills. As a result, the Wilsons were dragged deeper into debt. Ruth Ann had financial acumen, but despite her best efforts, the folders with bills and past-due notices from the mortgage company grew fatter. When they failed to pay local taxes, the county threatened to foreclose on their home. Finally, Ruth Ann decided that they had to see a bankruptcy attorney. Filing for bankruptcy would give them time to repay bills and prevent the bank from foreclosing on their home. James was so upset by the prospect of filing for bankruptcy that he went out to his pickup truck, sat in the front seat, and cried. Ruth Ann and James Wilson filed for bankruptcy in 2001 in northern Texas.

The Wilsons were a typical American family; they worked hard, paid their bills, and played by the rules. Yet when disaster struck, they stood to lose everything. As Warren and Tyagi point out, most people who file for bankruptcy are parents with children. They are more likely to be late making credit card payments, and more often experience the repossession of their cars and home foreclosures. Most are middle-class people who are laid off from work or whose business fails. Most have both parents working. Their poverty may be temporary, but the experience is all too painfully real, like being branded with a red-hot iron. It takes time to return to a state of security.[1]

The Working Poor. David K. Shipler introduces his readers to the working poor, those who maintain faith in the American Dream even as they struggle to keep their heads above economic ruin. One such person is Caroline Payne, who has worked hard to make the American Dream a reality in her life. The first person in her family to graduate from high school, she eventually earned an associate's degree because she knew the importance of a good education. Caroline married after completing high school, and she and her husband built a log cabin house where they raised their three children. After fourteen years of marriage, Caroline faced the reality of divorce, emerging with an agreement that removed her from her home, and forced her and her daughters to live in a small apartment with only $400 a month in child support.

Despite personal problems, Caroline had a cheerful outlook and made the best of situations that might have stopped many others. Her second marriage lasted only two years because her husband physically and mentally abused her. Caroline loved her daughter from the second marriage, Amber, and worked very hard to cope with her daughter's learning disabilities and a diagnosis of epilepsy. By the time Amber was ready for high school, Caroline had lived in many places in three states, owned a small home of her own (with the bank that held the mortgage), and worked a series of low-paying jobs. As she reviewed her situation, the fact that she was earning almost the same hourly wage after many years of work upset her the most. Despite working hard and getting additional training and education, Caroline was stuck earning barely above the minimum wage. Some work conditions, such as the rotating schedule required by Wal-Mart, prevented her from working other jobs to earn additional income, as she had done over the years. Amber's health problems also prevented Caroline from taking certain jobs because the girl needed supervision but suitable care was too costly. A back problem prevented Caroline from standing for long periods. Bouts of depression not only saddened her but also clouded her judgment so that she made errors at work. Poverty prevented her from caring properly for herself, as evidenced by a lack of dental care. Since Medicaid would pay for full dentures, she was forced to lose all her teeth. The new teeth never fit properly, and this effectively killed one of her major assets, her smile.

Overall, Caroline Payne has had a difficult life: a deprived childhood; living in many places and attending different schools; having to make friends over and over again; two failed marriages; having to sell her house for no profit, which prevented her from moving to a more affordable area where she could get better services and an adequate education and job training. Her accomplishments—raising four children, earning a college degree, surviving an abusive relationship, moving from a homeless shelter to her own home—were overshadowed by the fact that a job that paid a living wage always seemed out of reach. While Caroline Payne tried her very best, she still moved in and out of poverty. Despite her best efforts, the American Dream was just out of reach for Caroline.[2]

Welfare to Work. Jason DeParle followed the lives and fortunes of women who were poor as they lived the transition from welfare to work. He introduces his readers to Angela Jobe. Angie had lived in a Chicago ghetto where her mother worked two jobs to send her to parochial school with the hope that the school environment would counter negative forces in the neighborhood and within the family, especially her alcoholic father. Despite her mother's best efforts, Angie was attracted to Greg, who became her best friend and then her lover. When Angie became pregnant at seventeen, she left school. By age twenty-five she and Greg had three children. Life in the ghetto became tougher when Greg was arrested for defending his friends and sentenced to prison when he refused to testify against his friends.

Unable to support her children with the low payments from welfare and her low-paying jobs, Angie moved to Milwaukee to get higher welfare and lower rent. As a temporary worker at the post office, Angie enrolled in a class with the hope of earning a GED, a high school equivalency diploma. Things were looking up until she discovered that she was pregnant. She considered an abortion, but decided against it because in her mind it was murder. By age thirty, when Milwaukee sent out its first notices for a mandatory work program, Angie found a job on her own, as a nursing aide. Angie found satisfaction helping the elderly; she was empathetic with the patients and a natural caregiver. She had chosen backbreaking work that paid barely above the minimum wage; she also now had no health insurance. Angie was generous to a fault. When her cousin Opal arrived, she took her in. Opal promised to help pay for food, but she soon became addicted to crack cocaine. When it was evident that Opal's addiction was harming Angie and her children, she had the unpleasant task of putting her out.

While Angie struggled to survive on low wages and few benefits, the city of Milwaukee was claiming success at reducing welfare dependency. The word spread that welfare was ending, so clients had to fend for themselves. The number of people receiving welfare decreased significantly. Officials had privatized welfare, using companies like Maximus. Such companies hired caseworkers who were paid low wages and who were ill-prepared to counsel those in need of competent counseling. The process of applying for help involved a maze of paperwork and forms. Those whose education was limited and whose life was consumed by working more than one job to feed their children often became discouraged and had little time to battle the bureaucracy, so they stopped applying for welfare benefits. The law emphasized getting clients to work; if they worked at a dead-end job or soon left a job that proved impossible, the company still got credit for moving the clients off welfare.

The officials who stressed the traditional work ethic failed to see that welfare recipients had always worked to supplement welfare payments, and that they also had to turn to family and friends for help. As more poor women went to work, who would care for their children? Families suffered, as is evident from Angie's family. Her children were absent from school more frequently when she worked full time at the nursing home. With little or no supervision beyond their older siblings, the children had poor study habits and soon lost their desire to attend school. Angie was realistic in thinking that none of her children would graduate from high school. There were added pressures on her children: Her oldest daughter, Kesha, had to care for her younger brothers and sisters, so her chances of doing her own schoolwork were diminished. By age seventeen Kesha repeated the pattern by getting pregnant and dropping out of school. Angie's son Redd had dropped out of school when he was fifteen; by seventeen, with no job prospects, selling drugs looked like his only opportunity. While Angie's family suffered from her absence, the private companies that oversaw welfare clients wasted taxpayer money on misleading advertising campaigns and on managers who bilked money for themselves. Individuals, such as Angie, and their families suffered greatly while government officials bragged about success in decreasing the number of people receiving welfare benefits.[3]

Random Family. The insidious and very ordinary nature of poverty comes to light in the story of teenagers caught in the thicket of life in the South Bronx from the late 1980s through 2001. Adrian LeBlanc spent eleven years with the young women about whom she wrote. As a journalist, she first entered their world when she reported on the trial of George Rivera, commonly called Boy George, a notorious drug lord. Over time, LeBlanc won the confidence of Jessica, George's girlfriend, and Coco, her sister-in-law. She recorded the tangled relations among the boys and girls, men and women who lived in the Tremont section of the Bronx. Poverty was their companion even when there were brief respites from hunger, the struggle to pay rent, and the lack of medical and dental care. The values that emerge in this intimate tale are the constant search for love, fierce fidelity to friends and family, the joy of life in the midst of enormous suffering, and a constant lack of resources. These persons create a life in the midst of poverty. Searching for happiness in relationships is the daily drama of life. They treasure life and are proud of their children; babies are a source of pride, though their teenage mothers are sorely pressed to care for them as they grow into toddlers. Parenting skills reflect their upbringing; dressing their children well for the world to see is important. With little or no space to study, and with family situations that often prevent children from attending school, education is a low priority.

The drug trade attracts youth; it is the main way to earn money and respect in their neighborhood. Those involved in selling drugs are on a collision course with the law. Oftentimes the father of many children is imprisoned for years, leaving children without a father, and mothers to provide for their children alone. With few resources the mothers and girlfriends have the added burden of visiting their children's fathers who are often imprisoned upstate at a great distance from their homes in the Bronx. Visiting is time-consuming, expensive, and an emotional roller coaster. The mothers write to their husbands and boyfriends regularly and the letters are full of love, anger, recriminations, and admonitions. Still, the women and men caught in these destructive patterns of life often have compelling insights. For example, Cesar, after many years of imprisonment, wrote to Coco about their oldest daughter, Mercedes, age eleven. He noted that her problems in school are related to poverty. In his words, "Poverty is a subculture that exists within the ghetto. It goes beyond black or Hispanic, at least in my mind. Overworked teachers. Run-down schools. It looks like they designed this system to make our children fail. Socio-economic conditions. Why are we so passive? We accept conditions that don't benefit us—economic oppression we've been suffering for years. That's the primary condition."[4] As LeBlanc noted, Mercedes has experienced a lifetime of hardship, fear, and humiliation. Poverty has shaped almost all her memories: "nights in unsafe buildings; cold waits on the hard benches of homeless shelters, police stations, courtrooms, and welfare offices; she's been uprooted eight times in eight years. Her mother struggled every single day of her life. Her father was in prison. Terrifying seizures plagued her little sister."[5] She has seen adults and family members involved in drugs and violence. With all the responsibilities that she shouldered as the oldest of Coco's children, it is no surprise that Mercedes acted out in school.

True stories reveal the reality of poverty. They bring to light the women, men, and children whose lives have been scarred by the consequences of poverty. These people open our eyes to poverty in real lives and they embody the data that reveal the extent and depth of poverty in the United States. Their stories also reveal how economic, social, educational, and political structures place limits on their lives. The ecology of poverty is truly a complex web that holds people hostage.

THE U.S. CENSUS BUREAU REPORT ON POVERTY

Since 1959 the U.S. Census Bureau has issued a report on poverty in the United States. Released in the fall, it provides poverty data for the previous year, including the number of people in poverty and the percentage of the population living in poverty. The report issues data and graphs about poverty; it looks at people as individuals, as families, and as members of groups by age, sex, race, nationality, and locale. The data show the extent of poverty as well as who is most affected by it.

Figure 1

Number in Poverty and Poverty Rate: 1959 to 2005

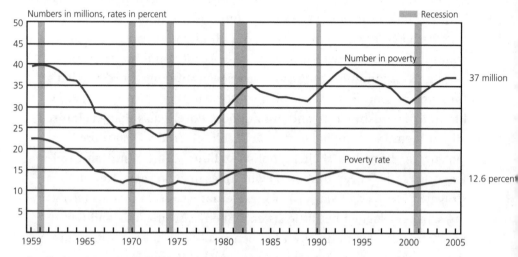

Note: The data points are placed at the midpoints of the respective years.

Source: U.S. Census Bureau, Current Population Survey, 1960 to 2006 Annual Social Economic Supplements.

The U.S. Census states that in 2005 there were 37 million people in the United States, 12.6 percent of the population, living below the official poverty level. In Figure 1 it is evident that there has been a steady increase in poverty for four years beginning in 2000 when there were 31.6 million poor people and a poverty rate of 11.3 percent; by 2004 there were 37 million poor people and a poverty rate of 12.7 percent. Since 1959, when this measure of poverty was first taken, 2005 has the third highest number of people living in poverty, just below 1959 and 1993 when almost 40 million people lived in poverty.

What is worth noting is that children are at greater risk than adults of being in poverty. In 2005 there were 12.9 million children under the age of eighteen who were considered poor. Overall, in 2005 children had a poverty rate of 17.6 percent. Children who live with only their mother are at a greater risk of being poor than those children who live with both parents. This is evident by considering the fact that 4.8 million children under the age of six live in poverty; these are related children under the age of six living in families whose poverty rate is 20 percent. Meanwhile, the poverty rate for related children under the age of six living in female-headed households with no husband present is 52.9 percent. Overall, children in the United States have a greater chance of being poor, as evidenced by the fact that while children are 25 percent of the total population, they are 34.9 percent of those who are poor.[6]

The data show that in 2005 the poverty rate and the number in poverty decreased for non-Hispanic whites. Non-Hispanic whites, like Caroline Payne, are 66.7 percent of the total population in the United States and 43.9 percent of the people in poverty; they have a poverty rate of 8.3 percent and 16.2 million in poverty. For blacks and Hispanics, the rate of poverty stayed the same as the previous year, but for Asians there was an increase in the poverty rate and the number in poverty. Blacks, like Angela Jobe and Greg, have a poverty rate of 24.9 percent with 9.2 million in poverty. Hispanics, like Coco and Cesar, have a poverty rate of 21.8 percent and 9.4 million in poverty. Asians have a poverty rate of 11.1 percent, or and 1.4 million in poverty.[7]

Working Families. Most working-class families rely on the income of all able-bodied members of the family. It is common for poor adults, like Caroline Payne, to work two or more jobs to meet financial and social obligations.[8] Individuals from ethnic groups that experience income disparities need to work more than one job to survive. The reality is that lower income directly affects families in terms of hunger, housing, and health care. Families with low incomes cannot cover the costs of necessities. Because their income is used almost as soon as it is earned, families often have no money for food. This is especially evident at the end of the month, before the next paycheck arrives. As a result, mothers with small children wait in line for hours, even in freezing weather, to get food from food pantries. Families with children are frequent visitors to soup kitchens, facilities that serve a hot meal. Senior citizens living on Social Security often have to choose between food and getting prescription medications for chronic health conditions. While food stamps and WIC (Special Supplemental Nutrition Program for Women, Infants, and Children) help many women and children, there are many others who are eligible for these services but do not receive the benefits because they are not aware that they are eligible, or cannot take time off from work to file the necessary forms, or find the extensive paperwork too difficult to complete. So hunger looms large for families with limited resources.

Housing, too, is a concern. When rising housing expenses consume well above the accepted 30 percent range, families have no money for other necessities. Affordable housing has decreased in urban areas, forcing families to live in less desirable neighborhoods or to live in areas far from their families and from their work. When families live in poorer neighborhoods there are fewer assets such as stores, schools, parks, and hospitals. Impoverished neighborhoods breed crime and violence, as seen in the lives of Coco and Cesar and their children. While some people have a social network of family and friends, there is also a strong counterculture of drug dealers and gangs. The presence of violent individuals results in people living in fear; they cannot be confident of their own safety or that of their children, who often have to stay indoors because it is not safe to play outside. Poor neighborhoods typically have schools that are overcrowded, with fewer services, and less experienced teachers. These factors result in inadequate education.

Health Care. Poverty also limits a person's access to health care. In 2005, 15.9 percent of the American population, a staggering 46.6 million people, had no health insurance.[9] The number of uninsured persons has increased steadily since 2000 as fewer businesses offer health insurance or require workers to contribute more than they can afford to qualify for health insurance. Of special concern is the fact that 11.2 percent of all children under the age of eighteen years—8.3 million children—had no health insurance in 2005. Children in poverty were even more disadvantaged; 19 percent of them had no health insurance in 2005.[10] Without medical insurance a person cannot afford to go to a doctor or dentist on a regular basis. When symptoms become severe, sick people will go to a hospital emergency room. Ignoring the early symptoms of an illness

increases the risk of serious illness and can make treatment more difficult and costly. A disease whose symptoms could have been treated in its
early stages can develop into a severe, life-threatening condition.

Lack of access to affordable health care has repercussions for the individual and for society. First, it is a threat to the sick person in terms of
health and comfort. It often means time lost from work and school and,
more importantly, it also threatens the fabric of the family, especially
when the person is the breadwinner, or when a child's life is at risk.
People who are uninsured also have to deal with the debt incurred for
treatment. Second, society stands to lose when a person does not seek
proper medical care. Of special concern would be a highly contagious
disease that could endanger the lives of others, for example, when there
is an influenza pandemic. In such a crisis all people, rich and poor, need
adequate health care. Persons without access to proper treatment could
inadvertently be carriers and spread a contagious disease.

Defining Poverty. To understand the true depth and extent of poverty
in the United States, we need to understand the poverty threshold and
how it came to be defined. The U.S. Census Bureau has a series of poverty
thresholds based on the size of the family and its composition, that is, the
number of adults and children. The official poverty threshold is defined
by the amount of income before taxes. It does not include capital gains
or noncash benefits such as Medicaid, food stamps, or public housing.
The poverty threshold, the total monetary earnings of all members of the
family, for a family of four (two adults and two children under 18 years of
age) in 2005 was $19,806; for a family of four (one adult and three chil-
dren under 18 years of age) the poverty threshold was $19,874. The pov-
erty threshold is the same for all geographical areas of the United States,
although some areas have higher costs of living. It is, however, adjusted
annually for inflation.[11] This official definition is a way of measuring poverty throughout the nation. Furthermore, the ratio of income-to-poverty
measures the depth of poverty and this is the way the government determines who are eligible for government-sponsored assistance, which includes Temporary Assistance for Needy Families (TANF), Medicare, food
stamps, and the Low Income Energy Assistance Program (LIHEAP).[12]

As originally developed by Mollie Orshansky of the Social Security Administration in 1963–1964, the poverty threshold was calculated by estimating the cost of the economy food plan, the cheapest of four food plans proposed by the Department of Agriculture for a family; this amount was then multiplied by three. This estimate assumed not only the most basic of food plans, but also minimal spending on other necessities.[13] Orshansky readily admitted that the poverty threshold represented "a measure of income inadequacy, not of income adequacy."[14] It is commonly recognized that the so-called absolute measure of poverty reported by the annual U.S. Census report falls short of what people and families actually need to live with minimal necessities. Moreover, while the poverty threshold is determined by the size of the family, it makes no allowances for the expenses associated with work, the cost of transportation, child care, and clothing needed for work; the cost of medical care; regional differences as reflected in housing/rental costs; rising living standards in the United States; and increases in the Social Security payroll tax.[15] Since 1969, the poverty threshold has been updated annually for inflation, using the Consumer Price Index. It is far removed from the income that a family needs to live. When compared to the median income, a better estimate of what people need to live, "the poverty line for a family of four was 48 percent of median family income in 1960; now it is 29 percent."[16]

Alternative Measures of Poverty. The average poverty thresholds have come under criticism because in focusing on income needed for food they do not give adequate consideration to the large proportion of income needed for housing, health care, and transportation. Nowadays it is recognized that food represents a smaller proportion of total living expenses, a fact that would raise the poverty threshold. Criticisms of the official poverty threshold led social scientists to search for alternative ways to measure poverty. In May 1995, the National Research Council (NRC) of the National Academy of Sciences proposed a measure of poverty that would consider factors that effectively increase or decrease a family's income.

Those factors that positively impact a family's resources include: food stamps, public housing and rental assistance (Section 8 vouchers), energy assistance, the Earned Income Tax Credit (EITC), and the child tax credit; and in-kind aid to children (Special Supplemental Food Program for Women, Infants, and Children, commonly referred to as WIC, school lunches, and Head Start). Those with a negative impact include: higher taxes (Social Security, federal, state, city, and property); work-related expenses such as transportation, child care costs, and clothing; and the cost of health care and medical insurance.

The proposed measure would also take into account differences between rural and urban areas. Since the cost of living for housing, health care, and child care varies by geographical location, the proposed measure would effectively shift the regional location with the largest number of poor children from the South and the Midwest to the Northeast and the West.[17]

The National Research Council's revised measure more accurately identifies the children who are impoverished. It also provides a way to measure the impact of recent federal government policies as well as anti-poverty measures at the state level. Experts have determined that methods of measuring poverty other than the official census report, including the proposed measure of the National Research Council, substantially increase the number of people who should be counted as poor.[18]

Comparing Measures of Poverty. Although the U.S. Census Bureau measurement of poverty is flawed, the official measures of poverty can still provide a sense of the depth and persistence of poverty in the United States. In a comparison of various measures of poverty from 1969 until 2000, Lawrence Mishel, et al. (2003) compared the official poverty rate with *one-half poverty*, *one-half median income*, and *twice poverty*. Those living at *one-half the poverty* rate, the deeply poor, form a fairly consistent segment of the population from slightly below to slightly above 5 percent of the population. In 2000, over 12 million persons were deeply poor. Research shows that they were less likely to benefit from periods of rapid economic growth as occurred between 1995 and 2000 and, while in need of a safety net, they were in fact in danger of losing benefits as social policy stressed welfare to work programs.

People living on *one-half the median income* comprised about 20 percent of the population. As the authors point out, the official poverty thresholds, while adjusted for inflation, do not actually reflect income growth. The official measure does not take into account rising standards of living. Even when families' income rose above the official poverty threshold, they made little or no progress. The authors estimate that since the early 1980s, 20 percent of the population has been below half the median income. The poor are worse off today because there is a greater divide between the majority of Americans whose income continues to increase and those considered officially poor.

Finally, families living below *twice the poverty threshold* in 2000 would have had an income of $35,200 for a family of four. Mishel, et al. estimate that this represented the income "families need to meet their basic needs for housing, food, health care, child care, and other necessities." Using this relative measure, they estimate that since the mid-1970s about one-third of the population has been poor or near poor.[19]

Depth of Poverty. The poverty gap is the difference in dollars between the actual income of a poor family and its poverty threshold. The poverty gap, which has risen consistently since the mid-1970s, measures the depth of poverty. In 2005, the average poverty gap was $8000. This is the highest since 1959 when the U.S. Census first reported family poverty rates and the family poverty gap. When families experience a lack of income in the thousands of dollars, they are bound to suffer. Necessities such as housing, utilities, and transportation are constant and cannot be ignored. Efforts to pay one bill and postpone payment on others can result in penalties, like late fees, or even services being cut. If poor people resort to local money lenders, they will have to pay even higher interest rates and this will impact their expenses for many months to come. Using credit cards to pay outstanding debts often results in penalties for late payments, a higher rate of interest on the amount owed, and ultimately a bad credit rating. In practical terms, families experiencing the poverty gap are often left with no money for necessities, especially food, as they near the end of the month. This is dangerous for babies and young children who need to eat nutritious food on a regular basis or they will suffer permanent brain damage and other preventable health problems and cognitive deficits.

Another disturbing fact is that 43 percent of those at the poverty threshold are actually below half the poverty threshold and this represents a record high mark. For a family of four with two children this would mean in 2005 a yearly income of just over $10,000. Social policy with its emphasis on work has not succeeded in lifting up those who have few resources. These families have so little income that they are far removed from the table of life where good things are enjoyed. What is evident from all sources is that the United States has many millions of individuals and families who are poor and that the depth of their deprivation is increasing.

Another fact about poverty in the United States is that families such as Ruth Ann and James Wilson, and Caroline Payne and Amber, move in and out of poverty. Some families spend a few months of each year in poverty. They are just able to meet their obligations and support family members until a mishap that more affluent families could absorb pushes them over the edge. This could include loss of a job, a hospitalization, an accident, or an extraordinary expense. They may take measures to rebound, but in some cases borrowing money or putting extra charges on a credit card may put them in an even more precarious position.

United States and Other Industrialized Nations. It is interesting to note that the United States has the highest level of poverty when compared with industrialized nations in Europe, Australia, and Canada. John Iceland (2003) compared the United States to these countries using both an absolute poverty level and a relative poverty measure. Although the United States has one of the highest average incomes in the industrialized world, it also has the highest absolute poverty rate and the highest relative poverty rate. The reasons for a higher proportion of people who are poor, according to Iceland, are that many jobs, even those that are full time, are low-wage jobs and, compared with European nations, the government benefits for the poor are lower and have a limited effect in alleviating poverty.[20] In another study, Mangum, et al., equate the United States tolerance for income inequality with its dedicated pursuit of individual wealth. They also attribute the high rates of poverty to an unequal income distribution, low earnings for workers who have less education and fewer skills, a lack of adequate income supports, a high proportion of single-parent families, a tax structure that favors the wealthy, and a widespread re-luctance to overcome poverty.[21] In a more scathing analysis, Mishel, et al, note that the United States is one of the richest nations in the world with the highest degree of inequality, a fact that they attribute to lower incomes for many and social policies that fail to provide access to health care and other social necessities. In their study they found that "The United States has the lowest life expectancy, the highest in-fant mortality rates, and the highest overall and child poverty rates of all the nations studied." They attribute all of these facts to "the high degree of economic inequality and unequal access to health care in the United States."[22]

Differences in Income. Another way to approach poverty is to con-sider income across the total population. Table One compares median income for the year 2005 with the previous year. *Income, Poverty, and Health Insurance Coverage in the United States: 2005* states that while the real median household income for 2005 was $46,326, there were signifi-cant differences among the races. A comparison of household income by race shows that black households had the lowest median income, $30,858, and Asian households the highest median income, $61,094. In terms of households, married couples had the highest median income, $66,067, while a female householder with no husband present had the lowest, $30,650.

Table 1: Income and Earnings Comparing 2004 and 2005[23]

Characteristic	2004 (Number, in thousands)	Median Income (Dollars, Estimate)	2005 (Number, in thousands)	Median Income (Dollars, Estimate)	Percentage Change in real median income (Estimate)
Type of Household					
Married couple	57,975	65,946	58,175	66,067	0.2
Female householder, no husband present	13,981	30,823	14,093	30,650	-0.6
Male householder, no wife present	4,901	46,526	5,130	46,756	0.5
Non-family household: Female householder	19,942	22,594	20,230	22,688	0.4
Non-family household: Male householder	16,543	33,083	16,753	34,048	2.9
Race and Hispanic Origin of Householder					
White	92,880	48,218	93,588	48,554	0.7
Black	13,809	31,101	14,002	30,858	-0.8
Asian	4,123	59,427	4,273	61,094	2.8
Hispanic	12,178	35,417	12,519	35,967	1.99
Shares of Household Income Quintiles					
Lowest quintile	22,669	3.4	22,877	3.4	-0.8
Second quintile	22,669	8.7	22,877	8.6	-0.7
Third quintile	22,669	14.7	22,877	14.6	-1.0
Fourth quintile	22,669	23.2	22,877	23.0	-1.6
Highest quintile	22,669	50.1	22,877	50.4	1.2
Earnings of Full-Time, Year-Round Workers					
Men with earnings	60,088	42,160	61,500	41,386	-1.8
Women with earnings	42,380	32,285	43,351	31,858	-1.3

Source: U.S. Census Bureau, Current Population Survey,
2005 and 2006 Annual Social and Economic Supplements

In addition to the differences in earnings by race and by the makeup of the family, Table 1 also compares the shares of household income across the population by dividing the total population into quintiles. Only the highest quintile with 50.4 percent of all the earnings had an increase in earnings, of 1.2 percent, for 2005. The lowest quintile, with 3.4 percent of all the earnings, had the lowest overall earnings for 2005, a decrease of .8 percent from the previous year. In terms of actual earnings, the U.S. Census states that "households in the lowest quintile had incomes of $19,178 or less in 2005. Households in the combined middle three (quintiles) had incomes from $19,179 to $91,705, and households in the highest quintile had incomes above $91.705."[24] If all earnings for 2005 were represented as a pie, the top quintile with the highest earnings would take more than half of the pie; the next highest quintile would take almost one-fourth; while the three remaining quintiles all together would only get a little more than one-fourth of the pie. The data in Table 1 show that the groups with the highest earned income include whites, Asians, males, and those living in a married-couple household. Blacks and Hispanics, females, and those living in a female-headed household have the lowest earned income and as a result are in the least favored positions.

Family Income. A family's income determines their economic well-being. This income pays for immediate needs, such as rent for housing, food, clothing, child care, and transportation, as well as long-term needs, such as a house mortgage, education, and health care. Since 2000, wages have not grown for middle- and lower-income workers, despite the fact that worker productivity has increased. The real median income for families declined 3 percent, about $1600, from 1999 to 2004. Between 2004 and 2005, the U.S. Census reported, the real median earnings of both men and women working full time, year-round declined; men earned $41,386 and women $31,858.[25]

Mishel, et al., have analyzed family income as recorded in the overall income scale. The richest families experienced the greatest income growth between 1979 and 2000. In those years, the authors note, "the real income of households in the lowest fifth grew 6.1 percent; the middle fifth was up 12.3 percent; the top fifth grew 69.6 percent; and the average income of those in the top 1 percent grew by 183.7 percent." Some factors that increased the wealth of those in the upper income scale include laws that lowered the tax burden on the rich and the enormous increase in capital income flowing from corporate profits. "Whereas the top 1 percent received 37.8 percent of all capital income in 1979, their share rose to 49.1 percent by 2000 and rose further to 57.5 percent in 2003." In their estimate, middle-income families maintained their income because wives entered the work force and worked over 500 hours each year between 1979 and 2000. This added to women's economic independence, but also was a strain in terms of balancing work and family.[26]

Income Disparity. Income disparity leads to a larger topic, the distribution of wealth. In a study of the persistence of poverty in the United States, Mangum, et al., explore both the distribution of income and wealth. Their analysis reveals that from 1947 to 1999 the bottom 60 percent of the population experienced a steady decline in income share. The top fifth of the population, and especially the top 5 percent, while experiencing slight declines through the mid-1970s, rebounded and had a lion's share of income by 1999.

Because income distribution favors those with the greatest income and puts the middle and lower classes at a disadvantage, it is also important to consider the distribution of wealth. A family's net worth equals the difference between the sum of their assets, such as savings, retirement funds, the value of their home, minus their liabilities, including debts for mortgage, credit card debts, and student loans. Their findings reveal that the distribution of wealth is even more inequitable than income distribution. The top 1 percent of households had over 33 percent of the wealth in 1983, and by 1998, over 38 percent of the total wealth of the United States. At the opposite end of the spectrum, the second fifth from the bottom had less than 1 percent of the wealth, and the bottom fifth registered as negative when measuring assets. This fact shows the reality of the life of the poor. The vast majority of the poor lacks resources and has nothing upon which to draw in times of social or economic crisis. One exception is the elderly poor who own their own home and who could use a reverse mortgage to insure a steady income for paying off debts. Renters, of course, cannot avail themselves of such an action.[27]

STUDIES ON THE EFFECTS OF POVERTY

In addition to the data and analysis of poverty by the U.S. Census, social scientists have researched poverty. These studies reveal the factors that contribute to poverty. Of special interest is the effect of poverty on women and children.

Studies on the history and administration of Aid to Families with Dependent Children (AFDC) discuss the benefits and limitations of this program. For instance, one study noted that the United States welfare system began in the mid-1930s as emergency aid for destitute families, and that for the sixty years prior to 1996, AFDC was a major part of this system, functioning as a cash assistance program for the poor. It assisted children whose parents could not support them financially. By 1992, 13.6 million individuals, including 9.2 million children, were receiving AFDC nationwide.[28] The percentage of the U.S. population that received benefits was relatively low, only about 5 percent, and this remained fairly constant in the years 1970–1992. Children were the primary recipients, with 14 percent of the nation's children receiving benefits in 1992. Despite an outlay of billions of dollars, one-third of children who lived below the poverty level actually received no help from AFDC in 1992. While AFDC was a federally mandated program, some states set income eligibility levels so low that many families did not qualify for, and therefore could not receive, needed cash assistance.

Women and Poverty. In terms of income, women are more likely to earn less income and to live in poverty. This results from a number of factors. In the first instance, women earn less than men for comparable work. While the rate of compensation has increased, the U.S. Census reported that in 2005 women earned 77 percent of what men earned for full time, year-round work. As can be seen in Figure 2, the median

Figure 2

Female-to-Male Earnings Ratio and Median Earnings of Full Time, Year-Round [29] Workers 15 Years and Older by Sex: 1960 to 2005

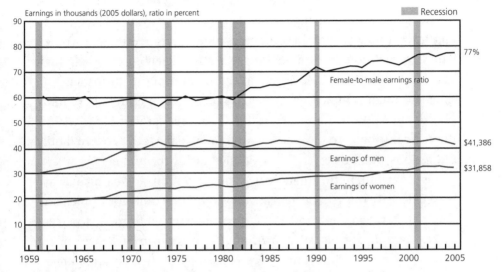

Note: The data points are placed at the midpoints of the respective years. Data earnings of full time, year-round workers are not readily available before 1960.

Source: U.S. Census Bureau, Current Population Survey, 1961 to 2005 Annual Social and Economic Supplements.

earnings of men were $41,386, while median earnings for women were $31,858, a difference of $9,528 for this one year.[30] Since this figure is a median, some women suffered even greater loss of income. Consider how such discrepancies add up over five, ten, or twenty years. Earnings are the primary source of income that a person uses to provide for the necessities of life. While men and women have similar dreams and plans for a good life, a lower income limits the aspirations of all women and their dependents. A woman's yearly income is affected, as well as her contributions to Individual Retirement Accounts (IRAs), and especially future benefits from Social Security and pensions. On the average, women live longer than men, so lower wages endanger their older years. Most women have to work many more years before they can retire or they will risk living in poverty at an advanced age when they are more vulnerable.

Women are also more likely to be the caregivers in the family. When a child or parent is ill or needs extended care, women often assume the duties of caring for the child or parent at home or overseeing care in the hospital and/or nursing facility. This can cause women caregivers to take leave from work and in some cases to resign from their job. Women who become mothers at a young age are less likely to complete high school or college, thus adversely affecting job options over their life-time. A woman's employment, then, is more often interrupted by family obligations and this has a major impact on her earning capacity. This directly contributes to the emotional strain of being torn between family obligations and the necessity of working outside the home.

It is also worth noting that divorce and separation, and ethnicity, have played decisive roles in the increase in poverty, especially for women and children. Between 1940 and 1960, divorce increased from 29.1 percent to 71.3 percent for blacks, and from 27.2 percent to 36.8 percent for whites.[31] In most cases women receive custody of their children after a divorce or separation, and their family income decreases substantially. Not until the 1980s were the laws made more responsive to enforcing child support. A small percentage of men are so poor that they are un-able to contribute to child support. A larger percentage of men remarry after divorce, with the result that it is often difficult for the father to con-tribute to the support of children from his former marriage. Beginning in California in the 1960s and spreading to other states, divorce reform shifted to strict equality in division of assets, with no provision made for the life conditions of family members. This represented a change from retributive justice, in which the guilty party paid, to distributive justice, entailing an equal sharing and division of assets between the husband and wife.[32] Race is another decisive factor. William Julius Wilson notes that "high rates of unemployment, homicide, and incarceration among young black men in underclass communities so substantially reduce the possibility of young women marrying employed men that female-headed households comprise up to 97 percent of some communities."[33] Thus, divorce and single parenthood effectively impoverish women and children.

Children and Poverty. A study by Betson and Michael on why children are poor makes distinctions that are helpful for understanding the extent of poverty for adults and children. An adult could be self-sufficient, but not family-sufficient, meaning that he or she lacked the resources to keep his or her family out of poverty.[34] Adults are considered self-sufficient when they have enough resources to maintain only themselves above the poverty threshold. Some adults do not even attain this level of sufficiency. In some cases, adults in families with children are so poor that they are able to survive only because they had children who received government welfare payments.

This study also shows how lack of education and earning capacity are two factors that contribute to poverty. Adults with less than or only a high school education have decreased earning power compared with those who have attended college, earned a bachelor's degree or an advanced degree. Those with less education are more likely to be affected negatively when there are economic downturns. Globalization has contributed to a loss of manufacturing jobs as companies move factories to countries that have cheaper labor and less restrictive laws. Technology has advanced to such a degree that information jobs are regularly outsourced to other countries. In its quest for profit, businesses are more apt to use temporary workers who do not get benefits such as health insurance and pensions. This in turn limits the income of American workers.

The causes of child poverty were studied in a particular year (1992) and then compared over a period of years (1979–1995) through a series of longitudinal studies (research in which the same subjects are observed repeatedly over a long period of time).[35] The study reported that in 1992 21.9 percent of children were poor; 9.8 percent of the children were poor because they lived with adults who lacked adult self-sufficiency; 4.6 percent of the children lived with adults who were personally self-sufficient, but not family-sufficient because they lacked the funds to support their children; and 7.5 percent were poor because of the demographic structure of their household. In terms of demographic structure, 55.7 percent of poor families with children had one adult. Poor families had a high divorce rate and a high rate of nonmarital births; poor families also had a higher number of children per family (an average of 2.24).

When income and poverty rates are compared from 1979 through 1995, the data show that poverty increased dramatically for children beginning in 1979. By 1983, the child poverty rate had reached 22 percent. Even when income increased by 16 percent from 1983 to 1989, the child poverty rate was still 20 percent. When there was a recession in the early 1990s, family income fell and the child poverty rate rose to 21 percent.[36]

The factors related to adult poverty include a lack of education, economic inequality, and an increase in female-headed families due to divorce, separation, and single parenthood. Children's poverty is also linked to an increase in ethnic and racial diversity. By 1990, two million of the 13 million poor children in the United States were foreign-born or born to immigrants.[37] The number of immigrants to the United States has spiraled as economic conditions in neighboring nations worsened. As a result, millions of migrants are working illegally in the United States so they can support their family here and send money to relatives in their country of origin. The American-born children of immigrant families are American citizens, but they are at risk because their undocumented worker-parents can be and often are forcibly removed from their work site, and families are sometimes divided by the detention and deportation of one or both parents.

Duration of Poverty. Longitudinal studies provide insight into the duration and dynamics of childhood poverty. A fifteen-year study of the economic circumstances of 1000 children between the ages of one and four found in 1968 that one-third of the children had spent at least one year in poverty. Two-thirds of the children had spent fewer than five years in poverty. For a small group—"five percent of all children and 15 percent of children who ever became poor—childhood poverty lasted ten years or more." Those who suffered long-term poverty experienced poverty continuously throughout their childhood or they were in and out of poverty on a regular basis. Long-term poor children were more likely to experience severe poverty, namely, living in a family whose average income was about half the income at the poverty threshold. Children in long-term poverty were more likely to live with a single parent throughout their childhood, have parents who were disabled, and live in the South or in rural areas.[38]

Consequences of Poverty for Children. Brooks-Gunn and Duncan did a survey of studies that establish the relationship between family income and child outcomes.[39] When a family's income is so low that it cannot supply basic needs of food, clothing, and shelter, the family is in poverty. The findings show the effects on children's physical health, cognitive abilities, school achievement, and emotional and behavioral characteristics. The studies also show that poor children experience diminished physical health as measured by a variety of factors. Low birth weight is a critical factor. Infants born with a low birth weight (2500 grams or less) were at greater risk of dying by the end of their first year of life. Those who survived were more likely to have serious physical disabilities, and as they grew often had learning disabilities, displayed lower levels of intelligence, and poorer achievement in mathematics and reading. The studies revealed that these negative birth effects were more prevalent among poor women, especially unmarried women, women with low levels of education, and black mothers.

Poverty appears to be the primary cause of health problems for children of all races. Children born to white women whose family incomes were below the federal poverty level in the year they gave birth had an 80 percent probability of having a low birth-weight baby. This was not the case for women whose family incomes were above the poverty level.

Poverty is a cause of poor nutrition for children. When nutrition is compromised, especially over a period of years living in poverty, children suffer from stunting, subnormal height for one's age. The environment in poor neighborhoods can expose young people to chemicals when their bodies and brains are developing and are especially vulnerable to their harmful effects. Children exposed to lead, for example, suffer serious health problems. Prior to birth and as infants and toddlers, poor children are likely to live in housing where lead-based paint, lead dust, and paint chips can be ingested or inhaled. Exposure to lead results in serious health risks such as stunted growth, hearing loss, and toxic effects on the kidneys.

In terms of cognitive abilities, children living below the poverty threshold are more likely to have learning disabilities, experience developmental delays, and are at greater risk of scoring lower on tests measuring cognitive ability, which is done by standardized tests for IQ, verbal ability, and achievement. Beginning at the age of two and continuing through the age of eight, children living in poor families scored lower on these tests as compared with children in higher-income families.

School achievement outcomes—completing grades and graduating—do not depend totally on the economic condition of the family. Once children enter school, there are factors other than the family that affect them, especially the school and the neighborhood. Achievement in school also depends on ability and behavior. Early childhood intervention is essential. A recent study found that an increase in family income from birth to age five insured that children would complete at least one more year of school.

Several studies have established the connection between poverty and emotional and behavioral problems. Emotional problems are evident in external behavior, including aggression, acting out, and fighting, and in internal behavior such as anxiety, social withdrawal, and depression. One study of low-weight five year olds showed that children from poor families exhibited more internal and external behavior problems than children who were never poor. Those who experienced long-term poverty, living below the poverty threshold for four consecutive years, had more problems than those who lived in short-term poverty, being poor for only one year. Two other studies of children 4 to 8 years old revealed that persistent poverty was related to internal symptoms, including dependence, anxiety, and unhappiness, while those experiencing current poverty exhibited more external behavior such as hyperactivity and headstrong behavior. Another study of children ages 3 to 11 confirmed that those who experienced one year of poverty had more behavioral problems than children who lived in long-term poverty. In many ways children are like barometers: In the early stages of income deprivation their behavior signals a malfunction, an intuitive reaction to family instability. As poverty persists or deepens, negative factors are internalized and the result is anxiety and unhappiness. For adolescents, it is not clear if there is a link between poverty and emotional problems. It appears that younger children are more affected by poverty and that adolescents are simply less willing to share their feelings with researchers.

Parents who are poor are less likely to be healthy, physically and emotionally. When parents become irritable or depressed, there is a greater chance of conflicts in their interactions with their children, especially adolescents. Such interactions have a negative effect on emotional, social, and cognitive development. When parents' health is poor or they suffer emotionally, their income can be adversely affected and their interactions with their children are also impacted negatively. In homes where adults suffer, the atmosphere is tainted to such an extent that children experience less emotional warmth, a higher level of stress, and decreased ability to learn and study.

Poverty is often reflected in the neighborhood. Poor people are limited in their choice of where they can live. Affordable housing is often out of reach in all but poorer neighborhoods. A poor neighborhood has homes or apartments that are often run-down, lack security, and have few or no services or maintenance. When problems such as lack of heat, holes in the walls, rodent infestation, peeling paint, and broken appliances arise, poor families are at the mercy of intolerable conditions. The neighborhood may reflect the socio-economic status of the residents: many unemployed adults and young people who have dropped out of school, stores that charge higher prices and offer fewer choices, and limited resources for children in terms of parks, playgrounds, libraries, child care and health care facilities. When young people drop out of school and cannot find work, they often gravitate to gangs for a sense of community and protection from violence. Poorer neighborhoods can be unsafe because of crime. They can also become a dumping ground for garbage and waste, some of which emit harmful chemicals that contribute to health problems, for example, asthma and lead poisoning.

Children's Views of Poverty. Jonathan Kozol, noted educator and author, has captured how poverty affects children. He researched schools in thirty communities between 1988 and 1990, observing and listening to the students and teachers. He recorded how children and their families suffer in schools that are underfunded and in need of extensive repairs; he also noted the impact of their neighborhoods and the poor quality of health care. In cities like New York there were schools for those with good incomes and for the gifted, and other schools in the ghetto for those who were poor. He was critical of how children living in the ghetto had to attend schools in need of repair, with teachers who were often not qualified. The schools were so overcrowded that some children had no desks, textbooks were outdated, and routinely there were not enough books for all the children. In effect, the United States has public schools, but they are separate and unequal. As Kozol wrote, "Equality of educational opportunity throughout the nation" is for many "more a myth than a reality."[40]

As a result of spending several years in the 1990s (1991–1993, 1997–1999) in Mott Haven, located in the South Bronx, one of the poorest neighborhoods in the nation, Kozol focused attention on what it is to live in poverty. Like many other poor neighborhoods, Mott Haven had become a dumping ground. For many years a medical waste incinerator spewed toxic substances into the air. Children and adults suffered from asthma and other respiratory diseases. Activists took steps to organize, but it took years before they were finally able to get the facility closed in 1998. The houses in Mott Haven, two-thirds of which were owned by the City of New York, were run down; many were freezing cold in the winter and hot and humid in the summer, with roaches crawling over every surface and rats popping out of holes. Kozol recorded one incident when rats climbed into the crib and attacked a seven-month-old boy.[41]

Homeless people were routinely relocated to this area, an area that had drug-infested buildings, overcrowded and understaffed hospitals and schools, and police who often failed to respond to calls for help. Health problems included asthma due to the highly polluted air, depression, and anxiety. Fear was a constant companion because gunshots rang out on a regular basis. Children described their neighborhood as "locked down." Adolescents felt that other people wanted them to re-main hidden and that they had been denied the power to decide.[42] What was the problem? They were poor and they were people of color. Poverty and racism were the factors that contributed to the ghetto existence of so many people.

In 2006, Jonathan Kozol was awarded the Puffin/Nation Prize for Creative Citizenship for "distinctive, courageous, imaginative, socially responsible work." He took this opportunity to turn people's attention to children—their suffering and their potential. When cities and schools are separated by race and income, children suffer the most. When public officials neglect their constituencies, children suffer the most. Children are open to the world; they are the future. Kozol believes that "the world would be a better place if black children and white children got to know one another early in life, when they are most open to learning from one another and their surroundings."[43] When children from all socio-eco-nomic levels become fellow learners, society will be enriched.

THE UNITED STATES RESPONSE TO POVERTY

In trying to understand how so many people in an affluent society like the United States could be poor, it is helpful to review how the United States has responded to poverty throughout its history. Since its earli-est days, there have been both private charities and government-funded welfare programs in the United States to try to alleviate poverty.

In the early days of European colonization the settlers' response to poverty reflected their experience and background. Many colonies drew upon the provisions of the Elizabethan Poor Law of 1601. Relief for the poor was administered and financed locally; it included, as John Iceland wrote, "direct aid to the unemployable, a policy of apprenticeship for the young, and work relief for able-bodied adults." Survival in the colo-nies depended on intensive labor devoted to clearing land, planting and cultivating crops, building homes, trading, and establishing businesses. Idleness was not just a disagreeable trait but also a threat to the life and well-being of other colonists. As a result, punishment was harsh for those who refused to work. "Vagrants refusing work could be committed to a house of correction, whipped, branded, put in pillories and stoned, or evicted from the community."[44] The colonies placed limits on who would receive help. Nonresident vagrants and strangers were effectively excluded from the community. Generally, the colonists would help only needy community members, with the expectation that those who were unable to work due to an illness or injury would return to work when they recovered.

Colonists were more willing to help children and the elderly who were poor. They considered their neediness to be more a product of unfortunate circumstances resulting from injury or the untimely death of a provider, and therefore judged them to be more deserving of charity. Because able-bodied persons were expected to work, the community labeled those who refused to work as undeserving of support. It was common for colonists to believe that an individual's misbehavior caused poverty.

By the nineteenth century the mechanization of agriculture and the production of goods resulted in rapid growth, industrialization, and urbanization. As a result, more laborers such as craftsmen, farmers, and the unskilled had to travel far and wide to find work. Those who sought relief or assistance when they were unable to find work were labeled as paupers, the undeserving poor. In fact, paupers bore a double burden: a lack of opportunities to earn a living by which they could support themselves and their families, and the added stigma of being labeled "dependent, defective, and delinquent."[45]

The Puritan ethos preached a "gospel of self-help" with an emphasis on personal responsibility. The early colonial settlers had a genuine desire to "relieve the misery of their less fortunate neighbors," but they were also reluctant to be overly generous lest it result in "socially destructive consequences."[46] In very real terms, the American ideal of equality of opportunity clashed with the reality of inequality of outcome. People were critical of poor, displaced workers and were quick to call them "lazy" and "degenerate."

In the eighteenth and nineteenth centuries the local community and state responded to poverty with various forms of "relief." These included "indoor relief" and "outdoor relief." Indoor relief for poverty began in the 1820s and continued until the 1930s. It was administered through institutions that included "almshouses, workhouses, orphanages, and mental hospitals," whose primary purpose was moral, namely, to "reform, rehabilitate, and morally educate the poor." These institutions had mixed results. Funded by the states but administered at the county level, they offered a dismal alternative for the poor. Eventually they lost popular support as the public learned that many poor houses were "places of degradation, disease, and near starvation." Outdoor relief allowed widows and families to live at home. This aid was administered through societies such as the African-American mutual aid societies in Philadelphia that used funds collected from their members to distribute money, clothing, and food to those in need.[47]

From 1860 until 1929, private agencies assumed responsibility for outdoor relief. Private charity was viewed as more reliable because it was "less vulnerable to corruption." One notable state program was the Widow's Pension. This provided cash assistance to women whose husbands had died in the war and it allowed widows to care for their children. Then efforts to counter poverty through outdoor relief reached a breaking point when the Great Depression overwhelmed individual charity and government resources. To remedy this situation, President Franklin D. Roosevelt's New Deal introduced the Social Security Act of 1935. This legislation had a two-tiered approach. It "protected workers from poverty caused by old age or disability, and protected children and widows from poverty caused by the death of a breadwinner."[48]

Aid to Dependent Children (1935). Aid to Dependent Children (ADC), signed into law by President Franklin D. Roosevelt on August 14, 1935, provided cash assistance "to families with fathers who were deceased, absent or unable to work." Later changed to Aid to Families with Dependent Children (AFDC), it then included aid for parents. This law was in effect until the 1960s. In 1964, President Lyndon Johnson declared a "War on Poverty." This was a comprehensive assault on poverty and it coincided with civil rights legislation that removed barriers to political participation, employment, and housing for African-Americans. The War on Poverty introduced programs to reduce poverty, hunger, and malnutrition, and to increase access to health care. The results were dramatic. Between 1964 and 1974, the percentage of people in the United States living in poverty dropped 60 percent. Between 1965 and 1972 there was a 33 percent drop in the infant mortality rate.[49] This was due in large part to Medicare and Medicaid, which provided access to health care for the poor. In addition, there were food stamps, housing assistance, and nutritional supplement programs. Also in the 1965 to 1972 time frame, amendments to the Social Security Act introduced the first work incentives for welfare mothers.[50] In 1967, the Work Incentive Program (WIN) "required states to establish employment and training programs for welfare recipients." Originally a voluntary program, WIN was expanded by the federal government and made mandatory for welfare recipients except where home responsibilities, namely, caring for preschool-age children, precluded participation. In the 1980s, there were cutbacks in welfare benefits. In 1988, Congress passed the Family Support Act (FSA), requiring states to operate the Job Opportunities Basic Skills (JOBS) training programs.[51]

Welfare reform stirred up considerable debate. Some working people whose taxes supported welfare recipients were critical of those who were not working outside the home and who had young children. It seemed like a free ride, especially since so many middle-class mothers had returned to full time employment after their own children's birth. Most American families relied on two incomes, and in some cases, one or both parents working more than one job to pay the rent or mortgage and provide the necessities of food, clothing, utilities, and health care. Many were critical of the lifestyle and immoral practices of welfare recipients. A common conviction held that welfare contributed to the increase of out-of-wedlock births. Meanwhile, Congress was considering the increased cost of welfare at a time when the economy was expanding. Lawmakers proposed to hardworking taxpayers that welfare recipients should be working.

The debate had deep, historical roots. It was, in effect, a continuation of the discussion begun in colonial times about the deserving poor and the undeserving poor. There has always been the suspicion that the poor did not deserve help; they needed to be prodded out of laziness and required to work for a living. Suspicions about the poor have been compounded by the American myth of rugged individualism. For many Americans, the socially accepted and honorable way to act is for everyone to "pull themselves up by their bootstraps" and do what is necessary to survive.

In his article on American attitudes toward the poor, H. Hugh Heclo notes that federal welfare reform occurred during the longest period of economic expansion in U.S. history. As the economy grew, policy makers had greater incentives to encourage women on welfare to join the work force. By 1994, the percentage of married mothers with young children who worked outside the home had risen to 60 percent from 10 percent in 1949. Public opinion was definitely in favor of poor women working.[52]

Heclo's research confirms that Americans remain ambivalent about helping the poor. While children are seen as needy and deserving, they are most often associated with adults whose neediness is less palatable. Americans expect adults to work and be self-sufficient. With declining trust in public institutions, especially the federal government, U.S. citizens still support programs of a more pragmatic nature, those upholding values of personal responsibility, such as parents' duties toward their children, and a belief that all should have the opportunity to achieve the American Dream through programs that encouraged job assistance.

U.S. Welfare Reform (1996). In 1996, President Bill Clinton signed into law the Personal Responsibility and Work Opportunity Reconciliation Act (PRWORA). This reform was forged in the public arena. Experts testified and bore witness to vastly different approaches to understanding the causes of poverty and to enacting anti-poverty public policy. Those who adopted the "individual behavior" perspective concentrated on behavioral causes, namely, "a low work ethic, apathy toward education, illegitimacy, and lack of self-control." In short, they tended to blame the poor for their poverty. Those who held the "structural" perspective viewed poverty as the result of social and economic forces. From this perspective, poverty is a national problem that requires national solutions. These include: "basic education, career development, health care, and child care resources for poor families. Some also called for...initiatives that improve wages and benefits."[53] While PRWORA incorporated dimensions of both the individual behavior and the structural perspectives, there was greater emphasis on reforming individual behavior.

PRWORA replaced the federal-state cash assistance of AFDC with Temporary Assistance for Needy Families (TANF). States received funds in a block grant that was to be used for the following purposes: 1) assisting needy families so children could be cared for in their own homes or in the homes of relatives; 2) promoting job preparation, work, and marriage with the aim of ending dependence of adults on government benefits; 3) reducing the number of out-of-wedlock pregnancies and establishing annual numerical goals for preventing and reducing these pregnancies: 4) encouraging the formation and maintenance of two-parent families.[54]

In its implementation PRWORA has instituted a rigorous and more complicated process for helping poor people. This is borne out by the following facts:

- The Block Grant shifted major responsibility from the federal to the state and local governments. Proponents hold that this allows greater flexibility. On the other hand, critics argue that there is less uniformity in available aid, that local governments have found the reporting procedures confusing, and that persons in need find it more difficult to complete the forms and follow the new, complex procedures.

- There is a maximum lifetime limit of five years for federal funds. States do have the option of offering aid after that time limit, but this would be at state expense. Word spread about the five-year limit, and needy people left welfare, but the high numbers of people living at or below the poverty threshold show that there are millions of needy persons without adequate means of support.

- TANF recipients must participate in a "work-related activity" leading to full-time employment. This sometimes causes difficulties for families. Many recipients have young children and this provision forces them to surrender their children to another's care; there is not adequate, affordable child care available; and attending college does not qualify as job training. Thus, one effect of the so-called reform was that women who were enrolled in college had to leave prematurely before completing their degree, adversely affecting future job prospects.

- This law decreased federal funding for the Food Stamp Program. It also changed eligibility requirements, making it more difficult for many persons to qualify. One example was restricting "benefits for unemployed able-bodied adults without dependents" by limiting the time they could receive food stamps to a total of three months every three years. "Previously, every person had a right to food stamps if their income and resources were low enough." As a result of the 1996 legislation, more poor people lacked nourishing food.

- A majority of non-citizen legal immigrants became ineligible for federal programs, such as food stamps and Supplemental Security Income (SSI), which is financial aid for the disabled and elderly. Even when Congress restored some benefits in 1998, federal benefits are routinely denied to a majority of those who lost eligibility in 1996.

- While the government has strengthened the law for collecting child support from the absent parent, there is a provision that seems punitive, for it uses a stricter definition of childhood disability to reduce the numbers of children who could qualify for disability aid.

- There were strong financial incentives for states to promote marriage, specifically two-parent families, and to reduce out-of-wedlock pregnancies. Federal funds could also be used for family planning and for abstinence education. Abortion was not to be promoted.[55]

Federal and state officials watched with great interest to see the effects of the 1996 welfare reform act. The employment rate for single mothers increased to 72 percent, up from 60 percent in 1994. However, many who left welfare had low-wage jobs. They may have left welfare, but poverty was their companion even as they complied with society's demands to work outside the home. For others, "a significant group of very disadvantaged women with few skills who had difficulty finding work or remaining employed and who suffered from poor physical and mental health,"[56] the situation became more desperate. Reducing dependency is not the magic bullet for reducing poverty.

Despite efforts to increase funding for job training and child care, both of which are essential for single parent householders, TANF was recently reauthorized at 1996 levels. Welfare reform is competing with issues of security: the Homeland Security Act first enacted in 2001, the War on Terrorism, the invasion (March 2003) and subsequent occupation of Iraq, as well as military encounters in Afghanistan. Tax reform, with tax cuts for the wealthiest Americans and large corporations, has added to a burgeoning deficit. The spiraling deficit combined with a widespread reluctance to fund social service programs will undermine the common good and short-circuit efforts to help the poor. These policies are effectively preventing the poor from having a place at the table and preventing them from participating in the forums of social discourse, at which decisions are being made about social priorities, and where the allocation of social resources and genuine community among persons is forged.

Meanwhile, there are advocates calling for the creation of a poverty-fighting system. They propose raising the federal minimum wage to insure that a full time, year-round worker's earnings would be above the poverty line. They call for creating living-wage jobs with benefits and suggest that health care should be guaranteed for all families. Advocates of poverty-fighting also encourage creating "a children's allowance and a caregiver's allowance (refundable tax credits for those caring for children or others—including elderly parents)."[57]

MODELS FOR RESPONDING TO POVERTY

Welfare-to-work, as the Personal Responsibility and Work Opportunity Reconciliation Act is commonly called, relies on the market economy to solve the ills of poverty. This is one more example of policies adopted by the United States that "reflect both its market economic orientation and its individualistic social bent."[58] In welfare-to-work the emphasis is on producing good workers. Individuals are free to promote their own welfare as they promote economic growth. The reasoning is that those whose income ranks at the top quintile of American society have benefited from equality of opportunity, so surely those in the bottom quintile will also benefit from full-time employment. However, there is a huge difference between the benefits access to savings and investments that those in the top quintile enjoy, as compared with the benefits gained through low-wage employment and lost by those giving up access to health care through Medicaid as they take on jobs that offer very few if any medical, retirement, and other benefits.

The first contemporary anti-poverty efforts with a market orientation were the 1980s programs that encouraged welfare recipients to seek employment. In the 1990s a market model was used to guide the dismantling of the federal administration of welfare. Then, through the implementation guidelines attached to federal block grants to states, a market model became the dominant approach in local anti-poverty programs throughout the country. Moreover, block grants placed the states in direct competition with one another so they would reduce the welfare rolls, move welfare recipients into the work force, decrease out-of-wedlock childbearing, and decrease single parenthood by encouraging marriage. Transforming the "culture of poverty" and reducing dependency certainly appeared to be a goal soon to be achieved when "The nation's welfare caseload plummeted from 5 million families in 1994 to 2.2 million in June 2000." In terms of benefits for children, "In 1994, 62 percent of poor children received cash welfare; by 1998, the share had fallen to 43 percent."[59] Ending welfare as we knew it, as President Clinton had advocated, seemed to be yet another market success.

Michael Katz explains how "market logic" favors private agencies for distribution of benefits and competition among providers as the optimal way to improve service. He notes that according to market logic, authority for providing benefits should rest with state and local authorities because they can recognize and respond more quickly to changes in local markets. Benefits are to be earned by individuals competing for work in the job market. Thus, the burden of achieving economic security rests with "individuals taking charge of their lives." Katz raises questions about the efficacy of market models in resolving poverty: "Whom do market-based policies really serve? What are the forms of capital and who controls them? Who participates in the exchange, and who suffers?"[60] Reliance on a market model, Katz asserts, has so entangled receiving benefits with employment that it has effectively "stratified Americans into first- and second-class citizens and undermined the effective practice of democracy." Reliance on the market has effectively "superseded social justice."[61] He bases this evaluation on the fact that when democracy is portrayed as a consumer choice, then those who are poor and severely limited in their choices by reason of poverty are effectively excluded from participating fully in democracy.

Critics of the Market Model. Judith Goode and Jeff Maskovsky (2001) have edited a collection of essays on poverty in the United States that give insightful critiques of the market model. In their introduction the editors state that the authors' perspective is to view poverty as a "political, economic, and ideological effect of capitalist processes and state activity." They identify the "new poverty" as resulting from "three interconnected processes—*economic polarization, political demobilization,* and *market triumphalism,*" all of which they regard as contributing to "the growing social and political disorder affecting the poor."[62] They define economic polarization as the widening gap between the rich and poor.

Since the 1970s, U.S. policies have become increasingly pro-business, favoring the private sector over the public sector. Corporate leaders launched ideological assaults on unions, and union membership diminished drastically in the latter part of the twentieth century. In an effort to lower labor costs, corporations downsized firms, relocated to low-wage, non-union areas, first the south and southwest of the United States, and then overseas. Corporations subcontracted work and created part-time jobs. All of these well-planned actions resulted in the decline of low-skill and semi-skilled jobs.

Social problems formerly addressed by the government were labeled as criminal matters. As welfare and social services decreased, the prison industry increased. The welfare state was moving to a law-and-order state where the state's role was to "regulate the poor through surveillance and incarceration, not through supportive services."[63] One very real example of the criminalization of the poor was the Rockefeller Drug Laws (1973) that waged war on drug abuse by mandating draconian sentencing on those involved in possessing or selling even small quantities of controlled substances. This is one example of criminalizing the poor, especially people of color and women, who have been sentenced to years of prison far beyond penalties for violent felonies. As a result, the prison population expanded enormously. Families have been disrupted and children abandoned by a parent guilty of a non-violent offense.

Political demobilization is a dedicated process of protecting the benefits of those who have succeeded as a result of the market economy by vilifying those who have not succeeded. In other words, it blames the poor for their misery and misfortune. The undeserving poor are even portrayed as a moral threat to the middle class. The deserving poor, on the other hand, are those who respond to market-based models. The goal is to re-educate the poor, using the rules of the market with the purpose of eliminating dependency. "The deserving poor are now those who embrace the spirit of entrepreneurship, voluntarism, consumerism, and self-help." The undeserving poor, on the other hand, "remain dependent on the state."[64]

Market triumphalism is linked to neo-liberalism, whose main tenet is that the primary function of good government is the promotion of a free market. Neo-liberals are proponents of unhindered competition and unregulated markets. Also, based on neo-liberal doctrines, the private sector assumed functions formerly performed by the state; for example, private firms have taken over public health and the welfare systems. As a result, the poor are disempowered, since they have no contact with the state and no recourse when private companies put profit ahead of service. When government has abdicated its role and responsibility for the poor, there is no reasonable way to resolve tensions that arise among communities. In fact, the poor are increasingly marginalized and in some cases, erased from memory.

The research presented in Goode and Maskovsky reveals how current economic and state policies that are built on market-based models "create new boundaries and tensions between the poor and other groups."[65] For example, Frances Fox Piven's essay explains the effects of cuts in welfare on the labor market. She points out that wages for low-skilled workers have decreased since the 1980s, and that with the advent of large numbers of welfare recipients into the job market, wages decreased even further as the poor were made to compete for low-wage jobs.[66] Government policies offered financial incentives, such as tax deductions and direct subsidies to employers, to hire welfare recipients. Employers effectively had enormous power over these employees: If workers failed to comply with employers' rules and regulations, they faced sanctions, such as a reduction or loss of benefits. The market model directly affects the well-being of welfare recipients, making them more materially vulnerable.

Robert Asen considers the market as "a misguided metaphor for political institutions and interpersonal relations." He begins by pointing out that the market seeks profits. He notes that privatization preempts government because it transfers government functions and responsibilities to "private agents and market forces." In a market model, citizens are considered consumers. The far-reaching effects of this model are evident when "a consumer orientation transfigures public interest into consumer desire and social goods into available products." In the final analysis, "a market model undermines the legitimacy of public intervention into pressing social problems and reduces interpersonal relations to purchasing decisions."[67]

The market ideal offers new approaches and possible benefits for those who are needed by society: healthy, well-educated, motivated, and skilled citizens. Those with problems of an enduring nature need professionals and institutions willing and able to take a long-term perspective to multifaceted problems. The market ideal is limited in what it can offer for eliminating poverty.

A Tilted Table. A review of the data for income and the data on poverty in 2005 reveals that poverty has increased at a steady rate since 2000. Wealth is also growing—for those in the top 1 percent of the highest quintile. U.S. welfare reform with its emphasis on welfare-to-work has resulted in more people working. Yet, those working for minimum wage have little to show for their efforts. With an unrealistically low income and having been denied a viable safety net, the poor have no place at the social table. In fact, the table is tilted away from the poor. The harder they work, the more benefits slide bountifully to the richest members of the population. In this regard, the poor are like children, too little and insignificant even to reach the table, let alone enjoy the munificence the table holds.

In contrast to the market model, John Iceland cites those most concerned with reducing poverty; they hold that government benefits are consistently too low to insure that the poor can escape poverty.[68] These critics offer alternative models for responding to poverty. Michael Harrington, for example, contends that poverty is the result of structural causes and that joblessness is the built-in reality of the American economy. More fully, he argues that a certain level of unemployment encourages competition for jobs and that there are a number of structural factors in society that help to foster and maintain this level of unemployment. The structural factors include economic trends that encourage an unwillingness to sacrifice to benefit the poor, disregard for those who lost jobs as a result of recessions, political and ideological trends that result in underestimating the numbers of people in poverty, the justification of poverty in an officially acceptable number of millions of unemployed people, discontinuation of programs that benefit the poor, and placing business interests before those of workers. Harrington concludes, "The poor are the most sorely tried and dramatic victims of economic and social tendencies." Overcoming poverty is a matter of morality and justice; he holds that "it is intolerable that the richest nation in human history should allow such needless suffering."[69]

There is something intrinsically unfair about a tilted table. While extolling the virtues of hard work, the market ideal has overlooked the need for community. In Robert Asen's words, "Community signifies mutual regard and concern which resist translation into calculations of profit and loss. In their individual and collective visions, a community's members look out for one another." It is precisely this sense of community that builds on "common experiences and interests among all members." Community effectively recognizes "a need for cooperation to attend to the consequences of human actions."[70]

Those who are poor often prove to be hardworking, dedicated workers who share the core values of American culture. They are part of our American community and deserve recognition and proper remuneration for their hard work. Race, sex, age, or class need not isolate those who are working to support themselves and their family. Continuing to disregard the poor is a dangerous option for all Americans because "the increasing economic isolation of poor Americans further jeopardizes a sense of national community."[71] For individuals to thrive, all people need access to community life which guarantees each one's well-being. Individuals' ability to secure the basic necessities of life—adequate food, shelter, education, health care, and so on—will enhance society as a whole. The greater the participation by healthy, motivated persons, the more our society will be able to achieve the American Dream of justice for all.

THE ECOLOGY OF POVERTY

A positive alternative to the market model is presented by David K. Shipler. He suggests that we need to focus on the ecology of poverty, that is, the complex web of interlocking factors that create an environment of poverty within which the poor are separated from the broader society. Shipler's model is based on explorations of the lives of the working poor who believe in the American Dream even when they are far from realizing its benefits. In his work, Shipler introduces us to the working poor whom he interviewed and studied over a five-year period. A majority are unmarried women with children, of all races and national backgrounds. The ecology of poverty affects every aspect of their lives. Living in poverty translates into low pay for menial jobs, lack of job security, substandard health care, substandard housing, and inadequate educational opportunities. Stress factors resulting from living in poverty are magnified in the complex web of poverty. When one thing goes wrong, it often precipitates a series of unwanted events. Without a cushion of wealth and access to professionals, the poor are easily overwhelmed. The humanity of poor people is tested and often stretched beyond its breaking point. Shipler is convinced that we need to attack all of the problems associated with poverty at once. The complexities demand a multi-pronged approach by professionals who approach problems holistically. "Hospitals, schools, housing authorities, police departments, welfare offices, and other critical institutions" need to be "well enough financed" that "they could reach far beyond their mandates, create connections of services, and become portals through which the distressed could pass into a web of assistance. It is a question of skill and will."

Shipler is also firmly committed to the concept of the poor claiming their own power. He notes that the poor have yet to claim their power in the marketplace and, more importantly, in politics; he contends that inequities in wages, health insurance, and education cry out for special attention. In Shipler's words:

> Opportunity and poverty in this country cannot be explained
> by either the American Myth that hard work is a panacea or by
> the Anti-Myth that the system imprisons the poor. Relief will
> come, if at all, in an amalgam that recognizes both the society's
> obligation through government and business, and the individ-
> ual's obligation through labor and family—and the commit-
> ment of both society and individual through education.[72]

CONCLUSION

Poverty is a pervasive socio-economic problem that is too often ignored. Statistics show that poverty has increased in the United States of America. At greatest risk are women and children. Research reveals the depth of poverty and its consequences for children and ultimately for adults. The richest nation in the world has had limited success in counteracting the negative effects of poverty. As a result, millions of children are growing up in conditions that hamper their physical development, limit their mental capacities, and add to the burdens of women struggling to raise their children. Poor parents, and especially women, try to balance the responsibilities of full time employment with the daily demands of child rearing. When basic resources, such as a safe, affordable living situation, access to nourishing food and basic health care, child care, education, and financial security, are lacking or jeopardized, the injustice rebounds from child, to parent, to the community, and ultimately to the nation. Impoverished children are an indictment of society. Burgeoning poverty is a serious threat to American society. The growing gaps between rich and poor are evident in gated communities and neighborhoods with substandard housing. Poverty creates an unhealthy environment where we are more likely to see adults and children who are undernourished, poorly educated, depressed, sick, and threatened by violence and crime.

Poverty is an impediment to achieving the goal of the American Dream. Restoring faith in the American Dream will require humane consideration of the needs of the poor and a renewed effort to include them at the table of social resources and decision making. Americans need to appreciate all members of the community. Undoing the imbalance of the tilted table requires knowledge of justice in the American sense, and for Christians, a commitment to justice in the biblical sense.

QUESTIONS FOR REFLECTION AND DISCUSSION

1. After reading the stories in A Portrait of the Poor in the United States, create a chart in which you list the persons in each story. List their positive characteristics, the difficulties they encounter, and how they survive. Which social, economic, and political factors helped or disrupted their lives? How would you describe the ecology of poverty that affects each person or family?

2. As you review the U.S. Census Bureau data on poverty, what patterns emerge? Who are most at risk of living in poverty? How does this affect families in terms of hunger, housing, and health care?

3. If you were in charge of communicating the extent and depth of poverty in the United States, what would you emphasize and how would you communicate this information?

4. What is your personal reaction to the extent of income disparity? Is this fair? How and by whom can this issue be addressed to achieve greater equity?

5. Discuss the studies on the effects of poverty. What surprised you? How are women and children affected by poverty? What are the consequences of poverty for children? How do children view poverty? What would you like to share with a community leader or elected official?

6. As you review the history of U.S. response to poverty, what patterns emerge in terms of how the poor were viewed, how they were treated, and how they received help? Why are many people ambivalent about helping the poor? If you were poor, how would you view the U.S. Welfare Reform of 1996? How could this legislation be improved?

7. Explain how welfare-to-work is related to a market model. Who benefits from a market model approach? Who suffers from a market model approach?

8. Discuss the thinking of the critics of the market model. What is meant by "economic polarization, political demobilization, and market triumphalism"? How is their critique similar to the idea of "a tilted table"?

SUGGESTED READINGS

Bane, Mary Jo, and Lawrence M. Mead. *Lifting Up the Poor: A Dialogue on Religion, Poverty and Welfare Reform*. Washington, DC: Brookings Institution Press, 2003.

Brooks-Gunn, Jeanne and Greg J. Duncan. "The Effects of Poverty on Children," *The Future of Children: Children and Poverty*. 7.2 (Summer/Fall 1997).

DeParle, Jason. *American Dream: Three Women, Ten Kids, and a Nation's Drive to End Welfare*. New York: Viking, 2004.

Duncan, Greg J., and Jeanne Brooks-Gunn, eds. *Consequences of Growing Up Poor*. New York: Russell Sage Foundation, 1997.

Duncan, Greg J., P. Lindsay Chase-Lansdale, eds. *For Better and for Worse: Welfare Reform and the Well-Being of Children and Families*. New York: Russell Sage Foundation, 2001.

Ehrenreich, Barbara. *Nickel and Dimed: On (Not) Getting By in America*. New York: Henry Holt and Company, 2001.

Goode, Judith, and Jeff Maskovsky, eds. *The New Poverty Studies: The Ethnography of Power, Politics, and Impoverished People in the United States*. New York: New York University Press, 2001.

Hays, Sharon. *Flat Broke with Children: Women in the Age of Welfare Reform*. New York: Oxford University Press, 2003.

Iceland, John. *Poverty in America: A Handbook*. Berkeley: University of California, 2003.

Katz, Michael B. *The Price of Citizenship: Redefining the American Welfare State*. New York: Henry Holt and Company, 2001.

Kozol, Jonathan. *Amazing Grace: The Lives of Children and the Conscience of a Nation*. New York: Crown Publishers, 1995.

LeBlanc, Adrian Nicole. *Random Family: Love, Drugs, Trouble, and Coming of Age in the Bronx*. New York: Scribner, 2003.

Mangum, Garth L., Stephen L. Mangum, and Andrew M. Sum. *The Persistence of Poverty in the United States*. Baltimore: Johns Hopkins University Press, 2003.

Mishel, Lawrence, Jared Bernstein, and Sylvia Allegretto. *The State of Working America 2006/2007*. Ithaca, NY: Cornell University Press, 2007.

Quigley, William P. *Ending Poverty as We Know It: Guaranteeing a Right to a Job at a Living Wage*. Philadelphia: Temple University Press, 2003.

Schwartz-Nobel, Loretta. *Growing Up Empty: The Hunger Epidemic in America*. New York: HarperCollins Publishers, 2002.

Shipler, David K. *The Working Poor: Invisible in America*. New York: Alfred A. Knopf, 2004.

Wilson, William Julius. *The Truly Disadvantaged: The Inner City, the Underclass, and Public Policy*. Chicago: University of Chicago Press, 1987.

NOTES

[1] Elizabeth Warren and Amelia Warren Tyagi, *The Two-Income Trap: Why Middle-Class Mothers and Fathers Are Going Broke* (New York: Basic Books, 2003), 1-7.

[2] David K. Shipler, *The Working Poor: Invisible in America* (New York: Alfred A. Knopf, 2004), 50-76.

[3] Jason DeParle, *American Dream: Three Women, Ten Kids, and a Nation's Drive to End Welfare* (New York: Viking, 2004).

[4] Adrian Nicole LeBlanc, *Random Family: Love, Drugs, Trouble, and Coming of Age in the Bronx* (New York: Scribner, 2003), 378.

[5] Ibid., 374.

[6] Carmen DeNavas-Walt, Bernadette D. Proctor, and Cheryl Hill Lee, U.S. Census Bureau, Current Population Reports, P60-231, *Income, Poverty, and Health Insurance Coverage in the United States: 2005*, U.S. Government Printing Office, Washington, DC, 2006, 13-15.

[7] Ibid., 13, 15.

[8] For a deeper understanding of the working poor, describing the work experience of the poor and non-poor, the annual earnings of heads of poor families, and the extent of the work experience of the poor, see Bradley R. Schiller, *The Economics of Poverty and Discrimination*, Ninth Edition (Upper Saddle River, NJ: Pearson/Prentice Hall, 2004).

[9] DeNavas-Walt, 20.

[10] Ibid., 25.

[11] Ibid., 45.

[12] Ibid., 17-18.

[13] In 1963, the poverty threshold for a family of four (two adults and two children) was about $3,100. Constance F. Citro and Robert T. Michael (eds.), *Measuring Poverty: A New Approach* (Washington, DC: National Academy Press, 1995), 2.

[14] Gordon M. Fisher, *The Development and History of the U.S. Poverty Thresholds—A Brief Overview*. Department of Health and Human Services, 1. http://aspe.hhs.gov/poverty/papers/hptgssiv.htm

[15] Citro, 2-3.

[16] Lawrence Mishel, Jared Berstein, and Sylvia Allegretto, *The State of Working America 2006/2007*. An Economic Policy Institute Book (Ithaca, NY: ILR Press, imprint of Cornell University Press, 2007), 11.

[17] Garth L. Mangum, Stephen L. Mangum, and Andrew M. Sum, *The Persistence of Poverty in the United States* (Baltimore: Johns Hopkins University Press, 2003), 36.

[18] Fisher, 3.

[19] Lawrence Mishel, Jared Bernstein, and Heather Boushey, *The State of Working America 2002/2003*. An Economic Policy Institute Book (Ithaca, NY: ILR Press, imprint of Cornell University Press, 2003), 325-27.

[20] John Iceland, *Poverty in America: A Handbook* (Berkeley: University of California Press, 2003), 61-65.

[21] Mangum, 48-49.

[22] Mishel, 2007, 14.

[23] DeNavas-Walt, 6.

[24] Ibid., 10.

[25] Ibid., 5.

[26] Mishel, 2007, 2-3.

[27] Mangum, 51-55.

[28] Stephen B. Page and Mary B. Larner, "Introduction to the AFDC Program," *The Future of Children: Welfare to Work* 7.1 (Spring 1997), 24.

[29] DeNavas-Walt, 11.

[30] Ibid.

[31] William Julius Wilson, *The Truly Disadvantaged: The Inner City, the Under-class, and Public Policy* (Chicago: University of Chicago Press, 1987), 199.

[32] Pamela D. Couture, *Blessed Are the Poor?* (Nashville: Abingdon Press, 1991), 57, 67.

[33] Wilson, 36.

[34] David Betson and Robert T. Michael, "Why So Many Children Are Poor," *The Future of Children: Children and Poverty* 7.2 (Summer/Fall 1997), 28.

[35] Ibid., 25-39.

[36] Mary E. Corcoran and Ajay Chaudry, "The Dynamics of Childhood Poverty," *The Future of Children: Children and Poverty* 7.2 (Summer/Fall 1997), 42.

[37] Ibid.

[38] Ibid., 45, 47.

[39] Jeanne Brooks-Gunn and Greg J. Duncan, "The Effects of Poverty on Children," *The Future of Children: Children and Poverty* 7.2 (Summer/Fall 1997), 55-71.

[40] Jonathan Kozol, *Savage Inequalities: Children in America's Schools* (New York: Harper Perennial,1991), 80.

[41] Jonathan Kozol, *Amazing Grace: The Lives of Children and the Conscience of a Nation* (New York: Crown Publishers, 1995), 4-5, 114.

[42] Ibid., 35, 40.

[43] Emily Lodish, "Jonathan Kozol: Listen to the Children," *The Nation On-line*. December 9, 2005. www.thenation.com

[44] John Iceland, *Poverty in America: A Handbook*. (Berkeley: University of California Press, 2003), 119.

[45] Ibid., 12 (quoting Herbert J. Gans, *The War against the Poor* [New York: Basic Books, 1995], 15).

[46] Thomas Massaro, S.J., *Catholic Social Teaching and United States Reform* (Collegeville, MN: Liturgical Press, 1998), 64.

[47] Iceland, 120.

[48] *Welfare Reform: A Primer*. The Bertram M. Beck Institute on Religion and Poverty (Bronx, NY: Fordham University Press, September 2001), 4-5.

[49] Ibid., 5-6.

[50] Massaro, 72.

[51] *Welfare Reform*, 6-7.

[52] Hugh Heclo, "Values Underpinning Poverty Programs for Children," *The Future of Children: Children and Poverty* 7.2 (Summer/Fall 1997), 142.

[53] *Welfare Reform*, 9-10.

[54] Ibid., 14.

[55] Ibid., 14-16. The U.S. Department of Agriculture: Food and Nutrition Service is the source for Food Stamp eligibility and benefits. Since 2002 food stamps are issued as an Electronic Benefit Transfer similar to a debit card. http://www.fns.usda.gov/fsp/. For the most current information on TANF and its reauthorization in the Deficit Reduction Act of 2005, see the U.S. Department of Health and Human Services: Administration for Children and families http://www.acf.dhhs.gov/programs/ofa/.

[56] Iceland, 132.

[57] *Welfare Reform*, 37.

[58] Iceland, 115.

[59] Ibid., 132.

[60] Michael B. Katz, *The Price of Citizenship: Redefining the American Welfare State* (New York: Metropolitan Books/Henry Holt, 2001), 30-31.

[61] Ibid., 2.

[62] Judith Goode and Jeff Maskovsky (eds.), *The New Poverty Studies: The Ethnography of Power, Politics, and Impoverished People in the United States* (New York: New York University Press, 2001), 3-4.

[63] Ibid., 6.

[64] Ibid., 8.

[65] Ibid., 16.

[66] Ibid., Frances Fox Piven, "Welfare Reform and Low Wage Labor Markets," 141.

[67] Robert Asen, "Including the Poor in the Political Community," *Focus* 22.2 (Summer 2002), 34.

[68] Iceland, 135.

[69] Michael Harrington, *The Other America: Poverty in the United States* (New York: Penguin Books, 1981), 203-14, xxviii-xxix.

[70] Asen, 35.

[71] Ibid.

[72] Shipler, 286, 299-300.

CHAPTER 3

Poverty: A Concern of Christian Faith and Social Justice

"Liberty and justice for all…" These words so familiar to Americans are often quoted and serve as a mantra of hope. They cause the heart to beat with pride and raise high expectations. If only there were liberty and justice for all, how wonderful life would be for all men, women, and children. The reality is that justice eludes the grasp of millions of poor people in a nation that prides itself on offering liberty and justice for all.

A prominent symbol of justice often sculpted on the façade of public buildings is the representation of Justicia, a woman holding high the scales of justice, blindfolded to ensure fairness and impartiality. Justicia represents a system based on law that guarantees equal treatment for all people. No one is meant to be higher than, greater than, or outside the jurisdiction of the law.

"Justice" is a word that has many meanings. In American society, justice is often linked with criminal justice and the penal system. It brings to mind trials where the prosecutor presents evidence with the express purpose of convicting the defendant. In the prosecutor's mind the defendant is a perpetrator who deserves to be convicted and punished for misdeeds. Meanwhile, the defense lawyer(s) present witnesses who tell the story from the point of view of the defendant with the express purpose of exonerating the person on trial. Hence, justice is commonly linked to crimes and punishment. Moreover, the criminal justice system depends on the truthfulness of witnesses as well as the competence of police, investigators, and lawyers in uncovering and presenting the evidence so that a jury can evaluate and pass judgment on the defendant. Despite people's expectations that their case will be handled fairly and impartially, there is no guarantee that justice will be served. Rather, this is a system of winners and losers. The winners are rewarded with financial settlements, or at the very least pronounced innocent of the charges; the losers are found guilty and punished. Sometimes, as we have seen in high profile cases, there is a miscarriage of justice which results in innocent parties losing their freedom and serving years of a prison sentence they did not deserve, and for some, facing the ultimate penalty of being condemned to death and waiting long years for a final determination on death row.

GOD'S VIEW OF JUSTICE, IN SCRIPTURE

Justice, however, is a concept broader than criminal justice. In the Bible, justice is a constant theme. In addition to viewing justice as fairness and fair treatment before the law, another view of justice emerges: caring for orphans, widows, and aliens. These are people who suffer the most: orphans, who have lost their primary caregivers, their parents; widows, who have no one to support them and their children after the death of their husbands, a primary responsibility of the man in a patriarchal society; and aliens who are strangers easily overlooked and even excluded from work and social contacts in a community where family and tribal connections determine who lives, what the quality of their lives will be, and who dies, depending on whether they are vitally connected to people who could welcome them and treat them as persons worthy of attention and care.

For a clearer sense of biblical justice John R. Donahue can guide us to texts that explain the importance of justice throughout the Bible. These texts reveal the nature of justice, God's sense of justice, the importance of justice for the community, how a just person acts, and how essential justice is to living a life acceptable to God. The biblical sense of justice is more inclusive and comprehensive than criminal justice, for it focuses on the good of the whole community, not just considering the guilt of the accused. Biblical justice addresses real-life issues of poverty, loss, exclusion, and ultimately the quality of life in society.

At the heart of a discussion on biblical justice is Isaiah's statement that "the Lord is a God of justice" (30:18), a clear indication of God's position in a world of conflict. The prophet Jeremiah shares a message for those who wish to know who God is: "I am the Lord; I act with steadfast love, justice, and righteousness in the earth, for in these things I delight, says the Lord" (9:24).

Because God identifies so directly with justice, people can rely on God when others fail or hurt them. The opening words of Psalm 11 state clearly that a person hounded by troublemakers can cry out, "In the Lord I take refuge" (verse 1). Despite the fact that evil and violence abound, there is hope, for "the Lord is righteous; he loves righteous deeds" (verse

7). As Donahue notes, justice is equated with integrity, the sense of how things should be if all were right, as things were meant to be. Justice is intimately connected with *salom* (peace), *hesed* (loving kindness) and fidelity.[1] In Psalm 85 these ideas come together:

> Steadfast love and faithfulness will meet (*hesed...'emet*);
> righteousness and peace will kiss (*sedaqah...salom*). (verse 10)

In Isaiah justice is once again identified with righteousness:

> The effect of righteousness will be peace;
> And the result of righteousness (*sedaqah*),
>   quietness and trust forever. (32:17)

In the New Testament Jesus places justice at the heart of what is right when he criticizes the Pharisees who prided themselves on their meticulous observance of the law of God, "Woe to you, scribes and Pharisees, hypocrites! For you tithe mint, dill, and cumin, and have neglected the weightier matters of the law: justice and mercy and faith. It is these you ought to have practiced without neglecting the others" (Mt 23:23).

The Just Person. Justice is not only God's domain, or responsibility. People are expected to act justly. It is the basis for the way individuals are to relate to God and to other people. God's total dedication to justice is a model and inspiration for the just person. Psalm 112 praises those who are "gracious, merciful, and righteous"; they will triumph, for "they have given to the poor; their righteousness endures forever" (4, 9). Those blessed by God with wealth are expected to act like God, the God who created and shared the goodness of creation with all people. God shares the goods of the earth with humanity with the expectation that people will then share with one another so that the needs of the human community are met. The good things of life, gifts from God, are reason to rejoice because they provide the means to be gracious. Justice refreshes relationships, restoring order and bringing a renewed sense of well-being. The rewards are obvious for the present, but justice also touches the future, especially in how one will be remembered. Psalm 112 states clearly that the righteous, those "who conduct their affairs with justice...will be remembered forever" (5–6).

Justice, in effect, restores right relationships and benefits individuals as well as the community.

Biblical justice is solidly on the side of the poor and oppressed. Deuteronomy describes God as "the great God, mighty and awesome...who executes justice for the orphan and the widow, and who loves the strangers, providing them food and clothing" (10:17–18). When someone in the community is in need, the advice is clear: "Do not be hard-hearted or tight-fisted toward your needy neighbor." In practical terms, "Since there will never cease to be some in need on the earth," God commands us, "Open your hand to the poor and needy neighbor in your land" (15:7, 11). Exodus clarifies God's command by stating, "You shall not wrong or oppress a resident alien," along with the reminder, "for you were aliens in the land of Egypt. You shall not abuse any widow or orphan" (22:21–22). The penalty for ignoring this warning is straightforward: Oppressors will die by the sword, effectively making their wives widows and their children orphans (24).

God deals harshly with those who act unjustly. The prophets, in particular, challenge those who oppress the poor, mincing no words when describing what God wants. Isaiah (58:5–7), for example, has this to say:

> Will you call this a fast,
>> a day acceptable to the Lord?
> Is not this the fast that I choose:
>> to loose the bonds of injustice,
>> to undo the thongs of the yoke;
> to let the oppressed go free,
>> and to break every yoke?
> Is it not to share your bread with the hungry,
>> and bring the homeless poor into your house;
> when you see the naked, to cover them,
>> and not to hide yourself from your own kin?

The prophet Amos (8:4, 7–8) directs God's message to those who take advantage of the poor by making their life more oppressive:

> Hear this, you that trample on the needy,
>> and bring to ruin the poor of the land,...

The Lord has sworn by the pride of Jacob:
Surely I will never forget any of their deeds.
Shall not the land tremble on this account,
    and everyone mourn who lives in it…?

Biblical justice is much more inclusive and sensitive than most understandings of justice in modern secular societies. According to Donahue, the differences between the two can be symbolized by the contrast between the "two women of justice": Justicia, the Roman goddess of justice, and Mary of Nazareth. Justicia symbolizes fairness and equality before the law; it reminds us that justice is to be administered without partiality or preference for those who are more powerful. We know from experience that Justicia is limited in her concern for humanity. There is no way to guarantee that truth and integrity will prevail over corruption and ignorance. Human law and justice are limited in their scope and outcome.

On the other hand, Mary of Nazareth aligns herself with God. Using the psalmist's words (Ps 138, Ps 75, and Ps 107), she displays a breadth of vision and a depth of compassion as she proclaims (Lk 1:51–53) that God

…has shown strength with his arm;
he has scattered the proud in the thoughts of their hearts.
He has brought down the powerful from their thrones
    and lifted up the lowly;
he has filled the hungry with good things,
    and sent the rich away empty.

Biblical justice reveals a God who is both generous in gifting and consistent in holding people responsible for themselves and one another. God consistently defends the poor and advocates merciful care and active, practical service on behalf of those in need. The rich are held to a high standard; their wealth and status are meant to be power for and with those of lesser means.

The Early Christian Community. Jesus and the early Christian community were guided by the Hebrew Scriptures and had a deep, even compelling, concern for the poor that was grounded in a scriptural sense of social justice. This section will provide an overview of Jesus' response to the poor and marginalized and discuss how his disciples related with the poor and the rich in the first through the fourth centuries of the Christian community.

Jesus was an observant Jew sensitive to the needs of people. When someone was sick, that person's healing was more important than an exact observance of the Sabbath. When people were caught up in the wonder and power of Jesus' message of love and repentance, he eagerly embraced them and welcomed them as those seeking the living God. Forgiveness and healing went hand in hand and Jesus was utterly inclusive in his guest list that included sinners, tax collectors, and lepers.

At the beginning of his ministry in Galilee Jesus used the words of Isaiah to proclaim, "The spirit of the Lord" is upon him "to bring good news to the poor, ...to proclaim release to the captives and recovery of sight to the blind, to let the oppressed go free, to proclaim the year of the Lord's favor" (Lk 4:18–19). People's response was divided: some were "amazed at the gracious words that came from his mouth" (verse 22) while others "were filled with rage" (verse 28). Crowds clamored for his attention even as Jesus shared a sense of urgency when he told them, "I must proclaim the good news of the kingdom of God to the other cities also; for I was sent for this purpose" (verse 43). So Jesus moved about, calling disciples to share in his lot, curing lepers, forgiving sin, and healing those beset by physical ailments and "those who were troubled with unclean spirits" (6:18). Jesus welcomed those who were poor, hungry, and sorrowful, calling them blessed (verses 20–21). Word of such deeds must have spread through the countryside and made people jump for joy as they were passed from lips to lips.

Jesus spoke in parables, stories with characters familiar to his listeners but with surprising, often paradoxical outcomes. In one parable the father welcomed back the repentant younger son who had squandered his inheritance, and then pleaded with the angry elder son saying, "We had to celebrate and rejoice, because this brother of yours was dead and has come back to life; he was lost and has been found" (Lk 15:32).

Jesus' followers were well acquainted with a society with enormous inequalities. The Romans ruled Palestine and Jewish leaders scrambled for some semblance of power. Poverty was a fact of life for most of the people. Against this backdrop, Jesus told the story of the rich man and Lazarus (Lk16:19–31). The contrast could not be greater: rich man, fine clothes, feasts galore versus poor man, looking for crumbs to satisfy his hunger, invisible to all except some dogs who licked his sores. Eventually both men die and the rich man suffers for his misdeeds, while Abraham welcomes Lazarus, the poor man, embracing him like a son. The rich man pleads for some relief, begging for Lazarus to bring even a drop of water to relieve his torment. Apparently he still looked upon Lazarus as a servant. But no, there is no relief granted. And when the rich man pleads for his brothers, the story ends with the admonition that they need to heed the warnings of Moses and the prophets.

Jesus appealed to people of all social classes. Witness the tax collector, Zacchaeus, climbing a sycamore tree to see Jesus. Jews were critical of Zacchaeus, a tax collector who cooperated with the ruling class and kept a percentage of what he collected from the poor. The common opinion was that tax collectors were like vultures living off the flesh of the people. Despite criticism, Jesus goes to eat at Zacchaeus' house. The tax collector says, "Half of my possessions, Lord, I will give to the poor; and if I have defrauded anyone of anything, I will pay back four times as much"; to which Jesus replies, "Today salvation has come to this house, because he too is a son of Abraham" (Lk 19:8–9). Jesus encouraged openness of heart in all people.

The gospels portray Jesus as a compassionate Jew who healed those afflicted by infirmities and preached the good news of the reign of God to the public. By day he moved about with a group of followers as he taught individuals and groups and healed the sick. By night he retired to pray to his Father. No doubt Jesus appealed to the poor and the disenfranchised. His message, though, also attracted leaders such as Nicodemus who came by night to learn (Jn 3:1–21). Jesus' life of service and his message of forgiveness were attractive to all people: men and women, rich and poor.

The early disciples of Jesus included many poor people. There is evidence that in the first century Judea had been especially hard hit by famine. This fact is recorded in Acts 11:27–30 and noted by Josephus and the Roman historians, Tacitus and Suetonius.[2] It is clear that the Christian community in Jerusalem was relatively poor when we read that the church in Jerusalem advised Paul to "remember the poor" (Gal 2:10).

Despite the existence of poverty in the early church, severe destitution was not evident because the Christians practiced almsgiving along with prayer and fasting. In other words, Christians cared for one another. As needs increased, the apostles appointed deacons to care for the poor in an orderly and equitable manner (Acts 6:2–6). In addition to these men, women were actively involved in offering hospitality (Lydia in Acts 16:15) and serving as leaders in house churches (Rom 16:3–5; 1 Cor 16:19). Widows were active not just in prayer, but also in helping those in need.

The expectation that the poor would be cared for as a matter of justice is shown by the murmuring of the Hellenists when the Hebrews neglected their widows in the daily distribution of food (Acts 6:1). We also read in Acts 4:32, 34: "The community of believers were of one heart and mind. None of them ever claimed anything as his own; rather, everything was held in common…nor was there anyone needy among them, for all who owned property or houses sold them and donated the proceeds." Yet this statement contrasts with the story of Ananias and Sapphira who plotted to keep the proceeds from the sale of property (Acts 5:1–11). There was an ideal: Everything was to be held in common. But there were people who did not or could not follow the ideal.

Early Christian response to the poor is related to *koinonia*, the sense of community as described in Acts 2:42; this was evident in their generosity, their prayerful sharing of the Eucharist, and the growth of the community. More than good feelings or a sense of partnership, *koinonia* "is a total sharing that includes the material as well as the spiritual."[3]

Amid such desperate need, many early Christians thought the Second Coming of Christ would happen during their lifetime, a fact that could have encouraged an otherworldly view and a disregard for ordinary time, that is, the necessities of everyday life. As Henry Clark states, "All these factors—the ubiquity of misery, the political impotence of the average citizen, and otherworldliness in religious belief—are important for an understanding of early Christian teaching on poverty."[4] Eschatology, beliefs related to the Second Coming of Christ at the end of time, is evident in the Last Judgment narrative in Matthew 25:31–46. Entrance into the kingdom of God is the direct result of feeding, clothing, and comforting those in need. Welcoming anyone in need is equated with welcoming Jesus. While most Christians today no longer adhere to Matthew's vision of the nearness of the end times, Christianity continues to emphasize God's love and concern for the least fortunate. Matthew's story will be shared throughout the ages to remind believers that the community has a responsibility to respond directly to those who struggle to satisfy their basic human needs.

Paul became totally committed to the Lord Jesus and he presented a vision of radical equality of the rich and poor. He called Christians to account when this ideal of equality was not realized. Paul's teaching about the Lord's Supper revealed the tensions that would arise among believers from different economic backgrounds. In Corinth he noted the factions that existed and he complained that "one person goes hungry and another becomes drunk" (1 Cor 11:21). He pointed out the contradiction of gathering to share the Body and Blood of the Lord Jesus even as some "humiliate those who have nothing." He labeled such behavior as "contempt for the church of God" (1 Cor 11:22). At the conclusion of this epistle Paul instructed the believers to do as the churches in Galatia had done, "On the first day of every week, each of you is to put aside and save whatever extra you earn…" (1 Cor 16:2). In effect, Christians had a weekly collection for those in need.

As an example of giving, Paul described the generosity of the churches in Macedonia. "For as I can testify, they voluntarily gave according to their means, and even beyond their means, begging us earnestly for the privilege of sharing in this ministry to the saints…" (2 Cor 8:3–4). Paul reminded the Corinthians of "the generous act of our Lord Jesus Christ, that though he was rich, yet for your sakes he became poor, so that by his poverty you might become rich" (2 Cor 8:9). He encouraged their cooperation: "For if the eagerness is there, the gift is acceptable according to what one has…it is a question of a fair balance between your present abundance and their need, so that their abundance may be for your need, in order that there may be a fair balance" (2 Cor

8:12–14). In this manner Paul urged moving beyond the pettiness and selfishness of some, to realize the glory of a community's joyful giving and receiving.

POVERTY AND JUSTICE IN THE FIRST FOUR CENTURIES

In addition to Scripture, there are writings from the first and second centuries that address concerns of poverty and riches. The *Didache*, or the *Doctrine of the Twelve Apostles*, often quoted by Christian writers from the second to the fifth centuries, was discovered in Istanbul in 1875. Reminiscent of the early days of the Jesus movement, the *Didache* reinforced the concepts of charity. Christians were to share all things in common. Those who turned away from someone in need followed the "way of death."[5] The teachings of the *Didache* reflected much of Acts 2 and 4. Since God is the giver of all gifts, sharing material goods is more important than possessing material goods.[6] One notable addition was that "what is given serves also as a ransom for the giver's sins."[7]

The Shepherd of Hermas, a work of the second century, proposed a new approach: a "concern for the welfare of the rich as well as of the poor."[8] In an analogical story that compared the growth of the church to the construction of a tall tower using stones of various shapes, William Walsh and John Langan explain how the rich were described as "'white round stones' which have to be chiseled into the proper size before they can fit into the building. The rich must become detached from their wealth before they can be genuine Christians. One proves that he is detached from his wealth by his willingness to help all who are in trouble financially, emotionally, and spiritually."[9] *Hermas* spelled out how the rich needed to realign their priorities: "Instead of fields, then, buy souls that are in trouble....Look after widows and orphans and do not neglect them. Spend your riches and all your establishments you have received from God on this kind of field and houses!"[10] In *The Shepherd of Hermas* the welfare of the rich was tied to their concern for and caring for the poor. The real treasure, the souls of those in need, was unseen. It emphasized the necessity of using material goods to aid the needy.

While the Hebrew and Christian Scriptures clearly state the obligation of welcoming and caring for the poor, how did this mandate continue in the centuries that followed? To get a sense of how the Christian community cared for the poor, it is helpful to study the actions and homilies of the Fathers of the Church, the Christian teachers and writers of the early centuries renowned for their learning and holiness, whose writings are a valuable resource for Christian tradition. Three of these leaders of the Christian Church—Clement of Alexandria, Cyprian, and John Chrysostom—open our eyes to the lives of the poor and the attitudes and actions of the larger community in caring for the needy.

Clement of Alexandria in the early third century examined attitudes toward riches. From his sermons we learn that there were Christians whose pursuit of wealth was tantamount to an addiction. As a result of loving wealth, they became hard-hearted toward those in need. They were so fixated on owning property that they cared little for the kingdom of heaven. Clement urged the wealthy to embrace the gospel message to be "poor in spirit," which he argued would require that a wealthy Christian be detached, and be prepared, if need be, to suffer the loss of his wealth cheerfully.[11] Clement realized that one's relationship to Christ is crucial. Conversion from addiction to riches to being poor in spirit is possible only if one is "altogether in love with God, with Christ, and with his fellow man."[12] Clement presents God's love in glowing terms: the love of the Father in the greatness of his being, the love of a mother in begetting the Son, and as a Lover offering his life as ransom for all people. Compared to such overwhelming love, he hoped that the rich would view their property and wealth as transitory pleasures and be moved to share their wealth with the poor.[13]

Cyprian, who lived in the third century, was both wealthy and well educated. He converted to Christianity at age fifty, sold much of his property, and gave the proceeds to the poor. Within three years of his conversion he was elected bishop of Carthage, in present-day Tunisia.[14] Cyprian had harsh words for the pagans who hoarded money and possessions, even buying more land so as to exclude the poor, "Their possession amounts to this only, that they can keep others from possessing it;

oh, what a marvelous perversion of names! They call those things good which they absolutely put to none but bad uses."[15]

Cyprian also called to account the many Christians whose faith withered when the Roman Emperor Decius mounted a persecution of the Christians in the year 250. At that time, many bishops abandoned the poor and went in search of wealth, while the laity valued wealth more than faith. When faced with the loss of their property if they left the country to avoid persecution, many wealthy Christians apostasized. Cyprian considered their apostasy a "shocking betrayal of Christ" and said, "They think of themselves as owners, whereas it is they rather who are owned; enslaved as they are to their own property, they are not the masters of their money but its slaves."[16]

Cyprian's most impressive work regarding wealth is his treatise *On Works and Alms*, written in 252 in the midst of a plague that claimed thousands of lives. According to Justo González, Cyprian argued that almsgiving was vitally important because almsgiving "is a means to atone for sins committed after baptism." Christ has saved each person, a reality for those who are baptized, but persons who sin after baptism can cleanse themselves through almsgiving. Cyprian also pointed out that almsgiving "increases the power and efficacy of prayer and fasting." He wrote that "those who give alms will not suffer physical want," which he relates to rich persons who need not be held captive by their wealth, for themselves nor for the sake of their own family. Finally, Cyprian contends that almsgiving "has been commanded by Christ," by far the strongest argument for it, since it flows from faith in Jesus, a faith that Luke witnessed when he recorded in his gospel how Jesus encouraged the rich young man to sell all that he owned, "distribute the money to the poor" so he would "have treasure in heaven" and then follow Jesus (Lk 18:22).[17]

John Chrysostom, born in Antioch where he was educated and then baptized as an adult, was attracted to the life of an ascetic. Six years devoted to the life of a monk in prayer and ascetical practices afforded him the opportunity to memorize the Old and New Testaments, but ill health forced him to return to Antioch. Ordained a deacon and then a priest, John became a great preacher. In 398, John was called to be bishop of Constantinople, the center of eastern Catholic churches as well as the imperial city for the eastern Roman Empire.

According to González, Constantinople was a city of great contrasts. The wealthy and those who lived at the imperial court were absentee landlords who lived supremely luxurious lives. Their lifestyle was made possible by the backbreaking labor of those who worked the land and the skilled workers who were poorly paid. While the wealthy and powerful had every luxury imaginable as evidenced by their highly decorated residences and feasts fit for the gods, "the vast majority of the population lived in wretched tenements often several stories high and leaning on each other." The poor included peasants "who had been uprooted by the land-grabbing greed of the powerful," laborers who had come to the city to work on construction projects but who found few jobs at low wages with horrid working conditions, sailors and others attracted by the city, and women who were forced into prostitution as their only available livelihood.[18]

Because of their size and importance, both Antioch and Constantinople attracted many visitors, some of whom were in poor health and unable to support themselves once they reached the city. Among those who lived in either city on a permanent basis, those who were most vulnerable to poverty and disease were "children, women and the elderly who became deprived of the support of immediate or extended family." Mayer and Allen record that by the time John was ordained a priest in 386, the church responded to the needs of the poor by administering orphanages, hostels, and hospitals. There is ample evidence that as bishop John allotted funds to construct and staff hospitals.[19]

John Chrysostom used his exceptional skills as an orator to encourage the rich to accept responsibility for the poor. When met by the indifference of the rich toward the poor, he admonished the rich, as he did in a sermon on 1 Timothy:

> Tell me then, how did you come by your wealth?…the beginning and root of wealth must lie in injustice of some sort! And why? Because, in the beginning, God did not create one person wealthy and another to go wanting.…He gave one and the

> same earth to all alike...the earth is a common possession....Is
> wealth something good? Not at all....It is not something evil—
> so long as it is not hoarded and is shared out with those in
> need. Unshared, wealth becomes something evil, a trap....It
> is rather the state of common property that is our inheritance
> which is more in keeping with our nature....How can a rich
> person be a good person? He is a good person when he shares
> his wealth....[20]

Chrysostom presented two basic ideas about wealth. The first was an understanding of the commonality of goods, which was contrary to how the rich viewed property, as their right and privilege according to Roman law. According to Chrysostom, the gifts of creation are meant for all people, not for a special few. The second was the assumption that the rich were obligated to share their wealth with the poor. Chrysostom thought that sharing wealth is natural and that hoarding is evil and against nature. Wealth, then, is seen in terms of proper use, not exclusive ownership.

Chrysostom uses an interesting comparison when he asked his hearers to imagine two cities: one in which only rich people lived and in the other, only the poor. With equal resources he contends that the city of the rich would be hard-pressed without field hands, carpenters, bakers, and so on. The city of the poor would lack the traditional trappings of wealth: no gold or silver, no jewels, and no expensive fabrics. He asks who is better able to grow food, bake bread, build and repair a building, or weave cloth? Obviously, when it comes to the tasks of daily living, the poor are in a better position. The rich are at a disadvantage when they no longer have servants, slaves, and workers. In such a situation the rich seem useless. The point of the story is that accumulating wealth is pointless; rather, the purpose of wealth is to share it with those in need.

One might also add that wealth creates problems when people are willing to do anything to maintain and increase their status. For Chrysostom, dependence is a normal part of living. The rich, he argued, are in greater need, for only poverty brings independence. In a homily on 2 Corinthians, Chrysostom observes,

For every day and in every thing, so to speak, do we stand in need of one another....If thou be rich, thou wilt stand in need of more....For just in proportion to thy wealth dost thou subject thyself to this curse....For if thou art desirous of being exceedingly independent of everyone, pray for poverty; and then if thou art dependent on any, thou wilt be so only for bread and raiment.[21]

John Chrysostom was less judgmental of the faults of the poor than those in our time who prefer to give only to the "worthy poor." Rather than neglecting someone truly in need, "Alms are to be given, not to the way of life, but to the human being; we must have compassion, not because the poor are virtuous, but because they are needy."[22]

In summary, the biblical sense of justice for the poor was at the heart of Jesus' life and mission. His seeking out the marginalized, his interactions with those considered outcasts, and his healing actions and words of hope touched people and showed God's deeply felt and all-embracing love. So, too, the disciples of Jesus responded to people's needs by providing for the poor among them. Throughout the early centuries Christian communities embraced the tradition of justice and charity for the poor. Today we can identify our heritage as one of loving service to the widow, the orphan, and the stranger, for loving service is how Christians connect with their God.

WOMEN AND POVERTY IN THE EARLY CHURCH

The contributions of women in a patriarchal society and in a religious movement dominated by male leadership reveal their faith and fidelity in times of need, and their absolute courage when faced with persecution for their beliefs. Women were certainly present and appreciated in Jesus' life. They accompanied him and the apostles as they journeyed through towns and villages and "provided for them out of their resources" (Lk 8:1–3). In the early days, women were an integral part of the Christian community. No doubt they played an active role in the prayer and worship in the home communities. Widows not only received help when they were in need, but also ministered to those in need. Eventually an order of deaconess arose, but while these women generously gave of themselves to the community, the order of widow and deaconess in the West, according to Gerard Sloyan, did not include ordination, that is, women were not ordained, but assigned.[23] Paul reminds Christians, "As many of you as were baptized into Christ have clothed yourselves with Christ. There is no longer Jew or Greek, there is no longer slave or free, there is no longer male and female; for all of you are one in Christ Jesus" (Gal 3:27–29). The thought that we are equal before God is especially appealing to our twenty-first-century sensibilities, but the reality for the early centuries was that as Christians became accepted by secular society, they were more likely to reflect the prevailing patriarchal practices. Gender equality would be a long time coming.

As Christians, women could escape the conventions of patriarchal control through celibacy. Women who embraced a virginal or celibate life achieved some freedom from society's strictures. Within the Christian community it was virtuous to abandon all to follow Jesus. But as JoAnn McNamara observes, "The message that women, for the sake of chastity, should deny themselves children, defy their parents, and even forsake their husbands struck a potentially mortal blow to the ancient order."[24] Patriarchy, based on established hierarchical norms according to which men held positions of power outside the home and exercised power over women within the home, was threatened by women who, in choosing celibacy, escaped from male-dominated family life and gained some measure of independent status within the broader social world. After all, women were expected to provide children and heirs and oversee the home for the pleasure and comfort of their husbands. Celibacy called into question time-honored traditions.

Martyrdom was another way in which women achieved equality. The early Christian martyrs included women: Blandina, Perpetua, Agatha, Lucy, and many others. Perpetua's prison diary is compelling reading. Her visions of heaven sustained her as she awaited a brutal death. At one point when she had been stripped, she said, "And I became a man."[25] Willing to surrender her infant son and to sacrifice her own life, she envisioned her female body reshaped into the form of a man's body. Society placed a premium on being a male and so she imagined herself in the more perfect male body ready to combat the devil himself, an encounter from which she would emerge victorious.[26]

A surprising feature of the poverty/wealth saga is that there were also women of means in the first centuries of Christianity. Women of faith who earned or inherited substantial income often placed their money and fortunes at the service of the church. Their generosity provided food and shelter for the poor, enabled bishops and church leaders to assist those in greatest need, and even dedicated funds to build monasteries and abbeys. Women were faithful partners in working with the Christian community to alleviate the needs of the poor and establish institutions where visitors, the poor, the sick, and the elderly and infirm would be welcomed and treated with care.

CHARITY FOR THE POOR

The early Christian communities practiced justice and charity toward the poor. Over time the Christian response to the poor became centralized in the cities where most poor people lived. Traditionally the bishop was the protector of the poor; he was responsible for distributing church funds from contributions and legacies and delegating authority to provide food, shelter, and medical care. When more people settled in rural areas the church's social ministry was decentralized. Parish priests assumed responsibility for caring for the poor in their local parishes.

By the fourth century, when Christianity became the official religion of the Roman Empire, the church acquired more assets, and by the seventh century, more civil power. Church leaders modified the early practice of property held in common as advocated in Acts 2 and 4; assuming responsibility for the social order required a different mindset. They reasoned that "private property and coercive human authority…were required by God as a consequence of sin." In an effort to make the best of an imperfect human condition, the church gradually developed "rules governing social and economic activity…oriented toward the efficient distribution of scarce resources."[27]

From the fourth century there were social and political forces that effectively shifted the care of the poor from justice to charity. As the church grew in numbers, greater resources were available, as evidenced by the foundation of monasteries and abbeys. These provided opportunities for individuals to band together under the guidance of a spiritual leader and follow a rule for a common life based on prayer, discipline, and good works. Monasteries and abbeys were also known for their dedication to the study of the Scriptures. Since they were far from large urban centers, they had to function as separate entities by growing their own food, constructing and maintaining buildings, and caring for their members. They offered hospitality to pilgrims and travelers, with guest houses for those of means and hospices for the poor and infirm. In an age when epidemics and plagues were commonplace, they built hospitals to care for the sick. They became centers of learning and places where liturgy and prayer were at the heart of their everyday routine. The arts and sciences were pursued even when cities and countries were ravaged by invasions, wars, and pestilence. A large portion of their budgets was devoted to caring for the less fortunate. The monks and sisters were motivated by charity, as were many individuals who lived in cities and who also responded with compassion to the needy, the sick, and the elderly.

When war and pestilence ravaged cities, the wealthy moved to estates in the country where they formed feudal societies. Feudal lords attracted and protected the workers and servants who supported their society. The lords assumed responsibility for caring for the poor on their estates. Problems arose when secular leaders usurped church assets or put relatives in positions of ecclesiastical power. This resulted in the perennial conflict between a love of wealth and the needs of the poor. Those in power were often supremely selfish, acting on their own behalf and ignoring the poor.

When the economy of Western Europe expanded after 1100, tension developed between the gospel ethic of charity and social responsibility for the poor. According to David O'Brien and Thomas Shannon, "the money economy, the growing importance of trade, and vigorous competition all challenged the harmonious organic theories of the earlier era," which presupposed a smoothly ordered hierarchical structure in society and the universe. There were still proponents of "primitive gospel simplicity" (for example, Francis of Assisi), but the later Middle Ages was a time of upheaval because of "the growing chasm between Christianity and economic practice."[28]

By the thirteenth and fourteenth centuries, with the rise of city-states, charity became a concern of the state. However, rivalry and the quest for wealth and power diminished the practice of charity, and the poor suffered as a result. Society had long been organized according to a hierarchy both within the church and in government. When leaders claimed exclusive prerogatives to wealth and privilege, as often happened, the poor were like Lazarus, wishing they had crumbs from the table of the rich man. Charity was limited by the motivation and lifestyle of the rich and powerful.

The Reformation, beginning with Martin Luther and continuing with John Calvin, placed great importance on the individual, his or her relationship with God, and on the individual Christian's responsibility to contribute to society. In Rebecca Prichard's analysis, Martin Luther held to a "theology of justification by grace through faith. His (*Ninety-five*) *Theses* (1517) clearly link theology and social concern; charitable works are not meritorious, but demanded by the gospel of grace."[29] Luther favored a "two kingdoms approach" where believers contributed to a community chest that would be used to help those in need. Donations were also made to civil authorities, since the city council bore responsibility for the temporal welfare of the community. The needs of the poor were so great that both private individuals and public officials had to work to satisfy their needs.

John Calvin became the religious leader of Geneva, a city to which the poor had flocked in great numbers. Believers donated money for the needs of the poor, and Calvin provided for the administration of the fund to be in the hands of deacons, who had the responsibility of caring for the poor, the sick, and the needy. Calvin spoke of the law of God in a positive way when he exhorted believers to live the spirit-filled life. As Prichard notes, "The law of God is written in the hearts of believers for Calvin; the faithful are indwelt by God's spirit, who offers them a life of obedience and sanctification." According to Ernst Troeltsch, this showed that "there was definitely talk of the common good in Calvin's Geneva."[30]

The Anabaptist movement, which was founded in Zurich, Switzerland, in 1525, and then spread to the Low Countries in 1533, is a primary expression of Radical Reformation faith. The Radical Reformers tried to go beyond the changes suggested by Luther, Calvin, and others to follow early Christianity's norms and practices, especially caring for one another. This is evident even today in the Mennonite movement, the largest form of Anabaptist faith. From its founding, their central beliefs included viewing Christianity as discipleship and defining discipleship in terms of concrete practices of caring for others, a conception of the church as brotherhood and love among the members, and a new ethic of love and non-resistance. Accepting Christian baptism as an adult entailed, for Anabaptists (and later, Mennonites), a total commitment to obey Christ. They understood brotherhood as "the actual practice of sharing possessions to meet the needs of others in the spirit of true mutual aid."[31] Those who possessed property were truly stewards, for when any community members were in need, they had a right to the property.

The Hutterian Brotherhood in 1528 went even further when they completely repudiated private property, believing that "private property is the greatest enemy of Christian love." The Anabaptists pledged themselves to "create a Christian social order" within their own community. Because they challenged social inequalities and offered a radical critique of existing social institutions, fellow Christians who benefited from established social relations often condemned Anabaptists and even killed them. As many of their members suffered and died at the hands of other Christians, Anabaptists came to view the church as a suffering church. Despite their suffering, they viewed love and non-resistance as an ethic that was to be applied to all human relationships.[32]

Generally, the practice of charity underwent changes in the fifteenth and sixteenth centuries. Changes in agricultural methods made people vulnerable to poverty; industrialization put even craftspeople at risk. While the economy expanded, wages were low. Natural disasters like crop failures and human disasters, such as war, as well as cultural changes caused by colonization and evangelization, resulted in the newly poor flocking to the cities in search of relief. Quite simply, there were so many poor people that the voluntary resources of the cities were often overwhelmed. People asked how they could assist the deserving poor, the widows, orphans, and the sick and crippled, and exclude those who were undeserving, especially those strong enough to work.

Religious belief entered into solving this problem. Protestant religions had the expectation that each individual would live a life of piety based on discipline. The individual was viewed as the locus of power and control in social and political obligations. On the one hand, individuals were seen as having certain rights that could not be overridden by the state. On the other hand, each person was regarded as having certain responsibilities, including working and contributing to society. People who did not live up to these responsibilities were sometimes seen as unworthy of social support. The Catholic Church, though, resisted these "new ideas of individual autonomy and popular participation, and... almost always...chose to assert the need for order and hierarchy."[33]

The problem of poverty in the fifteenth century was so great that it required the energies of many intelligent and caring people to find solutions. Since resources for charitable purposes were overwhelmed by the huge influx of the poor and newly poor, both Catholics and Protestants had to devise methods of helping those who were most in need, hence the use of the terms the "deserving poor" as opposed to the "undeserving." Communities sought to develop systems that guaranteed "greater efficiency in the administration of...resources and greater accuracy in the selection of recipients."[34] Protestants passed laws concerning the poor, such as those of Nuremberg (1522) and Ypres (1525), which placed charitable institutions under "a single administrative authority, financial resources were disbursed from a 'common chest,' [and] specialization of services was introduced to avoid duplication."[35]

The major difference between Protestant and Catholic care for the poor was their attitudes toward begging. As a result of the Reformation, begging was no longer considered a religious work; thus, begging became a concern of the government. Protestant governments prohibited begging, based on the premise that the poor needed to learn to work. While Catholic authorities also opposed begging, there was still the belief that giving money to beggars was a religious act. Essentially, begging could be forbidden, but it could not be controlled.

Relief for the poor soon came to rely on the principles of discrimination and exclusion. Authorities examined those who were poor to determine if they deserved help. Exclusion was determined according to a variety of factors. First, relief was based on the ability of the person to work; second, membership in the community was considered, and a person's religion and his or her residency determined a person's membership. Thus, Catholics could be excluded in a Protestant town. Foreigners and transients could also be denied aid. Relief was also denied on the basis of morality, that is, if a person did not conform to the community's moral standards, she or he could be denied relief.

The Protestant Reformation not only fractured the Catholic Church into reformed Christian churches, but also provided the opportunity for leaders in countries that adopted Protestant beliefs to confiscate Catholic monasteries and other church properties. Monks and nuns were sent packing, and their communal work discontinued. Communities then had to devise new ways to help the poor. Still, these efforts were often an inadequate substitute for the concerted efforts of monasteries and local churches.

When pauperism became a severe problem during the sixteenth and seventeenth centuries, civil authorities prohibited begging and threatened punishment. Many persons disregarded these punitive laws, especially St. Vincent De Paul (1580–1660), who became a powerhouse for helping and inspiring others to assist the poor. He encouraged home visitation of the poor and the building of hospices to shelter beggars. Women responded by banding together in newly founded religious congregations whose aim was to serve the poor. In the eighteenth century the French Revolution (1789) led to seizing church property and assets, and even disbanding religious congregations. When the revolution banned private charity, the poor suffered even greater destitution. By the nineteenth century the works of charity rebounded with the rebirth of religious congregations and the institution of many new ones. During this time, the United States witnessed an upsurge in the foundation of congregations of women and men religious, some an outgrowth from Europe, others founded in the New World. These religious congregations responded to the urgent needs of the poor by providing food and shelter for needy women and children, opening orphanages for infants and children whose parents had died, establishing hospitals, and founding schools and colleges.

When the Industrial Revolution resulted in wealth for a select few and misery for many, it was a challenge for charity to meet the needs the poor. Dedicated people like A. Frederic Ozanam (1813–1853) worked tirelessly to organize groups to serve the poor; such efforts paved the way for Catholic socialism. However, it became evident to many that charity alone could not solve the problems of the poor and so was born the concept of social justice. Initial attempts to promote social justice included: Ozanam (1840) who advocated "a 'natural wage' that would assure the workingman and his family enough money to live and be educated"; the Union of Fribourg (1886), a core group of Catholics from many countries that examined social problems with the express purpose of finding a just solution; and church leaders like Bishop Ketteler of Mainz, Germany, and Cardinal Manning in England who also sought solutions to pressing social problems.[36] Then the encyclicals of Pope Leo XIII, *Rerum Novarum: The Condition of Labor* (1891), and Pope Pius XI, *Quadragesimo Anno: After Forty Years* (1931), presented two essential principles: social justice and social charity. As explained by Pius XI, social justice began with "the spirit of justice." Social justice needed to erect "a juridical and social order able to pervade all economic activity." Meanwhile, social charity would be "the soul of this order." For social justice to prevail, government needs to fulfill its role "to safeguard effectively and to vindicate promptly this order" (*Quadragesimo Anno*, #88).

In her commentary on *Quadragesimo Anno*, Christine Firer Hinze distinguishes between social justice and social charity when she writes, "Social justice refers to the central and necessary set of conditions wherein each member is contributing, and thus enjoying, all that is needed for the common good." Social justice will only become a reality when it is "leavened by the virtue of social charity or love."[37] Social justice, then, establishes social, economic, and political foundations that uphold the common good, while the virtue of social charity or love inspires people to work for justice.

MODERN CATHOLIC SOCIAL TEACHING

Modern Catholic social teaching responds to the problems that people encounter in life. It establishes a moral compass to determine direction, but more important, it provides a broader approach to issues. Grounded in Scripture, disciplined by philosophy, and informed by centuries of the Judeo-Christian tradition, Catholic social teaching is both a product and a critic of history and current socio-economic thought with the potential for bridging the gaps among the people of the world caused by injustice and oppression. Catholic social teaching offers principles that provide a broad perspective for discussion, analysis based on theology and the social sciences, and most important, hope for transformation and change. Rooted in Catholic Christian beliefs, Catholic social teaching seeks to engage people of good will across many traditions, cultures, and systems of belief. In a very real sense it is both the legacy of Catholics and a gift to all people in a world where millions of people and nature itself struggle for survival even as people seek a better life grounded in peace and justice.

In a succinct statement Peter Henriot defines Catholic social teaching as "the body of social wisdom, about human individuals in society, and about the structures of that society that enable humanity to come to its fullness, that can be found in Scripture, writings of theologians, documents of churches, and witness of just persons and communities." In describing modern Catholic social teaching as a body of social wisdom, Henriot goes beyond describing it merely in terms of basic principles. It is rooted not only in Scripture and church documents but also in the work of theologians and those working for justice. In Henriot's words, "The authority and the authenticity, the relevance and the credibility, of the documents come from their foundation in scripture, their clarification in theological reflection, and their evidence in lived experience."[38]

Modern Catholic social teaching emerges like a chick pecking its way outside the frail, but protective covering of its shell. As a preliminary observation, it is important to note that modern Catholic social teaching is based upon an intentional effort within the church to move away from a sectarian posture and to address pressing social issues. It reclaims the sense of social ministry and concern for justice that marked the early church and that to some extent had been carried forward into the modern era within Catholic traditions. Modern Catholic social teaching emerges after a period of social, economic, and political upheaval during which the Catholic Church had become more and more removed from the center of Western culture. Enlightenment ideas inspired revolutions as well as the founding of a new nation. As an increasingly industrialized society embraced political ideals of liberty and freedom, the preeminence of science, and a dedication to progress, the Catholic Church was skeptical and reacted as if sinister forces were actually driving many of these ideals. People who welcomed Enlightenment ideas emphasizing critical thought and the pursuit of civil freedoms encountered resistance by the Catholic Church. Over time, church authorities became more insular, opposing ways of thinking that they deemed dangerous because they were fearful that religious values and rights would be compromised or trampled by liberals, revolutionaries, and socialists. As a result many were highly critical of the church and there arose "an anti-Christian secularism and...virulent anticlericalism"[39] that labeled the church as out of date and out of touch with popular thought.

The Catholic Church reacted negatively to liberalism and economic individualism. For example, it saw how ordinary people suffered when nineteenth-century *laissez-faire* attitudes led to economic individualism that favored the rich over the poor, and effectively created a powerful elite and a majority of disenfranchised, dependent people. Catholic thinkers also identified secularism as the cause of economic and social problems because political authority was allowed free rein and seemed divorced from God, while the economy operated freely without moral and ethical foundations. In the world of ideas, theorists like Marx and Darwin were a direct challenge to the church. Both questioned fundamental Catholic Christian suppositions about life, the nature of the human person and the social world. Both were criticized and rejected by the church. Overall, modern life and the church seemed to point in opposite and opposed directions, and as a result, by the end of the nineteenth century few expected the church to engage the realities of modern life in meaningful ways. Most expected it to retreat more and more from the world.

Few people had high expectations for Pope Leo XIII when he became pope in 1878. Most expected him to remain, like his predecessor Pope Pius IX, secluded within the Vatican while tides of change swirled around him. Yet, Pope Leo did engage the world. He entered the spotlight with a cry of protest. In 1891, Pope Leo issued *Rerum Novarum: The Condition of Labor*, the first encyclical to focus attention on the misery of the poor and the plight of workers. In it Pope Leo condemned both liberal capitalism, which isolated workers and placed them at the mercy of rich owners whose greed imposed working conditions that were effectively modern-day slavery, and socialism for depriving individuals of their right to private property and essentially disregarding human rights and people's religious rights. Pope Leo criticized modern trends that had increased disparities in wealth and led to the impoverishment of many people throughout the world. Drawing on the teaching of Thomas Aquinas, Pope Leo also cleared the way for future writers who would draw more deeply from the biblical and historical traditions of the church in order to defend the dignity of the human person, the common good, and other social and moral values that were often overlooked in the name of progress.

On the fortieth anniversary of *Rerum Novarum*, Pope Pius XI issued *Quadragesimo Anno: After Forty Years* (1931). Building very carefully on his predecessor's work, Pope Pius criticized capitalism for exalting individualism, contrasting its excesses with principles that benefit workers, namely, social justice and social charity (#88). Once again he rejected socialism, and now Communism for its "merciless class warfare and the complete abolition of private ownership" (#112).[40]

The body of social wisdom that we know today as Catholic social teaching developed over time. It is grounded in Scripture, tradition, and an understanding of natural law as applied to the human condition and problems in society. Its major contribution is its insights into human nature and the human condition. Written for believers, Catholic social teaching offers a deep understanding of human nature and broad views of a catholic, that is, universal nature, since it is meant for people of all beliefs throughout the world.

OVERVIEW OF CATHOLIC SOCIAL TEACHING RELEVANT TO SEEKING JUSTICE FOR THE POOR

Justice for the poor is a theme that grows incrementally in Catholic social teaching. An exploration of the papal documents issued since 1891, the documents from Vatican Council II (1962–1965), the letter from the Synod of Bishops (1971), and the U.S. Catholic bishops' pastoral letter on the economy, provides an overview of contemporary church teaching about the poor and stresses the responsibility of Christians and all people to care for the poor as a matter of justice.

Catholic social encyclicals and pastoral letters emphasize concern for the poor as a matter of justice, and as Catholic social teaching develops, the scope of this concern expands. In *Rerum Novarum* Pope Leo XIII responded to the exploitation of European and North American workers by stressing the need to remedy the misery that was the experience of the vast majority of the poor (#2). He upheld the rights of the individual and the just use of property and wealth; he also examined the rights and duties of workers/poor and employers/wealthy in society. This encyclical advocates for a just wage and working conditions conducive to promoting the welfare of workers. Workers' rights are a matter of justice and need to be protected by the government (#34). In fact, the state has the obligation of protecting "the poor and helpless (who) have a claim to special consideration," for they often have "no resources of their own to fall back upon, and must chiefly rely upon the assistance of the State" (#29).

Forty years later Pope Pius XI addressed social injustice in the midst of a worldwide economic depression in *Quadragesimo Anno*, reaffirming the church's right and duty "to deal authoritatively with social and economic problems" for the simple reason that these are moral issues (#41). To curb the excesses of the marketplace, that is, unregulated competition, social justice and social charity are needed as guiding principles. For the spirit of justice to permeate all institutions of public and social life, "this justice must be truly operative. It must build up a juridical and social order able to pervade all economic activity. Social charity should be...the soul of this order" (#88).[41] Social justice is to serve as the norm for public institutions as they strive to provide for the common good (#110).

Pope John XXIII reiterated the call of his predecessors in *Mater et Magistra: Christianity and Social Progress* (1961), as he addressed the enormous gap between rich and poor—among nations and even within economically developed countries. Like Pope Pius XI, he maintained that "economic undertakings be governed by justice and charity" for the simple reason that these are "the principle laws of social life" (#39). Pope John also upheld the principle of subsidiarity, which holds that higher authorities should not perform functions that rightfully belong to individuals or smaller communities (#53, 152).

Essentially, cooperation is needed to balance the rights of individuals with the activity of the state (#66). Justice would always be the norm guiding not only the distribution of wealth, but also the conditions under which workers functioned (#82). Pope John was optimistic about development as a way of extending prosperity to nations worldwide. He warned that mistrust leads many people and nations to direct valuable resources to destructive actions, and that aggression prevents people from sharing the basic necessities of life. In an age when science and technology seem to open up "almost limitless horizons," leaders and governments need to find ways for these advances to "prove useful as instruments of civilization" (#211). Pope John reminded us that "the church's teaching on social matters...has truth as its guide, justice as its end, and love as its driving force" (#226). To achieve the goal of applying Catholic social thought to life, he suggested a practical, three-stage process that consists of observing the situation, judging by careful evaluation, and acting based on the norms of Catholic social teaching (#236).

The Second Vatican Council (1962–1965), as Marvin Krier Mich points out, was "an event and a process that redefined the Roman Catholic church's self-identity and its relationship with contemporary societies."[42] First called by Pope John XXIII in January 1959, the council opened on October 11, 1962, at St. Peter's Basilica in Rome. Meeting over a period of four years, first under the guidance of Pope John and then his successor, Pope Paul VI, the council included nearly three thousand Catholic churchmen from all nations of the world who worked on schemata, or draft documents, prepared by commissions. The Council Fathers were painfully aware of a world suffering from broken dreams and promises—the Holocaust in Europe, the threat of atomic warfare, regional strife and hatred—and yet, they drew upon their faith to approach the world with openness and optimism. The Second Vatican Council produced sixteen documents that testified to a sense of new life and renewal. *Gaudium et Spes: Pastoral Constitution on the Church in the Modern World* (1965) is notable for emphasizing the church's willingness to engage the world.

As Donal Dorr relates, *Gaudium et Spes* "expresses the consensus that emerged after three years of private and public dialogue, debate, and even controversy."[43] Lone voices, such as Dom Helder Camara, archbishop of Olinda and Recife in Brazil, reminded the council to look beyond church issues; he was soon joined by other bishops who worked with groups of experts to educate themselves about issues of concern to the world. The document went through six drafts before its final approval, but one could argue that such intense interaction on the part of church leaders produced a more universal—catholic—document worthy of the attention of all people. It is also worth noting that the pastoral constitution had wider appeal, much like a mirror that reflects the viewer as well as the background or a microphone that encourages participants' comments that broaden the discussion. Dorr mentions its "dialectical approach: the ideal is contrasted with reality—a reality marred by social evil."[44] This approach appeals to people who are skeptical of good news because they suspect that it is contrived like some news stories in the media.

As the church identifies with "the joys and the hopes, the griefs and the anxieties" of all people (#1), she is energized to scrutinize "the signs of the times...interpreting them in the light of the gospel" (#4). These include humanity's "social and cultural transformation," even as people experience difficulties attributed to the extreme contrast between "an abundance of wealth, resources, and economic power" and the millions "tormented by hunger and poverty" (#7–8). Created in the image of God,

men and women can abuse their liberty, as we see in their lifelong struggle between good and evil, bearing witness to "the call of grandeur and
the depths of misery" (#13). The human person, by reason of his or her
inherent dignity, is entitled to a broad range of rights, including the right
to food, clothing, and shelter; the right to education and employment;
the right to privacy and respect, rights that are meant to guarantee a truly
human life. Social order "must be founded in truth, built on justice, and
animated by love" (#26). Equality and social justice are essential. When
people's rights are trampled or ignored, the dignity of persons cries out
for redress. "For excessive economic and social differences...cause scandal, and militate against social justice, equity, the dignity of the human
person, as well as social and international peace" (#29). Against a backdrop of people's growing interdependence, and "a mutual respect for the
full spiritual dignity of the person" (#23), the council called for solidarity, "social unity" based on "mutual service" (#32).

The welfare of society is at stake when economic development inten-
sifies social inequalities. Economic development has all too often led
to "a decline in the social status of the weak and...contempt for the
poor" (#63). The wealth/poverty contrast is so great that "while the few
enjoy very great freedom of choice, the many...often subsist in living
and working conditions unworthy of human beings." Economic development is meant to be under human control with many people having
"an active share in directing that development"; such power is not to be
restricted to a select few or to the state (#65). The gifts of this earth are
not predestined for a fortunate few; they are actually "common property" as needed for the benefit of others (#69). Since good working conditions are far from the norm, reforms are necessary "if income is to grow,
working conditions improve, job security increase, and an incentive to
working on one's own initiative be provided" (#71). Christians working
for socio-economic development and defending justice and charity contribute to prosperity and to peace. Seeking God's kingdom in the spirit
of the beatitudes will increase love of neighbor and perfect "the work of
justice under the inspiration of charity" (#72).

Pope Paul VI wrote *Populorum Progressio: On the Development of Peoples*
(1967) after traveling to many countries where he learned directly about

poverty and the many problems that threatened people throughout the world. He had addressed the United Nations General Assembly in October 1965, where he pleaded the cause of poor peoples. As a result of his direct experience and years of studied concern, Pope Paul approached poverty as a problem that needed to be solved not just for one's area or country, but for all nations where people suffer the consequences of poverty. He was clearly aware of the misery and oppression that poor peoples and nations suffer: the disparities between peoples and among nations, "the scandal of glaring inequalities" not just in material possessions but also in "the exercise of power" (#9). His approach was to advocate development in its fullest human and spiritual sense: for all people "to seek to do more, know more and have more in order to be more," so that people can enjoy political freedom, social and economic growth to guarantee that they enjoy full participation in society (#6).

Pope Paul identified the church's mission: to contribute "a global vision of man and of the human race" based on the teaching of Jesus whose primary mission was to preach the gospel to the poor and the need to enter into history as a positive force for human progress (#12–13). His approach was reminiscent of his experience at the Second Vatican Council where dialogue forged consensus and resulted in documents that addressed the needs of the church and the world. His method was essentially that of a consensus builder and a teacher. As a teacher, he shared the facts about the excesses of capitalism: the drive for profit, competition as "the supreme law of economics," greed in owning and controlling the means of production that results in "excessive suffering, injustices, and fratricidal conflicts" (#26). There was a sense of urgency because of the cries of injustice on the part of the many who were suffering. Pope Paul advocated programs and agencies to plan and work together to improve the lot of the poor (#29–30, 33). He encouraged programs to "reduce inequalities, fight discriminations, free man from...servitude"; in short, to work for social progress, a concept that depends on educating people. Illiteracy can be as devastating as hunger for "an illiterate is a person with an undernourished mind"; education can fill the void by enabling people to act capably on their own behalf (#35). Pope Paul reminded nations that it was their moral duty to help those in need, out of a sense of shared humanity. This sense of brotherhood is based on human solidarity which binds nations to give aid to developing countries; on social justice whereby trade relations between powerful and weak nations could be resolved more equitably; and on universal charity where the habit of giving and receiving will prevent the progress of one group at the expense of another (#44). Contributing to poor nations will benefit the rich just as surely as greed will "call down upon them [the rich] the judgment of God and the wrath of the poor" (#49).

As a consensus builder, Pope Paul called upon the rich and powerful to activate planned programs and to collaborate at the world level with organizations such as a World Fund whose assets would come in part from abandoning armaments (#50–52). When countries work together it will result in "a system of cooperation feely undertaken, an effective and mutual sharing, carried out with equal dignity on either side, for the construction of a more human world" (#54). Pope Paul considered collaboration as essential for world unity, a unity that "should allow all peoples to become the artisans of their destiny" and where mutual respect and friendship will be a mark of interdependence (#65).

As he envisioned development, the real benefit is world peace. When nations "wage war on misery and…struggle against injustice" they will improve the life of all people, lead to progress, and achieve "the common good of humanity" (#76). Pope Paul appealed to all people of good will to live a more human life where justice and love will prevail; to achieve this end, he encouraged the privileged members of society, educators, journalists, government officials, and delegates to international organizations to use their unique talents to effect this new world (#82–83).

To commemorate the eightieth anniversary of *Rerum Novarum*, Pope Paul VI issued an apostolic letter, *Octogesima Adveniens: A Call to Action* (1971). The world is a paradox: The pope heard both "cries of distress" and "cries of hope" as he moved among people as he visited different continents. The economic, cultural, and political development of nations had led to "flagrant inequalities," the contrasts between industrial and agricultural areas, prosperity and starvation, and high standards of culture versus illiteracy (#2). World problems had become so complex and diverse that Pope Paul urged Christian communities "to analyze with objectivity the situation which is proper to their own country, to shed on it the light of the gospel's unalterable words and to draw principles of reflection, norms of judgment and directives for action from the social teaching of the Church" (#4). Action for social justice begins in a particular place where people who are more familiar with their own situation can then use the wisdom of the gospel as well as reflection on the principles of Catholic social teaching to determine how best to address their problems and work for a just solution. New social problems have been created by the modern economy: "professional or regional unemployment, redeployment and mobility of persons, permanent adaptation of workers, and disparity of conditions in the different branches of industry" (#9).

Despite severe social problems, men and women still aspire to equality and participation, a natural outgrowth of their dignity and freedom. Aspirations do not always translate into deeds and structures; human rights are often disregarded and stifled to satisfy the interests of those in power. For equality to overcome discrimination, exploitation, and contempt, there is a need to move beyond entrenched individualism by educating for solidarity. Pope Paul stated clearly that the gospel "instructs us in the preferential respect due to the poor and the special situation they have in society," a mandate that calls for the more fortunate to "renounce some of their rights so as to place their goods more generously at the service of others" (#23).

Pope Paul realized that equality and participation are related to and depend upon people's ability to take an active role in the political life of society. Education for political participation includes information regarding one's rights as well as one's duties toward others (#24). The church's role is to encourage people in their search for answers to life's questions, to move beyond general principles by sharing the gospel message, and to respond with a "will to serve and attention to the poorest" (#42).

Pope Paul VI had the foresight to convene the bishops of the world on a regular basis with the goal of implementing the teaching of the Second Vatican Council. In 1971, the Synod of Bishops produced a document, *Justice in the World*, to examine justice as "the mission of the People of

God." The bishops who represented dioceses throughout the world stated that they were saddened by serious injustices worldwide as evidenced by "a network of domination, oppression, and abuses" that effectively prevented people from enjoying the benefits of lives enhanced by justice. "The cry of those who suffer violence and are oppressed by unjust systems and structures" is in stark contrast with the church proclaiming as did Jesus, "Good News to the poor, freedom to the oppressed, and joy to the afflicted." And yet, as the bishops stated in their introduction, "Action on behalf of justice and participation in the transformation of the world fully appear to us as a constitutive dimension of the preaching of the Gospel." Working to achieve justice is raised to new heights; it is identified as a mandate of the gospel. Action for justice is on a par with a communal effort to transform the world; these will guarantee that the good news comes to people in this time and place in history (#1–6).

Justice in the World addresses the paradoxes of wealth and poverty in the world: a unified world society where there are divisions between nations, races, and classes; economic growth while there is underdevelopment and "pockets of poverty" within wealthier areas; a world rich in resources yet riddled by pilfering and pollution (Chap. 1: #7–19). The document refers to Scripture where God is "the liberator of the oppressed and the defender of the poor," where faith in God is demanded, as is justice toward one's neighbor. *Justice in the World* notes that Jesus, who united the human to God and humans with one another, spoke of God as father and worked tirelessly to bring justice, God's mandate, to the needy and oppressed. It declares that preaching the good news of the gospel leads to liberating men and women in their "present existence in this world," and that, "action in the cause of justice in the world" will reveal the true power of the Christian message (Chap. 2).

The bishops conclude that justice must begin at home—within church structures and communities. Specific recommendations then follow regarding fair wages and the right to participate, freedom of expression, and a share in decision making. The bishops address the need to educate for justice. They note that the gospel is like leaven meant to permeate all aspects of life: family, school, work, social and civic life. This "truly human way of life in justice, love, and simplicity" requires "a renewal of heart," as well as "a critical sense," and a willingness to renounce values that contradict justice. In effect, "knowledge of the concrete situation" will lead to "transformation of the world." The bishops state that the gospel message is also practical, for "it comes through action, participation, and vital contact with the reality of injustice." They add: "Our mission demands that we should courageously denounce injustice, with charity, prudence, and firmness, in sincere dialogue with all parties concerned." They also encourage reliance on liturgy. "The liturgy of the word, catechesis, and the celebration of the sacraments have the power to help us to discover the teaching of the prophets, the Lord, and the apostles on the subject of justice" (Chap. 3).[45]

In Pope Benedict XVI's encyclical, *Deus Caritas Est: God Is Love* (2005), he reminds us that the Acts of the Apostles showed how "charitable activity on behalf of the poor and suffering" was "an essential part of the Church of Rome from the beginning" (#23). Those committed to doing good for others need "a heart that sees," like the Good Samaritan who sees and responds with love to the needs of the wounded man (#31). In modern times the church has a role in working toward justice. While there are two domains, the church and the state, the church is concerned with "the promotion of justice through efforts to bring about openness of mind and will to the demands of the common good" (#28). Through its social teaching, the church uses "reason and natural law" in its desire to "help form consciences in political life and to stimulate greater insight into the authentic requirements of justice" (#28). Once again Pope Benedict reminds us that charity is the force that animates those who work in public life to achieve the common good (#29).

Pope Benedict XVI wrote about the Eucharist in *Sacramentum Caritatis: Sacrament of Charity* (2007). He reminds us that the crucified Christ calls Christians to share love with all people through acts of charity and working for justice. Since Christ shed his blood for all, "We must denounce situations contrary to human dignity…and at the same time affirm the inestimable value of each individual person" (#89). In a response to the untold numbers of refugees throughout the world, he reminds us that "The Lord Jesus, the bread of eternal life, spurs us to be mindful of the situations of extreme poverty in which a great part of humanity still lives;

these are situations for which human beings bear a clear and disquieting responsibility" (#90). For Christians to fulfill their social and political responsibilities to other people, they would benefit from being "adequately prepared through practical education in charity and justice" (#91).

Principles for Addressing the Issue of Poverty. An understanding of poverty and justice within Catholic social teaching was further developed when the United States Catholic bishops issued a pastoral letter on the economy, *Economic Justice for All* (1986). First proposed at the November 1980 meeting of the bishops, the pastoral letter was the result of a collegial process that involved church leaders and expert lay men and women who participated in intensive hearings. They read and analyzed thousands of written comments and reactions and attended numerous meetings, at which over a six-year period they discussed and debated proposals. The first draft in November 1984 underwent numerous revisions until the fourth draft earned almost unanimous approval (225 to 9 votes) at the November 1986 meeting of the U.S. bishops.[46]

The bishops addressed the economy to determine "how it touches human life and whether it protects or undermines the dignity of the human person." Their primary concern was how economic decisions "help or hurt people, strengthen or weaken family life, advance or diminish the quality of justice in our land" (#1). Based on Scripture and the social teachings of the church, the letter presented six basic moral principles:

1. "Every economic decision and institution must be judged in light of whether it protects or undermines the dignity of the human person." The human person is sacred, a reflection of God. Human dignity flows from God. "We judge any economic system by what it does *for* and *to* people and by how it permits all to *participate* in it. The economy should serve people..." (#13).

2. "Human dignity can be realized and protected only in community." The human person is social and relates to others within a community. Basic to the sacred/social quality of each person is the question, "Does economic life enhance or threaten our life together as community?" (#14)

3. "All people have a right to participate in the economic life of society." Each person has a right to work; this is how individuals satisfy their material needs, creatively use their talents, and "contribute to the larger community" (#15).

4. "All members of a society have a special obligation to the poor and…vulnerable." From Scripture we learn that the true measure of justice is how one treats the poor, that is, the widow, the orphan, and the stranger. Jesus proclaimed, "The Spirit of the Lord is upon me….He has sent me to bring glad tidings to the poor" (Lk 4:18). Jesus was on the side of the poor. His disciples must ask themselves, Do I accept the "option for the poor," namely, to speak for the voiceless, to defend the defenseless, to assess lifestyles, policies, and social institutions in terms of their impact on the poor? (#16)

5. "Human rights are the minimum conditions for life in community." Human rights include civil, political, and economic rights. As Pope John XXIII declared, "All people have a right to life, food, clothing, shelter, rest, medical care, education, and employment" (#17).

6. "Society as a whole, acting through public and private institutions, has the moral responsibility to enhance human dignity and protect human rights." Government has "a positive moral responsibility in safeguarding human rights and ensuring that the minimum conditions of human dignity are met for all" (#18).

Poverty itself is better understood by a close study of *Economic Justice for All*. This document defines poverty as "the lack of sufficient material resources required for a decent life" (#173). Poverty "entails a more profound kind of deprivation, a denial of full participation in the economic, social, and political life of society and an inability to influence decisions that affect one's life. It means being powerless in a way that assaults…one's fundamental human dignity" (#188). While poverty begins as lacking resources, it actually removes a person from mainstream society to such a degree that he or she is rendered powerless. Poverty robs a person of his or her sense of autonomy. The direct result of poverty is marginalization, a process that effectively isolates the person from the normal activities of society (#203). Poverty is more invidious than not having money or goods; it is evil, for it eats away at the very marrow of a person's worth as a human being.

Poverty conveys the sense of being deprived of something important, of something essential for daily living. It becomes real when we consider what it means to be poor. Poverty is then humanized and embodied in those who suffer its consequences. As Peter Henriot simply stated,

> To be poor is to be hungry, to be without decent shelter and clothes, to lack adequate educational and healthcare opportunities, to be unemployed, to be on the margin of society, to feel excluded from decisions that affect you, to feel controlled by outside forces, to be unable to deal with problems of daily existence, to be discriminated against.[47]

Poverty, then, isolates and undermines an individual by denying his or her fundamental human rights. It is a complex web of woes that prevents poor people from living healthy, normal lives by forcing them to work against great odds and diminishing their humanity. Poverty in the United States is truly "unfinished business in the American experiment in freedom and justice for all" (#9).

Justice and Participation in the Community. Since the economy is rooted in the community, the bishops explore how best to fulfill one's responsibilities as an individual and as a member of society. The commandment of love, love of God and of our neighbor, is the ideal that we see modeled in the life of Jesus (#64). Biblical justice is an ideal that would effectively result in a just society. But for those who need norms for living justly, the bishops restate the minimum norms of conduct for living in an imperfect world. Basic justice is built upon three dimensions known as commutative justice, distributive justice, and social justice.

Commutative justice is the justice called forth when individuals and groups interact, in situations that require contracts, sales agreements, and employment. Based on the dignity of the human person, commutative justice evokes a sense of fairness among individuals and in personal and communal agreements. This rests upon giving one's word and honoring agreements, as if all aspects of the agreement/contract concerned one's self.

Distributive justice looks at how income, wealth, and power are shared in society. This is essentially the right of all persons to share the goods of the world. In the words of the Second Vatican Council, "The right to have a share of earthly goods sufficient for oneself and one's family belongs to everyone. The Fathers and Doctors of the Church held this view, teaching that we are obliged to come to the relief of the poor and to do so not merely out of our superfluous goods" (see *Gaudium et Spes* #69) (#70).

Social justice, in the words of the U.S. bishops, "implies that persons have an obligation to be active and productive participants in the life of society" (#70). It stresses the duty of each person to participate in society contributing her or his abilities "to help create the goods, services, and other nonmaterial or spiritual values necessary for the welfare of the whole community" (#71). Social justice concerns the right to participate in society and in social decision making. This aspect of social justice will be more fully explored in Chapter 4.

POVERTY IN THE UNITED STATES: A CATHOLIC PERSPECTIVE

Poverty in the United States is an issue of social justice that has been addressed by Catholic social teaching. In *Catholic Social Teaching and United States Welfare Reform*, a study of the history, context, and content of the 1996 U.S. welfare reform legislation, Thomas Massaro presents principles for discussing poverty in a broader context so that people with different religious, political, economic, and social beliefs can more readily address poverty. Principles are like structural frameworks that once in place provide a solid basis upon which to build. They are essential, the bottom line, and the starting point from which agreement can build to a greater, more comprehensive consensus.

While people may share a basic belief, the actual translation of that belief into action will differ widely. As developed by Protestant ethicists, the concept of a "middle axiom" is a useful tool that has the potential of appealing to people from diverse backgrounds. According to Massaro, middle axioms are "provisional formulations of Christian social principles" that address areas of concern that "may serve as loci of overlapping agreement, holding the potential to build bridges among social observers of diverse backgrounds." Middle axioms that are more general can be applied to many societies throughout history and therefore "enjoy a higher level of moral authority." Three such middle axioms are applicable to justice for the poor: 1) Social membership must be universal. 2) No person is a surplus person. 3) There is a preferential option for the poor.[48]

Social membership must be universal. Scripture states clearly that men and women are made in the image of God and that God saw that all of creation is very good. All humans share an inherent dignity that flows from being created in the image of God. Humans long to be with persons who will enhance their joys and mitigate their sorrows. They are social creatures with the capacity to work together for common goals and struggle against common enemies. The friends, acquaintances, and loved ones who share their time and place make their lives memorable. The universal quality of social membership is worth examining from the vantage point of Catholic social teaching in a variety of documents.

Rerum Novarum presents a world view in which harmony and agreement between rich and poor is desirable, just as the human body enjoys symmetry and balance among its members. While good order is extolled, the dignity of each person is based on "moral qualities, that is, in virtue." Dignity requires that respect be accorded every human and that workers be treated justly in terms of working conditions and wages. In fact, "To defraud any one of wages that are his due is a crime which cries to the avenging anger of heaven" (#20, 15–17). Equality is presented as an ideal, the hoped-for reality based on rights from God, for "all men are equal; there is no difference between rich and poor" (#32).

Mater et Magistra: Christianity and Social Progress (1961) states unequivocally that human dignity flows from God. "Mutual relationships between [people] absolutely require a right ordering of the human conscience in relation to God, the source of all truth, justice, and love" (#215).

In his encyclical, *Pacem in Terris: Peace on Earth* (1963), Pope John XXIII extols a universal common good that flows from a person's dignity as a child of God and that involves rights proper to all humans (#11–27). Rights are linked with duties: toward oneself and toward others: "A well-ordered human society requires that [people] recognize and observe their mutual rights and duties" (#31). Essential to the inherent dignity of the human person is "the right to act freely and responsibly" (#34). Human society is best served when justice is the guide that motivates citizens to respect the rights of others and to carry out their duties; and charity motivates people to care about their neighbor and to share their goods (#35). Such a society would show that social membership is universal.

Participation is essential for universal social membership. Only when persons participate in society at a variety of levels can they feel that they are truly part of that society. The U.S. Catholic bishops explain in *Economic Justice for All* (#77) what happens when participation is limited or denied to people:

> Basic justice demands the establishment of minimum levels of participation in the life of the human community for all persons. The ultimate injustice is for a person or group to be treated actively or abandoned passively as if they were non-members of the human race. To treat people this way is effectively to say that they simply do not count as human beings.

The bishops give examples of persons who are excluded from social life, the marginalized: in the political sphere when free speech is restricted, power is limited to a select few, or the state resorts to repression. Marginalization can result from poverty when economic forces render the poor, the disabled, and the unemployed powerless. Stated more positively, "justice demands that social institutions be ordered in a way that guarantees all persons the ability to participate actively in the economic, political, and cultural life of society" (#77–78).

To participate in American society people need sufficient income, and for most people this comes from their work. The idea of society taking an active role in helping citizens find adequate employment was stated clearly in *Gaudium et Spes* (#67). *Economic Justice for All* expands this idea by saying that "All persons have a right to earn a living, which for most people in our economy is through remunerative employment" (#80). The U.S. bishops build on the concept of universal human rights as outlined in *Pacem in Terris* by stating that all persons have "a right to security in the event of sickness, unemployment, and old age." In fact, "Participation in the life of the community calls for the protection of this same right to employment, as well as the right to healthful working conditions, to wages, and other benefits sufficient to provide individuals and their families with a standard of living in keeping with human dignity" (#80).

As experience reveals, work is not always available or when available, work does not necessarily pay a living wage. Moreover, in times of distress, for example, the death of a parent or guardian who was the breadwinner or a divorce that reconfigures the family, family income may be drastically reduced. Women with children often have to apply for welfare as a way to survive. In the United States, welfare and most services for the poor depend on a means test, which determines eligibility for cash payments or benefits after examining the finances of the person(s) who apply for aid. Stated differently, a means test focuses on the means people have to support themselves financially. This contrasts with the Social Security system that is based on participation, namely, the contributions of the employer and employee over a required period of time. Welfare as we know it developed as a second-level response to the destitution of the Great Depression. While the United States welfare system has some ability to help the poor, it is not a comprehensive solution to poverty. Other industrialized countries, notably in Europe, have developed as welfare states. Some even provide cash allowances for all children. The United States offers assistance only on a limited basis. The challenge today is to work to develop a public consensus for the United States to provide greater public welfare benefits in order to ensure that all persons living in the United States share in the benefits of membership in our society.

No person is a surplus person. The call to universal inclusion flows from "...the aspiration to equality and the aspiration to participation, two forms of [a person's] dignity and freedom" (*Quadragesimo Anno*, #22). This second principle, the principle of participation, focuses attention on the fact that persons have been excluded. Historically there are examples of cultural exclusion; for example, castes that relegate people to lower or higher status based on accidents of birth. Socially and economically, people are often excluded: for example, the homeless and immigrants. Culturally, entertainment and advertising are aimed at certain groups. These people are worth a considerable expenditure of time and energy, because there is an expectation that they will purchase products to enhance their beauty and prowess. In the youth-dominated culture of the United States, older people sometimes seem superfluous. In particular the mentally ill, the handicapped, the poor have limited value in American society, so people often look beyond them or, even worse, through them.

In the United States the poor have traditionally been classified as "deserving" (widows and children) or "undeserving" (unwed mothers, non-working adults, and those with chemical or drug dependencies). Labels pose a barrier to inclusion; society will help those who are poor through no fault of their own, but resist helping those who do not observe accepted moral behavior and in some cases have not succeeded in a highly competitive society. The problem in ignoring those with problems is that children are often the first to suffer. The reality is that adults need help so that assistance may be provided for their innocent children.

U.S. workers are currently experiencing greater job insecurity and as a result are made to feel like "surplus persons." The globalization of the economy that brings inexpensive goods to American superstores has also meant that U.S. workers have lost jobs that pay a living wage and as a result millions of Americans no longer have or can afford health insurance. As their jobs are outsourced, they are made to feel that they are no longer needed in the work force, that they are in effect surplus commodities. Corporations routinely relocate to countries with fewer restrictions governing labor conditions, where they can pay lower wages and ignore environmental concerns. As a result, U.S.

workers are often left with no alternative except to work longer hours at jobs that pay lower wages. The idea of being retrained for different, well-paying jobs is more fantasy than reality. Many able-bodied adults worry that they will be jobless and left without health benefits or even a pension. The news reports these situations on a regular basis: corporate takeovers, downsizing, and more recently, businesses that file for bankruptcy and renege on union-negotiated pensions and benefits. Amid this turmoil, it is important to recall the words of Pope John Paul II in his encyclical *Centesimus Annus: On the Hundredth Anniversary of Rerum Novarum* (1991) (#27):

> Human work, by its nature, is meant to unite peoples, not divide them. Peace and prosperity, in fact, are goods which belong to the whole human race; it is not possible to enjoy them in a proper and lasting way if they are achieved and maintained at the cost of other peoples and nations, by violating their rights or excluding them from the sources of well-being.

Corporations by their very nature are on a constant quest for higher profits to reward their investors with greater returns. Despite their initiative, dedication, and hard work, American workers are at risk of being replaced by lower paid workers in other countries. This reality is a serious challenge to individuals and society alike. Overall, to protect the rights of American workers and their families we can argue that as a nation we need to embrace more fully the conviction that a person should never be excluded from the table of social discourse and economic and social decision making.

There is a preferential option for the poor. This phrase sums up all that the church has taught and done over many years in terms of caring for and caring about the poor, humbly acknowledging that each poor person is Jesus before us. Concern for the poor is rooted in Scripture and manifested in the Christian community's consistent ethic of care. *Gaudium et Spes: Pastoral Constitution on the Church in the Modern World* reminded us that the Fathers and Doctors of the Church taught that men and women are obliged to help the poor not merely from superfluous goods but at personal sacrifice (#69). This same document emphasized that we are the neighbors of each and every person and that we are obliged to actively help our neighbor (#27). The Latin American Conference of Bishops meeting in Medellín, Colombia (1968) and Puebla, Mexico (1979) emphasized this concern because their people were suffering intensely from a material poverty so deep and pervasive that they labeled it as "institutional violence." These bishops stated that the poor challenge the church to conversion, service, and solidarity (*Puebla Conference Document*, 1979, #1147). They also stated unequivocally that the option for the poor requires changes in unjust political, economic, and social structures (#1155). The universal church subsequently referred to the option for the poor. Pope John Paul II in *Sollicitudo Rei Socialis: On Social Concern* (1987) explained *the option or love of preference for the poor* when he wrote (#42):

> This is an option, or a special form of primacy in the exercise of Christian charity, to which the whole tradition of the Church bears witness. It affects the life of each Christian inasmuch as he or she seeks to imitate the life of Christ, but it applies equally to our social responsibilities and hence to our manner of living, and to the logical decisions to be made concerning the ownership and use of goods.

The U.S. Catholic bishops stated emphatically in *Economic Justice for All* that "the poor have the single most urgent economic claim on the conscience of the nation" (#86). They stressed that we have an obligation "to evaluate social and economic activity from the viewpoint of the poor and the powerless" (#87). Their pastoral letter

> repeatedly calls for a reorientation of economic structures and public policies so that the poor benefit in two ways: first, that their most basic and immediate needs be met; and second, that they are afforded enhanced opportunities to participate in all facets of the life of the mainstream, including dignified standards of living, healthy family life, and greater access to economic power. The bishops' letter...interprets the option for the poor not as an adversarial slogan which en-

dorses class conflict, but as an appeal for social cooperation
that will benefit all.[49]

The mandate to embrace the preferential option for the poor is a challenge for us as a society. It calls us to work with the poor so that they
may enjoy life and all the privileges that flow from their dignity. Once
again, it is not a case of doing for, but rather an opportunity for working
with, those in need. Only when all of us, rich and poor, have invested
ourselves can we become truly empowered as citizens of our nation and
of the world community.

THE ROLE OF THE INSTITUTIONAL CATHOLIC CHURCH IN U.S. WELFARE REFORM

The Catholic Church with its history of social teaching continued its
advocacy for the poor when it entered the debate over changes to the
U.S. welfare system. In John A. Coleman's analysis of American Catholic
organizations, he notes that these groups generally follow the lead of the
hierarchy in formulating Catholic public policy initiatives.[50] Coleman
considers this a re-active rather than a pro-active role. He describes the
institution responsible for producing public policy: the United States
Conference of Catholic Bishops (USCCB). The bishops function through
semi-annual meetings of their national conference and through committees whose membership is limited to the bishops. They are served
by a staff of over 350 lay people, priests, deacons, and religious. In 1986
the bishops' pastoral letter, *Economic Justice for All*, focused attention on
moral principles related to a just economy, a Christian vision of economic life, and a discussion of issues related to employment and poverty. It was a natural progression for these episcopal groups to join the
discussion on U.S. welfare reform by actively reminding Congress of the
principles of Catholic social teaching.

In addition to the national conference, there are some thirty state
Catholic conferences of bishops that also monitor their respective state
governments and legislatures and issue statements on public policy.
These state conferences are important lobbies, especially in the present

setting where responsibility for welfare has shifted dramatically to the states. About a hundred dioceses also sponsor peace and justice offices whose duties vary from educational efforts to encouraging engagement in policy and lobbying.

Catholic institutions include national federations that address issues related to education, health, and social services. These institutions are separate legal entities, but they are in contact with and follow the lead of the USCCB on policy issues. The Catholic institution that has consistently researched and lobbied on welfare reform is Catholic Charities USA.

Catholic Charities USA, founded in 1910, is "the largest single nongovernmental provider of social services in the United States."[51] Its primary mission is to provide direct service to the poor (such as food pantries; housing-related services; counseling and mental health services; services for immigrants, refugees, addiction, pregnancy, and adoption) and also to be an advocate to reduce poverty, support families, and empower communities. Catholic Charities agencies are incorporated as public charitable trusts; they evolved from groups originally concerned with helping poor Catholics to agencies dedicated to serve the poor of every race, creed, and nationality. As a result, they have valuable firsthand knowledge of the needs of individuals and families in their struggle to survive poverty. Catholic Charities has a real sense of people's problems and how best to help people in need. Over the years it has worked to improve the lives of the poor. These efforts have included working to influence policy at the local, state, and national levels.

In terms of U.S. welfare reform, Catholic Charities USA published an eighteen-page white paper, *Transforming the Welfare System*, on January 24, 1994. In it, Catholic Charities was attentive to the consequences of stressing work responsibility over financial aid for all welfare dependents. It raised concerns about rigid time limits that ignored the real needs of poor people: the fact that some welfare recipients would not be able to hold a steady job, for example, those with severe learning disabilities or serious health problems; and the punitive nature of some provisions, for example, refusing welfare to children of teenage mothers or of legal immigrants. Some of the proposed measures of the reform were punitive in nature and could cause women to choose abortion rather than face destitution.

As politicians debated changes to the US welfare system, Catholic leaders worked steadily through bishops' conferences and committees to bring to mind the poor children and their families whose lives were at stake. In November 1994, the bishops of Connecticut issued "Welfare Reform and Basic Human Needs," which stated clearly that caring for the vulnerable members of society is a primary concern. Governments, not just churches and non-governmental groups, have a responsibility "to ensure that no one lacks the necessities of life."[52] Bishop John Ricard, chair of the USCCB Domestic Policy Committee, wrote to the House Ways and Means Committee, the Senate Finance Committee, and the Department of Health and Human Services on January 13, 1995, to remind the lawmakers that they had the lives of the poor in their hands. In his words, "Reform should serve the human needs of poor children and their families, not just the political needs of public officials....Its target ought to be poverty, not poor families."[53]

On February 16, 1995, the bishops of Florida issued a statement that emphasized the dignity and worth of the poor and stressed the need for "positive reform." They urged a concerted effort on the part of "both the public and private sectors to generate jobs at a fair wage, which in turn will reduce the need for welfare programs and give individuals human dignity and self-worth."[54] The USCCB Administrative Board issued a statement on March 19, 1995, urging Congress to respect human life and human dignity, to value the family and work, and to protect the vulnerable. They stressed the dignity of poor children and their families and stated how welfare reform was a measure of who Americans are as a nation. "The target of reform ought to be poverty, not poor families. We believe our society will be measured by how 'the least of these' are faring. Welfare reform will be a clear test of our nation's moral priorities and our commitment to seek the common good."[55]

These statements are powerful testimonials based on moral principles that sought to remind policymakers to act in the best interests of the poor and vulnerable. They are compelling reading. Their message was directed at those responsible for developing welfare legislation, the senators, representatives, and their staffs. With minimal press coverage, the public had limited knowledge of the Catholic Church's position on the issue of U.S. welfare reform. With recent advances in technology it is relatively simple to access information using the Web site (www.usccb.org) of the United States Conference of Catholic Bishops. Updated information on Welfare Policy: TANF (Temporary Assistance for Needy Families) Reauthorization is readily available for those interested in the Catholic Church's position. For updates on issues related to welfare policy, Network, a Catholic social justice lobby, provides information on current legislation in the U.S. Senate and House of Representatives and it offers the option of sending letters to the elected officials before critical votes are scheduled (www.networklobby.org).

AN ANALYSIS OF THE CHURCH'S EFFECTIVENESS IN WORKING FOR JUSTICE FOR THE POOR

Biblical understandings of justice, Christian traditions in which concern for the poor are central, and Catholic social teaching are still embraced by Christians today and in many ways seem to be improving the conditions of the poor. Of special interest is the contribution of Catholic social teaching. Donal Dorr has summarized the strengths and weaknesses of Catholic social teaching. In his judgment Catholic social teaching provides:

1. A humanistic teaching with the potential of appealing to all people of good will by inviting those of other traditions to dialogue, especially through the language of human rights

2. An emphasis on the values of participation and solidarity by encouraging people to acknowledge their own power and to embrace solidarity, the ability to share responsibility for one another

3. The possibility of applying it to many situations in different countries

4. A reliance on social analysis to identify the root causes of poverty

5. A solid base in the Bible which encourages ecumenical dialogue

6. A prophetic call to challenge oppression and exploitation and to inspire renewed hope for all, especially the poor and oppressed.

Catholic social teaching also has weaknesses. Despite all the messages of hope and the presentation of moral principles, the documents are difficult reading because they are abstract and written in a dry and not readily accessible style. Modern Catholic social thought is also decidedly Western in outlook. This is evident in its reliance on and limited criticism of Western models of development that encourage competitiveness, consumerism, and often result in exploitation of workers and farmers, thus increasing the divide between rich and poor. It has also failed to appreciate values that are vital to other cultures, such as respect for elders, reverence for nature, cooperation, and gentleness. In its determination to expose the evils of Marxism and socialism, it fails to confront and oppose unjust political regimes that protect the interests of the rich and ignore the plight of the poor. In attempting to maintain good order, it seems to uphold the interests of the more powerful classes in society. As a result, it is often reluctant to pursue social analysis to uncover the root causes of social injustice. Catholic social teaching speaks with great authority, but such statements have far less appeal than actions that bear witness, such as the heroic acts of activists working for justice. Single issues, for example, birth control and respect for life, often preempt other concerns. The right to life needs to address the quality of life in issues such as housing, education, health care, and work. Women's issues are frequently misunderstood and misrepresented as when the documents speak of a woman's place in the home as if for centuries and especially in current times, women had not worked to support their families. Sexism is evident not only in issues, but also in language. Non-inclusive language makes women invisible and is a justice issue because it perpetuates patriarchy. Issues of race and class get an overly optimistic presentation; in the United States there are deep divisions in society as we see in the higher rates of poverty for blacks and Hispanics. Catholic social teaching needs to include input from all people, especially the poor, women, people of color, and other nationalities. Finally, there is an urgent need to present guidelines for addressing environmental concerns in the larger context of the unity of creation. The earth is spiraling toward extinction and it is the poor who suffer most severely in regard to failing health and diminished life expectancy due to a ravaged environment: noxious air, unclean water, polluted land, and poisoned food, to name a few.[56]

A PLACE AT THE TABLE

The U.S. Catholic bishops issued *A Place at the Table: A Catholic Recommitment to Overcome Poverty and to Respect the Dignity of All God's Children* (2002) as a pastoral reflection on poverty. They use the image of the table to capture the ordinary and extraordinary tasks of human life. The table is a place where people eat to satisfy hunger, a place where people meet to make decisions, and a place where people worship and celebrate the Eucharist. While most take these activities for granted, the poor among us often do not have enough food, are excluded from the process of decision making, and may feel unwelcome at their place of worship. The bishops focus on poverty as a moral scandal and on human dignity as the right of every human being. They contrast poverty—affecting millions of people in the United States and throughout the world by destroying lives—with breaking the cycle of poverty. This is evident when poor people have worked hard, organized for a living wage, and effectively sought their rightful place at the table. However, the reality is that as some people pull ahead, many are left behind.

Catholic social teaching provides the backdrop: the biblical vision of treating all people with respect, compassion, and justice; modeling human actions on those of the God of justice who protects and defends the poor and on Jesus who encourages people to serve the poor by recognizing Jesus in every person in need; the historical context of caring for the weakest with the conviction that the world belongs to all, not only the rich; practices that enhance human dignity and uphold economic justice as everyone's right; and the principle of solidarity that calls all people to act justly toward one another as neighbor.

The bishops propose a new direction as they enlarge the vision of the table by describing the four legs, or organization, upon which it rests. The first leg of the table identifies families and individuals and their role in serving the poor. While acknowledging that every person has a responsibility to respect the dignity of others and to work to insure their own rights as well as those of others, the bishops' emphasis is on the primacy of marriage and family. For children to thrive, families need support from society and public policy that would "reward, encourage, and support parents, including single parents." Investing in those who care for children will benefit the common good. The second leg of the table is community organizations and religious institutions and their role in helping families. Negative forces such as discrimination, injustice, and neighborhood problems prompt people to cry for help. Institutions have the power to confront structural injustice and work with individuals as they struggle to build community. The third leg of the table is the marketplace and institutions of business, commerce, and labor. The private sector needs to reflect values that contribute to the common good. Corporate responsibility includes the duty of both employers and labor to provide even the poorest workers a place at the table in determining just wages and working conditions. Work is meant to enhance human dignity by allowing those who work full time to escape poverty. Workers and farmers need "living wages; access to health care; vacation time and family and medical leave; a voice and real participation in the workplace; and the prospect of a decent retirement." The fourth leg of the table is the role and responsibilities of government. Government is a positive force when it serves the common good and defends the poor and vulnerable. When problems require efforts beyond what the individual and the community can do, then government needs to use its power to overcome structural injustice. Just as a table cannot stand without strong, supportive legs, so too the Catholic tradition recognizes that families, communities, the marketplace, and government have the responsibility to work together to overcome poverty.[57]

In summary, the poor have a claim on our hearts and on our resources. God's actions and words of concern as revealed in Scripture encourage individuals and the community to work for justice. Poverty in all its dehumanizing aspects needs to be countered by principles of justice and charity. In a world that suffers from injustice, Christians today still strive to live by the biblical mandate to care for the poor as a matter of social justice. Despite difficulties in seeking justice for the poor, including those who question or reject the biblical mandate, God's call to righteousness and faithfulness is clear and constant. It urges us to respond willingly and with generosity to our gracious God who is revealed in the persons of the poor and afflicted. This responsibility requires the concerted effort of individuals and families, communities, the marketplace, and government to effect justice for the poor.

QUESTIONS FOR REFLECTION AND DISCUSSION

1. Use biblical texts to explain how God is a God of justice. Who benefits from God's view of justice? How does God react to injustice? How does the Bible describe a just person? Describe the differences between the "two women of justice."

2. How does the life of Jesus reflect a concern for the poor? Which stories and sayings show Jesus' attitude toward the poor? How did the early followers of Jesus show their care for those in need? What is meant by "a vision of radical equality for rich and poor"?

3. Trace the concern for poverty in the first four centuries. Refer to the writings and the teachings of the Fathers of the Church.

4. How were women involved in addressing poverty in the early church?

5. Review the section Charity for the Poor. Create a table in which you list the persons or groups, the time they lived, their contributions, the problems they encountered, and the attitudes toward the poor.

6. Explain what is meant by Catholic social teaching. How may it be defined? Describe the various aspects of Catholic social teaching.

7. Trace Catholic social teaching related to seeking justice for the poor. Create a chart with the names of the authors, the title of the document and the year it was issued, and the most important ideas. What pattern emerges as you review these documents?

8. Cite the six principles stated by the U.S. Bishops in their pastoral letter, *Economic Justice for All* (1986). How does this document describe poverty? Define the terms: commutative justice, distributive justice, and social justice.

9. Use the section Poverty in the United States as an Issue of Social Justice to explain the meaning of a "middle axiom." Then discuss the three axioms used to address justice for the poor. Explain the meaning of each, especially "preferential option for the poor."

10. What was the role of the institutional church in U.S. Welfare Reform? How could the church's effectiveness be increased in working for justice for the poor?

11. Describe the analysis of the U.S. Catholic Bishops' pastoral, *A Place at the Table* (2002), in the use of the image of the table as a reflection on poverty.

SUGGESTED READINGS

Catechism of the Catholic Church. Second edition. Washington, DC: United States Catholic Conference, 1997.

The Church in the Present-Day Transformation of Latin America in the Light of the Council, II, *Conclusions.* Bogotá, Colombia: General Secretariat of CELAM, 1970.

Coleman, John A. "American Catholicism, Catholic Charities USA, and Welfare Reform," Hugh Heclo and Wilfred M. McClay, eds. *Religion Returns to the Public Square.* Washington, DC: Woodrow Wilson Center Press, 2003.

Coleman, John A., ed. *One Hundred Years of Catholic Social Thought: Celebration and Challenge.* Maryknoll, NY: Orbis Books, 1991.

Couture, Pamela. *Blessed Are the Poor?* Nashville: Abingdon Press, 1991.

Curran, Charles E. *Catholic Social Teaching, 1891-Present: A Historical, Theological, and Ethical Analysis.* Washington, DC: Georgetown University Press, 2002.

DeBerri, Edward P., James E. Hug, with Peter J. Henriot, and Michael J. Schultheis. *Catholic Social Teaching: Our Best Kept Secret.* Fourth Revised and Expanded Edition. Maryknoll, NY: Orbis Books, 2003.

Donahue, John R. *What Does the Lord Require? A Bibliographical Essay on the Bible and Social Justice.* Saint Louis: Institute of Jesuit Sources, 2000.

González, Justo L. *Faith and Wealth: A History of Early Christian Ideas on the Origin, Significance, and Use of Money.* San Francisco: Harper, 1990.

Gremillion, Joseph. *The Gospel of Peace and Justice: Catholic Social Teaching since Pope John.* Maryknoll, NY: Orbis Books, 1976.

Haughey, John C., ed. *The Faith That Does Justice.* New York: Paulist Press, 1977.

Heclo, Hugh, and Wilfred M. McClay, eds. *Religion Returns to the Public Square.* Washington, DC: Woodrow Wilson Center Press, 2003.

Henriot, Peter. *Opting for the Poor: A Challenge for North Americans.* Washington, DC: Center of Concern, 1990.

Massaro, Thomas. *Catholic Social Teaching and United States Welfare Reform.* Collegeville, MN: Liturgical Press, 1998.

Massaro, Thomas J., and Thomas A. Shannon. *American Catholic Social Teaching.* Collegeville, MN: Liturgical Press, 2002.

Massey, Lesley F. *Women in the Church.* Jefferson, NC: McFarland & Co., 2002.

Mayer, Wendy and Pauline Allen, *John Chrysostom.* New York: Routledge, 2000.

McNamara, JoAnn Kay. *Sisters in Arms*. Cambridge, MA: Harvard University Press, 1996.

Nolan, Albert. *Jesus Before Christianity*. Twenty-fifth Anniversary Edition. Maryknoll, NY: Orbis Books, 2001.

O'Brien, David J., and Thomas A. Shannon. *Catholic Social Thought: The Documentary Heritage*. Maryknoll, NY: Orbis Books, 1992.

A Place at the Table: A Catholic Recommitment to Overcome Poverty and to Respect the Dignity of All God's Children. Washington, DC: United States Catholic Conference, 2002.

Ramsey, Boniface. *Beginning to Read the Fathers*. New York: Paulist Press, 1985.

NOTES

[1] John R. Donahue, S.J., *What Does the Lord Require? A Bibliographical Essay on the Bible and Social Justice* (Saint Louis: The Institute of Jesuit Sources, 2000), 23.

[2] Justo L. González, *Faith and Wealth: A History of Early Christian Ideas on the Origin, Significance, and Use of Money* (San Francisco: Harper, 1990), 81.

[3] Ibid., 83.

[4] Henry Clark, *The Christian Case Against Poverty* (New York: Association Press, 1965), 19.

[5] González, 92-93.

[6] William J. Walsh and John P. Langan, "Patristic Social Consciousness—The Church and the Poor," John C. Haughey (ed.), *The Faith That Does Justice* (New York: Paulist Press, 1977), 114.

[7] González, 95.

[8] Walsh and Langan, 115.

[9] Ibid.

[10] Ibid., *Parables* 1.8–10.

[11] Ibid., 120.

[12] Ibid., 121.

[13] Ibid.

[14] González, 124.

[15] Walsh and Langan, 122. *To Donatus* 12, 80-81.

[16] Ibid., 123.

[17] González, 125-26.

[18] Ibid., 201.

[19] Wendy Mayer and Pauline Allen, *John Chrysostom* (New York: Routledge, 2000), 47-48.

[20] Boniface Ramsey, *Beginning to Read the Fathers* (New York: Paulist Press, 1985), 188-90.

[21] González, 207.

[22] Ibid., 211.

[23] Gerard S. Sloyan, "A Roman Catholic Perspective," John C. Raines and Daniel Maguire (eds.), *What Men Owe to Women: Men's Voices from World Religions* (Albany: State University of New York, 2001), 159.

[24] JoAnn Kay McNamara, *Sisters in Arms* (Cambridge, MA: Harvard University Press, 1996), 25-26.

[25] Ibid., 31.

[26] Ross Shepard Kraemer, *Her Share of the Blessings: Women's Religions among Pagans, Jews, and Christians in the Greco-Roman World* (New York: Oxford University Press, 1992), 160.

[27] David J. O'Brien and Thomas A. Shannon (eds.), *Catholic Social Thought: The Documentary Heritage* (Maryknoll, NY: Orbis Books, 1992), 2-3.

[28] Ibid., 3-4.

[29] Rebecca B. Prichard, "Health, Education, and Welfare in the Protestant Reformation: Who Cared?" *Encounter* 55.4, Autumn 1994, 363-64.

[30] Ibid., 370-71.

[31] Harold S. Bender. *The Anabaptist Vision* (Scottdale, PA: Herald Press, 1944), 29-30.

[32] Ibid., 30-31, 34-35.

[33] O'Brien and Shannon, 5.

[34] "Charity and Poor Relief" http:www.answers.com/topic/charity-and-poor-relief.

[35] Ibid.

[36] *New Catholic Encyclopedia*, 2nd ed., s.vv. "Works of Charity" [3.420].

[37] Christine Firer Hinze, "Commentary on *Quadragesimo Anno (After Forty Years)*," Kenneth R. Himes, O.F.M. (ed.), *Modern Catholic Social Teaching: Commentaries and Interpretations* (Washington, D.C.: Georgetown University Press, 2005), 167.

[38] Peter Henriot, S.J., *Catholic Social Teaching and Poverty Eradication: Key Concepts and Issues*, (CAFOD Policy Papers, November 2001), 4. <http://www.cafod.org.uk/archive/policy/henriot_prsps.shtml >

[39] O'Brien and Shannon, 9.

[40] Quotes from papal encyclicals, Vatican II documents, Synod of Bishops, and the U.S. bishops' pastoral letter are from David J. O'Brien and Thomas A. Shannon.

[41] Marvin Krier Mich draws out the meaning of "social charity" as distinct from "individual charity," for example, almsgiving, and social justice. "Social charity has structural and institutional dimensions....Whereas social justice may be seen as each receiving their 'due' and paying their 'debt,' social charity emphasizes a more positive orientation of benevolence...." Marvin L. Krier Mich, *Catholic Social Teaching and Movements* (Mystic, CT: Twenty-Third Publications, 1998), 80.

[42] Ibid., 120.

[43] Donal Dorr, *Option for the Poor: A Hundred Years of Vatican Social Teaching* (Maryknoll, NY: Orbis Books, 1992), 152.

[44] Ibid.

[45] John Paul II in his social encyclicals, *Laborem Exercens* (1981), *Sollicitudo Rei Socialis* (1987), and *Centesimus Annus* (1991), reaffirmed the principles of Catholic social teaching discussed in this section. John Paul II's social teaching provides a contemporary Catholic Christian perspective on seeking justice for the poor.

[46] Krier Mich, 314.

[47] Peter J. Henriot, S.J., *Opting for the Poor* (Washington, DC: Center of Concern, 1990), 24-25.

[48] Thomas Massaro, *Catholic Social Teaching and United States Welfare Reform* (Collegeville, MN: Liturgical Press, 1998), 38-55.

[49] Ibid., 53.

[50] John A. Coleman, S.J., "American Catholicism, Catholic Charities USA, and Welfare Reform," Hugh Heclo and Wilfred M. McClay (eds.), *Religion Returns to the Public Square* (Washington, DC: Woodrow Wilson Center Press, 2003), 246-68.

[51] Ibid., 250-51.

[52] "Welfare Reform and Basic Human Needs," Connecticut Bishops. *Origins* 24, no. 26 (1994), 435.

[53] Bishop John Ricard, "The Factors of Genuine Welfare Reform," *Origins* 24, no. 24 (1995), 566.

[54] Florida bishops, "Promoting Meaningful Welfare Reform," *Origins* 24, no. 37 (1995), 611.

[55] "Moral Principles and Policy Priorities on Welfare Reform," U.S.C.C. Administrative Board. *Origins* 24, no. 41 (1995), 677.

[56] Donal Dorr, *Option for the Poor: A Hundred Years of Social Teaching* (Maryknoll, NY: Orbis Books, 2001), 366-77.

[57] *A Place at the Table: A Catholic Recommitment to Overcome Poverty and to Respect the Dignity of All God's Children* (Washington, DC: United States Conference of Catholic Bishops, 2002), 1-16. <http://www.usccb.org/bishops/table.htm>

Liberation Theology and Justice for the Poor

Justice for the poor, a central theme throughout biblical literature, was also a central concern for the early Christians and Christian communities. Over time, a focus on charity (giving charitably to the poor) replaced a concern for justice (seeking justice for the poor). Then as Christianity became the established state religion in the Roman Empire in the fourth century and began to take its place as a major world religion, there was often less and less concern within Christian communities about charity for the poor as an expression or dimension of the Christian faith. When Christianity fractured and split into factions in the sixteenth century many Christians began to emphasize the importance of "right" Christian belief (orthodoxy) and to place even less importance on Christian morality (orthopraxis), including Christians' obligation to care for the poor in their midst. By the end of the medieval period and the beginning of the modern era, two other developments further diminished Christians' concern for the poor. First, as theology became a top-down activity by academics, clergy, and church leaders, it became even more disconnected from the actual social conditions of the masses. Second, as secular and theological reflection focused more and more on individual rights, less attention was paid to social conditions, such as poverty and the social forces and structures that contributed to the impoverishment of human life.

At the end of the nineteenth century and during the early part of the twentieth century, the focus of Christian thought and life began to shift and, with the development of modern Catholic social teaching, greater attention was paid to the social conditions of human life. In the mid-twentieth century the Second Vatican Council addressed world concerns and urged local Catholic churches to engage the world by once again addressing problems at the local and regional levels. Building upon the renewal of the Second Vatican Council, liberation theology emerged when people in small groups known as Christian base communities prayed and discussed the lived experience of their faith. They would begin with their own experiences of poverty and oppression, reflect on Scripture as a source of enlightenment and inspiration, analyze the issues they faced in daily life, and seek solutions. The deliberations of the Latin American bishops formalized a process for doing this new type of theology, which in effect worked from the bottom up. This was a way for the poor and dispossessed—persons who were invisible in society—to claim their dignity as sons and daughters of a loving and just God, and to work together as a community to see how social problems might be named, challenged, and ultimately overcome through prayer, social analysis, and their power as children of God and members of a Christian community.

This chapter explores the roots of liberation theology in the writings of Latin American theologians, specifically Gustavo Gutiérrez, and the deliberations of the Latin American bishops at Medellín and Puebla. The insights of Roger Haight and Letty M. Russell will show how liberation theology has broader appeal than its Latin American beginnings. Liberation theology, in effect, is a viable means to work with people as they confront sinful social structures and look for signs of hope in the midst of their struggle for wholeness. Liberation theology has the potential to address poverty in the United States and show both the oppressed and the well-off how to work toward liberation and salvation.

Vatican Council II was an energizing force that stirred the hopes of Catholics throughout the world. According to Alfred Hennelly, Latin Americans responded in a variety of creative ways. Priests and bishops deliberated to discern how they could embody the new theological insights. As early as March 1964, theologians such as Juan Luis Segundo, Lucio Gera, and Gustavo Gutiérrez were meeting to discuss a Latin American theology that would be grounded in the insights of Vatican Council II.[1]

The publication of *Populorum Progressio: On the Development of Peoples* in 1967 had a far-reaching impact. In response to it, eighteen bishops from ten third world countries issued "A Letter to the Peoples of the Third World" (August15, 1967) that upheld the rights of workers and the poor and identified socialism as compatible with Christianity;[2] a seminar for priests sponsored by the Social Department of the Latin American Bishops' Conference in Chile (October-November 1967) voiced concern about the injustices their people were enduring and expressed their commitment to building "a new social order that is more just and more human;"[3] a conference for priests and laity at Chimbote, Peru (July 21–25, 1968) featured Gustavo Gutiérrez, who concluded that "One cannot be a Christian in these times without a commitment to liberation."[4] In addition, the Jesuit provincials of Latin America at their meeting in Rio de Janeiro, Brazil (May 6–14, 1968), sent a letter to all the members of the Society of Jesus endorsing as their goal, "the liberation of persons from every sort of servitude that oppresses them."[5]

THE LATIN AMERICAN BISHOPS CONFERENCE AT MEDELLÍN (1968)

The Latin American bishops became actors in the development of liberation theology when they convened their Second General Conference at Medellín, Colombia (August 26–September 9, 1968). CELAM [*El Consejo Episcopal Latinoamericano*], the Latin American Bishops' Conference established in 1955 to link the national conferences of bishops from Mexico, Central and South America, would meet every ten years; each Latin American country would send representatives and they would meet over a two-week period. According to Marvin Krier Mich, the bishops and their representatives at the Medellín Conference entered into a process whereby they learned about poverty in Latin America through papers and slide presentations. Over the course of their meetings the bishops acknowledged both the global dimension and the depth of poverty for their people, a situation that had worsened over the years, despite efforts at fostering development.[6] In their deliberations they concluded that poverty violated human rights to such a degree that it had become "a situation of injustice that can be called institutionalized violence" (Medellín 2.16). They stated that the deficiencies of society's social and economic structures caused poverty and they also focused on liberation from poverty as a priority for the church.[7]

Historically the Catholic Church in Latin America was an ally of the government. From the fifteenth century when the Spanish conquistadors arrived on the shores of the Americas wielding cross and sword, Catholicism supplanted the beliefs of the indigenous people. When one visits towns and cities where Spanish forces were victorious, the central square has two imposing structures: the church or cathedral and the government palace. These buildings bear witness to the fact that for centuries Roman Catholic popes cooperated with and supported the efforts of the Spanish and Portuguese monarchs in their quest to conquer the Americas. While this agreement offered protection to the missionaries, it also set a precedent for the government to wield enormous influence, even to the point of approving bishops for their area. When the Latin American countries gained their independence in the nineteenth century, there were still vestiges of political control over the churches. In fact, the churches encouraged deference to the ruling party, even when the government was supporting policies that were harmful to the majority of the population, namely, the indigenous poor. For the church to side with the poor as it did at Medellín was prophetic and provocative. Those who benefited from the exploitation of the poor viewed the church's actions as a threat to governments and civil order.

The Document on Peace. A Medellín document, *Peace*, begins with Pope Paul's reference in *Populorum Progressio* (#87) to development as the "new name for peace." In effect, the bishops were drawing attention to the fact that Latin America was so severely and unjustly underdeveloped that this was a threat to peace. The bishops stated that there were tensions that threatened peace: between classes, at the international level, and among the countries of Latin America. They noted the extreme inequalities between the privileged few and the dispossessed masses. The privileged enjoy the blessings of "culture, wealth, power, prestige," while most people have little or nothing (Medellín 2.3). The rich and powerful exhibit "a lamentable insensitivity...to the misery of the marginated sectors," resisting any efforts to change the social system, which effectively guarantees their privileges (Medellín 2.5). International tensions are related, the bishops noted, to neo-colonialism, a system that establishes a state of dependency; Latin American countries are dependent on other nations that abuse their resources and thereby control not just their economy but also their very livelihood. These factors include the actions taken by industrialized nations to enrich themselves at the expense of poor countries: the removal of natural resources without adequate reimbursement, tax evasion, the practice of sending profits abroad rather than reinvesting in the development of the countries, and policies that cause economic dependence through international monopolies. The bishops pointed out that the Latin American countries risked being encumbered by debts to international organizations, the payment of which would consume the greater part of the countries' profits (Medellín 2.9).

In their analysis the bishops noted that in addition to economic factors resulting in misery for the masses, there were social, political, cultural, religious, and racial factors that had disrupted relations and increased tensions among several Latin American countries. The bishops identified nationalism and a build-up in armaments as the most significant factors contributing to Latin American political tensions. Quoting *Populorum Progressio* (#53), the bishops critiqued the arms race: "When so many communities are hungry, when so many homes suffer misery, when so many men live submerged in ignorance...any arms race becomes an intolerable scandal" (Medellín 2.11–13). Even as the bishops identified violence as perhaps the gravest problem in Latin America, they reaffirmed peace as a Christian ideal and as the means "to achieve justice" (Medellín 2.15). They stated unequivocally that unjust situations could be labeled as "institutionalized violence" where whole segments of the population lack what is necessary for life. Such a violation of fundamental rights demands "all-embracing, courageous, urgent and profoundly renovating transformations" (Medellín 2.16). Aware of the divisions resulting from disparities in wealth, culture, and power, they appealed to people to work for greater justice and peace, which "conquer by means of a dynamic action of awakening (*concientización*) and organization of the popular sectors" (Medellín 2.18). Overall, the bishops addressed the injustices of poverty because creating a just social order is "an eminently Christian task" (Medellín 2.20).

The Document on Poverty. In *Poverty of the Church* the bishops at Medellín responded to the criticism that the church herself was rich and primarily concerned about the rich (Medellín 14.2). They began by distinguishing three different meanings of poverty. First, material poverty causes people to be without the goods and services they need to thrive or perhaps even to survive, effectively denying them the right to live as humans with dignity. The biblical prophets denounced material poverty as "contrary to the will of the Lord" and the "fruit of the injustice and sin of men" (Medellín 14.4a). Second, spiritual poverty is the attitude of persons who are not attached to riches and who place their hope in the Lord in a spirit of openness. Third, voluntary poverty as a loving commitment to the needy models itself after Jesus who embraced poverty. People who choose to be poor with the poor "bear witness to the evil which it [material poverty] represents and to spiritual liberty in the face of material goods" (Medellín 14.4c). The Latin American bishops then acknowledged the overwhelming crisis of their people whose material poverty "cries out for justice, solidarity, open witness, commitment, strength, and exertion" (Medellín 14.7). They claimed that the crisis of their people was so urgent that the Latin American Church needed to model the spirit of poverty though "actions, attitudes and norms" so that power and finances would be used for the common good (Medellín 14.7). They also challenged all Christians to embrace voluntary material poverty as "a sign and a commitment—a sign of the inestimable value of the poor in the eyes of God, [and] an obligation of solidarity with those who suffer" (Medellín 14.7).

The Latin American bishops at Medellín argued in their document *Poverty of the Church* that love of the poor means allocating resources differently, showing preference for those who are poorest, and serving as the advocate for the poor with those who have the power to effect positive change. The bishops called the church to solidarity with the poor by identifying with those who are poor and acknowledging their problems and their struggles as the church's concern. They added that solidarity translates into "criticism of injustice and oppression, …the willingness to dialogue with the groups responsible for that situation in order to make them understand their obligations" (Medellín 14.10). With human advancement as the goal, the bishops added that actions toward this goal must always take into consideration the dignity of poor persons, as we work to have them help themselves (Medellín 14.11). The bishops concluded that all the People of God are called to a sincere conversion, one that will change "the individualistic mentality into another one of social awareness and concern for the common good" (Medellín 14.16).

The Document on Catechesis. When the bishops at Medellín considered catechesis, the process whereby Christians share their faith, beliefs, and practices within their community, they stressed in their document *Catechesis* the importance of the historical situation. At that moment the majority of the population lived at the margins of society; they were in such great need and suffered so many injustices that social change was a priority (Medellín 8.7). Among the many nations with diverse cultures and standards of living and education, the bishops identified the family as being at the heart of Christian development, worthy of attention and potentially the "most effective agent of catechetical renewal" (Medellín 8.10). Comparable to the family is the role of Christian base communities; both provide a community where love can be experienced and where faith can grow. In fact, the bishops encourage participation in a Christian base community as an expression of the family of God and as "the first and fundamental ecclesiastical nucleus" with the potential for human growth and advancement as well as growth in the riches of faith (Medellín 15.10).

The Medellín conference opened the door for dramatic change in Latin America. According to Penny Lernoux, "Medellín's commitment to the poor and oppressed was indeed prophetic" because the Latin American bishops broke with their political and social traditions in a number of ways. First, the Catholic Church effectively criticized existing social and political structures by stating that the structures needed to promote a transfer of power to the impoverished masses. Second, the church identified itself as a servant of the poor, renouncing privileges and riches that had come from centuries of state patronage. Finally, the bishops committed themselves to work for a community of faith as opposed to continuing the hierarchical model of authority with its pyramid power structure.[8]

Christian Base Communities. As we look back at the Medellín Conference today, one of the most noteworthy developments was the high priority the Latin American bishops placed on Christian base communities as a means of catechizing the poor. Their approval encouraged the acceptance of Christian base communities as part of the parish, and eventually their growth and development as an integral part of ecclesial structures.

A Christian base community was a small group of neighbors that met to pray, read Scripture, consider their lives in relation to God's word, and analyze the socio-economic realities they faced. When community members read the Bible as a story of liberation, they were encouraged to apply biblical stories to their own lives; as Penny Lernoux noted, they could then "perceive an essential parallel: if the God of the Bible was on the side of the poor and oppressed back then, God must be on their side, too."[9] While religious sisters and priests were instrumental in forming base communities, lay persons rapidly gained confidence and competence, assumed leadership roles, and related to the larger church structures.[10] Between 1968 and 1979 the *comunidades eclesiales de base* grew and provided a counterforce to the "conservative theologians and bishops in Latin America and Europe [who] attacked Medellín and liberation theology."[11] Overall, the base communities kept the church in Latin America focused on the needs of the materially poor and nurtured the growth of liberation theology.

The Challenge of Marxism. Liberation theology's use of Marxism to analyze political and economic realities met with great resistance. When the Group of Eighty Priests met in Chile in April 1971 and expressed their view that socialism was compatible with Christianity and that Christians need not fear participating in the socialist government led by President Salvador Allende, the bishops of Chile reacted swiftly with a working paper entitled "The Gospel, Politics, and Socialisms."[12] The bishops equated socialism with Marxism and in their estimation, "Marxism was not only a method but an all-embracing philosophy, an atheistic world view, and in practice, an ideological 'monolithism' that led to the imposition of totalitarianism and the single party."[13] Similarly, Pope Paul VI in his encyclical *Octogesima Adveniens* (1971) warned against Marxist ideology because it was "atheistic materialism" that espoused a "dialectic of violence," and effectively absorbed "individual freedom... denying all transcendence to man and his personal and collective history" (#26). Pope Paul also cautioned against accepting Marxist analysis when he stated that Marxism was an ideology that encouraged class struggle and that a Marxist interpretation of social issues would result in a totalitarian, violent society (#34).

Marxism was a cause of great concern for church leaders. It affected Latin American church leaders in much the same way as Communism affected the United States. As a result, liberation theologians that used a Marxist analysis came under scrutiny and were suspect. Alfonso López Trujillo, then bishop of Bogotá, Colombia, and the Secretary General (1972–1979) and later president of CELAM (1979–1983), reflected the thinking of conservative church officials in his criticism of liberation theology. During the tenure of López Trujillo, some of the leadership of CELAM moved from supporting the teachings of Medellín and the efforts of liberation theologians to consistent opposition, a position that Vatican officials supported, as evidenced by Alfonso López Trujillo's being named archbishop of Medellín (1979) and then cardinal (1983).[14]

THE LATIN AMERICAN BISHOPS CONFERENCE AT PUEBLA (1979)

The tension between advocates of a theology of liberation and more socially conservative factions of the church set the stage for the Third General Conference of the Latin American Episcopate at Puebla, Mexico, in 1979. Several hundred delegates (bishops, religious superiors, and lay delegates) met from January 27 through February 13, 1979, producing one major document, *Evangelization in Latin America's Present and Future*. The Puebla conference had commissions whose working papers were informed by input from position papers written by Latin American liberation theologians (Gustavo Gutiérrez, Juan Luis Segundo, Leonardo Boff, and Jon Sobrino), whose work had "melded together academic theology, critical social thought, and the lived experience of the poor."[15] As noted earlier, this new way of doing theology encountered stiff resistance from conservative politicians and church leaders who equated liberation theology with Marxism. These critics wanted to discredit liberation theology. Still, despite concerted opposition, especially by conservatives hoping for sanctions against or a condemnation of liberation theology, Puebla managed to chart a course for the future that reaffirmed both the main concepts proposed in the Medellín documents and the development of liberation theology.

The Latin American bishops at Puebla once again clearly and prophetically expressed their "preference for, and solidarity with, the poor" (#1134). Mindful of the distortions and resistance encountered in the years between Medellín and Puebla, the bishops called all the church to convert to "a preferential option for the poor, an option aimed at their integral liberation" (#1134). They acknowledged the misery and suffering of the poor, evident in the worsening conditions and repressive measures taken against them. The reality was that the majority of the people lacked even the basic necessities of life, while a small minority accumulated ever greater wealth. Such poverty, in the judgment of the bishops, was inhuman, for it disregarded "fundamental human rights as life, health, education, housing, and work" and violated the dignity of the person (#41). Human life had little or no value, and those who attempted to organize workers were threatened, kidnapped, and even terrorized. Such acts of violence denied each person his or her dignity as a child of God and also denied his or her basic human rights. Poverty was so entrenched in their countries that it was "the product of economic, social, and political situations and structures" (#30). Power had been abused; this was evident with regimes that resorted to repression and brute force. Justice was subverted so the rich and powerful could maintain control over the masses.

The bishops strove to put a human face on the poor, identifying them as children and young people whose health and development were compromised and severely limited; as indigenous peoples who were marginalized and among the poorest of the poor; as peasants who were exiles, driven from their land, and exploited by forces beyond their control; as manual laborers whose back-breaking toil was worth next to nothing; and as marginalized urban dwellers and the elderly whose poverty was in stark contrast to the powerful rich (#32–39). The bishops pointed out that women of these social groups were oppressed and marginalized to an even greater degree (#834). Still, it would be more accurate to say that while women are mentioned explicitly and the dual burden of their oppression noted, in fact, they are triply oppressed. First, women are poor and suffer all the adversities of material poverty. Second, women suffer the ill effects of *machismo* in societies where male privilege and power reign supreme. Third, indigenous women experience the negative effects of racism. Overall, the Latin American bishops conference at Puebla resulted in an affirmation of human rights, a condemnation of repressive regimes, and consideration of the concerns of the indigenous and women.

AN OVERVIEW OF THE LATIN AMERICAN CONFERENCES

The Latin American bishops' conferences at Medellín and Puebla made significant contributions to a discussion of justice for the poor. First, they not only consistently endorsed a preferential option for the poor; they used social science as well as theology to address the effects of poverty and to work to change oppressive structures. Second, the bishops identified salvation history and human history as one. They emphasized that God's gift of life in creation, mirrored in the goodness and dignity of each human, was extended by Jesus' loving concern for all people, especially those at the margins of society, and that in our lives today Christians are called to be the instruments of Jesus' love in human history, especially in outreach to the poor. The bishops noted that God's Spirit moves us to see God in all of humanity, and that distinctions based on poverty and riches fade when compared with the richness of God's call to seek fullness of life in both our embodied historical existence and in the life to come after death.

Third, the bishops affirmed in the Medellín and Puebla documents the importance of Christian base communities as places where the call to Christian conversion and everyday life are linked. They noted that small Christian communities offer a viable method for people of all ages, races, and nationalities to come together for prayer, reflection, and social analysis. In an age when the number of priests and religious brothers and sisters is rapidly declining, Christian base communities are one way of building community within a parish and evangelizing families by bringing people together, drawing on their experience, and providing inspiration and space for God's presence to be revealed in their lives as God's word opens their minds and hearts to a message of liberation.

Fourth, the bishops noted the enormous political and economic power of the privileged minority: the potential to abuse this power, and the equal potential to use this power to enrich the lives of all people. In today's terms, some will use their power and privilege to maintain their position at the head of the table and to limit access to power for others. History, after all, bears out that many of those who work to effect justice in socio-economic and political structures will suffer at the hands of repressive regimes. However, God's message of justice and peace urges us to welcome the disenfranchised. If those who are impoverished are empowered to come to the table of social decision making, the greater diversity of opinion and cultures could enrich our world, broaden our perceptions, and deepen our understanding of justice so that we are more fully able to focus on liberation as a goal for all people.

GUSTAVO GUTIÉRREZ AND THE THEOLOGY OF LIBERATION

Gustavo Gutiérrez, an indigenous priest born in 1928 in Lima, Peru, first began studies in Peru to be a medical doctor, and later studied psychology and theology in Europe. Gutiérrez has written numerous books and articles and has lectured and taught liberation theology in many universities in the Americas and Europe from the vantage point of one who lives among and works with the poor. In recent years he became a member of the Dominican Order. With the publication of *Teología de la Liberación* in Spanish (1971) and then in English translation (1973), Gutiérrez identified liberation theology as "a *new way* to do theology."[16] Like all theology, it presupposes wisdom and rational knowledge. The love of God is shared by using prayerful reflection on Scripture as it relates to the lived experience of people. Since poverty is the stark reality for the vast majority of the people in Latin America, liberation theology relies on the social sciences for its expertise in addressing and analyzing poverty as a political, cultural, and economic, historical reality.

Gutiérrez considered the three senses of poverty, the understanding of which helps Christians live out the gospel more effectively. He noted that Christians often place a positive value on poverty, even when this appears to be at odds with the actual lives of poor people. Gutiérrez then emphasized that material poverty is a "subhuman situation," because being poor means that people are illiterate, exploited by others, and often die of hunger. People who are poor may not even know they are being exploited, and even worse, they can be made to feel that they are not even human.[17] Furthermore, the misery of the poor increases when they are forced to do backbreaking work for meager wages. As Gutiérrez explained, "The exploitation and injustice implicit in poverty make work into something servile and dehumanizing. Alienated work, instead of liberating man, enslaves him even more."[18]

In addition to material poverty, Gutiérrez addressed spiritual poverty. Some consider material poverty as an ideal for spiritual perfection. This can lead to encouraging people to accept a life of misery because that is all they can expect in this life. In other words, spiritual poverty can lead to a justification of living conditions that are degrading and even discourage people from hoping or working for a better life.[19] Gutiérrez called upon all Christians to embrace spiritual poverty by recognizing that we all depend on God. Without God as the center of our lives, we are impoverished. Gutiérrez noted that when we place material possessions, success, or something else at the center of our lives we can be led away from or forget God. Based on the Beatitudes, Gutiérrez concluded that spiritual poverty reminds one of childhood. Those who are spiritually poor are like children who trust God and receive life's bounty as gifts from God. Gutiérrez also contended that while material poverty is dehumanizing, "The poor are blessed *because* the Kingdom of God has begun."[20] The kingdom of God is not restricted to the future, but rather enters present time. Gutiérrez also claimed that the poor are blessed when their poverty comes to an end; this happens when brotherhood replaces exploitation and people work in solidarity so that justice can prevail.

A Focus on the Poor. The needs of the poor is a major focus in Gutiérrez's writings. The poor had been "nonpersons," those who had little or no significance and were, in effect, absent from history. The poor only gradually became present as evidenced by the popular struggles for liberation and a new historical consciousness. It is this struggle of the poor to emerge from the shadows and take their place on the stage of life that is called the "irruption of the poor."[21] As communities organized around popular movements and struggled for justice, individuals came to realize their personal dignity and indigenous peoples rose up and defended their rights.

Latin America has had a long history of war, especially evident since the Spanish came to conquer, carrying the cross and the sword. In the second half of the twentieth century, there was civil unrest and armed guerrilla activity on the part of those seeking to gain their rights. In response, many governments became more authoritarian and repressive. It was a world where the perceived threat of Communism resulted in violent repercussions. Additionally, civil wars had dire consequences for the poor: indiscriminate killings, destruction of livestock, razing whole villages, the displacement of thousands of families (especially in Guatemala, El Salvador, and Nicaragua), and the disappearance of untold numbers of men and women (*los desaparecidos* in Argentina and Chile).

In the midst of social and political upheaval, liberation theology addressed the concerns of Christian faith raised by "subjugated peoples, exploited classes, despised races, and marginalized cultures."[22] Moreover, over the years liberation theologians became more aware of and sensitive to how "factors of race, culture and gender" contributed to poverty. Of particular concern was discrimination against women, a situation that was deeply embedded in their cultures and so common that families and communities accepted such discrimination as the norm.[23] Liberation theology, on the other hand, reminded people that, "the poor person is someone brimming over with capacities and possibilities, whose culture has its own values, derived from racial background, history and language." In the midst of personal and communal suffering and persecution, liberation theology indirectly helped poor people to emerge in history as people who work to "resist all attempts to mutilate or manipulate their hopes for the future."[24]

Drawing insight from Christian Scripture, Gutiérrez argued that how men and women relate to the poor is indicative of their relationship with God. He claimed that when anyone oppresses the poor, that person offends God for "to know God is to work justice" among people. Simply stated, "The existence of poverty represents a sundering both of solidarity among men and also of communion with God."[25] Gutiérrez claimed that for the predominantly Christian continent of Latin America, and in fact, everywhere, the poor emerge as the face of God: a face of material need, desperate suffering, and premature death. He noted that the poor are oppressed and thus they have a primary claim in charity and justice on the rest of the Christian community. Matthew 25:31–46 portrays the coming of the Son of Man as showing the intimate connection between commitment to the poor and welcoming God into our lives. This text teaches that the mystery of faith is beholding God in the faces of the poor. Citing Matthew 25, Gutiérrez pointed out that solidarity with the poor could open one's mind and heart to the God who dwells within them.

However, he also noted that standing with, fighting for, and committing oneself to improving the lives of the poor is a process that requires Christians to engage in critical theological reflection. Gutiérrez pointed out that the practice of doing good allows one to live in God's presence. He also claimed that contemplation and commitment are essential partners for living a Christian life, that is, practice is the first act that allows the mystery of God's presence to permeate all of life. Such a life inspires reflection, what Gutiérrez called "the second act." Generally, theology empowers people to see the intimate connection between the life of faith and the necessity of working to create a more just society. As Gutiérrez wrote, "in essence, theology helps the commitment to liberation to be more evangelical, more concrete, more effective."[26]

As the Bible makes plain, God is a God of justice whose presence is evident throughout history. The culmination of God's presence is Jesus, the incarnation of God, who lived among us as a poor man. Jesus' life and loving acts of healing and forgiveness model for Christians how they are to be among people. God in the person of Jesus Christ can motivate Christians to stand against the physical and cultural death that results from poverty. Then, confronting the historical reality of those suffering from poverty, Jesus can move Christians to act. Accepting and caring for the neighbor and seeking greater justice in the world can, in turn, enable disciples of Jesus to know God more fully. As Gutiérrez wrote, "solidarity with the poor and the oppressed is based on our faith in God, the God of life revealed in Jesus Christ."[27] Such solidarity with the poor can lead us to understand more fully Jesus' call to liberation from sin and injustice for all people.

Liberation of the Poor. Gutiérrez argued that injustices, including poverty, can be overcome by liberation and that a Christian understanding of liberation is rooted in biblical and theological tradition. Additionally, he distinguished between three simultaneous and interdependent processes of liberation. First, political and social liberation works to eliminate the causes of poverty and injustice. The goal is to achieve a society based on respect for persons, which encourages people to attend to the needs of the weakest members. Second, human liberation is an attempt to work at a deeper level, by "liberating human beings of all those things—not just in the social sphere—that limit their capacity to develop themselves freely and in dignity." This is what Vatican Council II called a "new humanism," in which men and women are defined by their responsibility to their brothers and sisters and to history (see *Gaudium et Spes* #55). Third, liberation from selfishness and sin will eliminate injustice at its very root. For this last process of liberation, "only the grace of God, the redeeming work of Christ, can overcome sin."[28]

Gutiérrez explained the connection between globalization and poverty. He noted that as the dominant policy, neo-liberalism raises the economy to an exalted plane and encourages globalization. Through multilateral trade agreements, global corporations supersede political power; as a result, local governments effectively lose control of business. Markets without restrictions have enormous power throughout the world. In the name of supplying goods cheaply, local businesses, including local farmers, are losers, for they cannot compete against huge international corporations. Economic neo-liberalism and globalization have resulted in growing inequality. The economy may thrive, but people suffer because there is little regard for human beings and a rapacious disregard for nature. As a result, people and the environment are treated like commodities to be used and thrown away. In Gutiérrez's words, globalization has led to "the exclusion of a part of humanity from the economic loop and from the so-called benefits of civilization."[29] Economic neoliberalism makes profits for owners and investors, but the vast majority of the population suffers as corporations show little or no respect for human life and for nature.

Gutiérrez observed that liberation theology emphasizes reflection on practice and is rooted in spirituality. Discipleship, following Jesus, requires both prayer and commitment. Prayer enables disciples to open their minds and hearts to the overwhelming beauty of God's love. It also unites love of God and love of neighbor. Commitment results from disciples responding to God's love and marching together on the journey toward justice. Gutiérrez wrote of the depth of this spirituality, rooted in faith in the God of life, as well as the willingness to surrender one's life for others.[30]

Proclamation of the gospel in Latin America has resulted in persecution and martyrdom. Like the early Christians, many who are faithful to the God of life and who live in solidarity with the poor have experienced both joy and sorrow. Their efforts to share the good news of God's love for every person have often been met with threats, slander, violence, and even death by those who seek to maintain the status quo. Martyrdom has been the fate of catechists, union leaders, peasants, priests, vowed religious, and bishops. Today, thanks to forensic science, the bones of children and adults who were massacred and seemingly forgotten are witnesses to atrocities visited upon their people. Gutiérrez noted that such suffering has resulted in "an ecclesial community, capable of stubbornly sustaining the hope of the dispossessed."[31] He also pointed out that this is a life and death struggle for believers who daily commit themselves generously and joyfully to share the good news of the gospel, as well as for those who place their lives at great risk, even martyrdom. Ultimately life will prevail, thanks to faith in Jesus who also suffered persecution, surrendered his life for others, and showed that God's love results in the new life of resurrection. In Gutiérrez's words, "Theology is done in a Church which must provide in human history the testimony to a life victorious over death. To be a witness to the resurrection means choosing life, life in all its forms, since nothing escapes the universality of the Kingdom of God."[32]

Liberation theology arose in the context of the struggle against poverty in Latin America. Based on faith in God and on commitment to the poor, it sees the human and the divine as united, especially in conditions of extreme need. Since its inception in the 1960s and as the poor and exploited raised their heads and claimed their power, suffering has escalated. Thousands of people have lost their lives. Prophets like Archbishop Oscar Romero have shared the fate of thousands of ordinary men and women. Speaking the truth and acting for justice met severe resistance on the part of those who did not want to share the gifts of this earth. Like the first Christians, priests and laity alike have offered their lives so that others might live. In the midst of suffering and death, liberation theology is a beacon of hope that focuses believers' minds and hearts on God. God is present. God is among the suffering. Death is not the final word. Resurrection, God's gift of salvation, is manifest in the lives of believers. When God calls all to judgment, those who have walked in solidarity with the poor, sharing their lives and fortunes, will be invited by God to enter the kingdom (Mt 25:34).

ROGER HAIGHT AND A NORTH AMERICAN PERSPECTIVE ON LIBERATION THEOLOGY

Liberation theology originated in Latin America as a reflection on God's guiding presence amid the poor, It has a particular claim on the peoples of Central and South America where many of their peoples face the crisis of poverty. From a North American perspective we can ask: Is liberation theology relevant to nations and areas of the world whose theologies deal with questions of meaning in a world of relative affluence, for people whose concerns are more existential, philosophical, and individualistic? Roger Haight's discussion of liberation theology from a North American perspective is helpful for exploring this question.

In 1985, Roger Haight, S.J., wrote of his experience of presenting liberation theology using specific theological categories. As a professor in a graduate program of theology, Haight has used the texts of liberation theology to discuss its interpretations of Christianity. He acknowledged the ambivalence of his students: the energizing effect of liberation theology's Christian vision for human life, and the difficulty of translating this vision within a culture and a world removed from the social and economic contexts of Latin America.

In the years since his book *An Alternative Vision: An Interpretation of Liberation Theology* (1985) appeared, conditions have changed: the vast immigration from the south to the north in the Americas may well make the translation less difficult. A growing number of Hispanics have traveled at great peril to the North (*el Norte*) to earn sufficient money to support themselves and their extended family; they embody the hope of creating a better life both in the United States and in their native country. Additionally, the United States is also facing increasing levels of poverty, and this may also make it easier for people in our country to understand liberation theology.

Themes of Liberation Theology. Haight points out that liberation theology is in its infancy, with many authors and different places contributing to its formation. He identifies commonalities by exploring themes. In his presentation of the basic themes of liberation theology, Haight began with the *experience of poverty*. Poverty with its destitution, suffering, and premature death is an experience that evokes outrage, condemnation of the decisions that cause poverty, and guilt for allowing it to continue. Moreover, the realization that human beings cause poverty raises questions about the connections between wealth and poverty. For liberation theology this connection is of *religious* significance. God opposes injustice, and consequently this presents a deep moral imperative for the Christian conscience. Generally, liberation theology reminds Christians that working to eliminate poverty is essential for being one with God.

Liberation theology arises among people with an acute *historical consciousness*. A historical consciousness means that persons living at this time realize that the present is not simply a repetition of the past, but is different from the past. Thus they also learn that the future can be different from the present. In discussing the importance of this, Haight notes that theology needs to become relevant by addressing the problems faced in ordinary human life, that the experience of *autonomy and freedom* is linked to historical consciousness. Humans are autonomous and responsible for human history. They work and plan in order to establish the structure of social life. Freedom is both personal and collective and means that the "exercise of choice and creative initiative…is not inhibited by external force or suppression." Poverty and other conditions that limit the freedom of humanity are dehumanizing. Secularization reinforces *the importance of this world* where human history unfolds and where life is lived. "It is the experience of 'being at home' in the world."

Haight points out that insofar as liberation theology is seen as *contextual and related*, its explicit goal is to understand God in relation to particular situations. Moreover, from a liberation theology perspective an analysis of the poverty and suffering of people requires faith-filled Christians to respond responsibly and be active participants in society. The *historical viewpoint* is not just seeking data and analyzing unjust structures; it also leads to a *method of correlation* whereby it seeks solutions to problems in light of Christian tradition. The *existential* aspect of liberation theology is related to the overriding concern to make sense of actual human existence. The poor are individual people, particular families. There is a sense of urgency in the face of suffering, and impatience with reliance on abstractions. Liberation theology will dispute and argue "not only against society but also against the Church and other theologies insofar as they fail to meet the exigencies of historical life."

Liberation theology opens up *a broader context for theological thinking*— the world, history, and human experience. This opens the horizon for the church and Christianity by placing them within the broader context of the world and history. Within this broader context liberation theology relies on social analysis or the social sciences. This reliance can be considered both a strength, because it integrates theology with life, and a weakness, because "it still is not clear methodologically how social analysis enters into theological understanding." What has come under criticism is liberation theology's acknowledgment of the challenge of Marxism, which is evident in the use of "Marxist social and historical analysis and language."

A constant theme of liberation theology that flows from social scientific study is *the social nature of human existence*. "The human person is constituted by society," that is, as a person learns, the process of socialization "governs human thinking and acting at every point." Society's influence in the formation of the human person is so powerful that one needs to question the "assumptions of any given social milieu since they determine our most basic ideas, values, and behaviors." As social beings, persons relate consistently with others, living lives of "radical interdependence." Finally, social sciences provide an understanding of the factors that support and sustain social structures, as well as the factors that diminish and destroy these structures. As they incorporated insights from the social sciences into their theological reflections, liberation theologians acknowledged the achievements of human history and the value of human experience. At the same time, they formulated understandings of institutional and social sin.

The power of the community is realized for liberation theology in the symbol and ideal of solidarity. As Haight observes, "The impetus of this ideal is a desire that more and more people take on and share the common experience, values, interests and problems of the greater proportion of the community." In our time we have witnessed the political power of solidarity; for example, Poland's effective use of solidarity to resist Communism and achieve independence. However, the symbol of solidarity has even greater implications for the possible unity of the human race. Liberation theologians envision solidarity as being even more comprehensive than the commonality of working together to improve the community. Solidarity moves beyond community and links liberation with unity among all people and union with God.

The focus within liberation theology on the *universal availability of God's saving grace* affirms both a positive view of human history and a confirmation of the importance of everyday life as revelatory of God's activity. Liberation theology establishes *the close relation between liberation and salvation*. Liberation considered as "social, economic and political release from oppressive structures" depends on the saving activity of God. While salvation is viewed as beyond history, "uniting the symbol and experience of salvation with historical liberation is a central element in liberation theology."[33]

Methodological Themes in Liberation Theology. Theology, according to Haight, is "reflection on reality in the light of Christian faith." As a disciplined inquiry, theology relies on method to develop and organize its structure for understanding faith. Liberation theology incorporates certain principles or themes that are basic to its teachings. Haight identified methodological themes for liberation theology. First, liberation theology is a "response to the problem of the non-person" evident in history and more specifically in "the social injustice and oppressive poverty that marks Latin America." A second theme is that of dependence. Latin America is dependent on capitalist nations. This dependence is internalized by the wealthy few in Latin America who have become the agents of industries and capitalist ventures. They in turn perpetuate a system that effectively locks the masses into a state of dependency and oppressive poverty. Another aspect of dependence is that liberation theology depends on social science and its disciplined analysis of the social, political, economic, and cultural aspects of historical reality in order to arrive at its theological understanding. A third theme is the centrality of the symbol of liberation in this theology. Liberation has many meanings, as Gustavo Gutiérrez so ably explained. Liberation as a religious symbol is essential for understanding the mystery of grace and salvation. In Haight's words, "Salvation is a form of liberation... inclusive of the other spheres of liberation. They all interact."

A fourth theme is the centrality of praxis as a method of liberation theology. The lived experience of acknowledging and caring for those living in dependence and oppression leads to a method of doing theology: a continuous circle of action-understanding-action, moving from praxis, to reflection, and returning to praxis. Liberation theology begins with contemporary human experience. Focusing on the experience of those whom society defines as "non-persons" and on the experience of those who have a wealth of resources requires analysis to grasp the psychological, social, and cultural dimensions of human life. In addition to human experience, liberation theology relies on Christian sources, namely, Scripture and tradition. The Christian message needs to be applied to the whole of human existence. Additionally, Scripture reveals justice as a challenge to all, especially "the wealthy few...[who]

maintain a system that keeps the masses in a dependent and oppressive poverty."

A fifth theme is the option for the poor. This is a powerful theme for liberation theology because an option for the poor establishes both a decisive attitude and a commitment. There is a clear focus on those who are excluded and oppressed, making them the center of attention, just as parents always have their children in mind and in their hearts. When the actions of individuals and groups are motivated by the option for the poor, their aspirations and work can lead to liberation, which Gustavo Gutiérrez defined as a response to dependence, a process of humanization, and a principle for interpreting and understanding Christian salvation. The dialogic method whereby human experience and revelation mutually relate and inform has power to inform, inspire, and move one to compassion and care for one's neighbor.[34]

Liberation Theology and Social Justice. Haight has noted that the viability of liberation theology flows from its emphasis on the social aspects of life: the absolute necessity of connecting with and relating with others, and the importance of interdependence in the lives of people. This emphasis can help to generate a new enthusiasm for life and can be an antidote to the numbing sense of isolation that too often plagues daily life. The theme of liberation resonates in our North American society where individuals are struggling to achieve or maintain their God-given dignity, where people work multiple jobs to provide for their families, and where structures are complicated and seem to conspire against families' well-being. While concern for justice informs Christian faith, concern for *social justice* for people who are suffering and oppressed is a relatively recent phenomenon. Haight stresses that social justice, "as an intrinsic form of faith is a new teaching corresponding to a new historical consciousness and social awareness characteristic of our time. [Social justice] depends on a realization of social interdependence, of social structures and situations as changeable human structures, of the ways in which all people participate in these situations."[35]

Liberation theology, Haight points out, fosters a spirituality that is rooted in this world, as was Jesus' life, and encourages one to work and pray for the coming of God's kingdom "on earth as it is in heaven." It is a Christian reflection on a way of life. It is contemplation in action: acknowledgment of our dependence on a loving God and our freedom to be in the world where we exercise and discover our freedom as human persons along with the members of our community, a community that begins with the family and is experienced at work, through participation in church events, as well as in activities in the town, city, or state. Liberation theology places a high priority on faith. To Haight, being in the world and yet oriented toward the kingdom of God can bring an ever greater awareness of the joys and sufferings of other human beings. We can reach out to assuage the pain of those who are oppressed and use our considerable talents to work to change the structures that unjustly limit and denigrate them. As followers of Jesus, we can seek forgiveness and healing so that we can experience conversion: a loving acceptance of others and an openness to the immanence of God in humanity and all of creation. We can accept our limitations in life, but place our hope in the transcendent God whose kingdom of love and justice will come at some point in the future in all its fullness.[36] For now, we can walk humbly with our God and our neighbors, seeking justice, and working mightily for the liberation of our world from sin, injustice, and oppression.

THE VATICAN AND LIBERATION THEOLOGY

Roman Catholic Church authorities have both endorsed and critiqued various aspects of liberation theology. Two Vatican documents addressed liberation theology and affirmed many of its values. The "Instruction on Certain Aspects of the 'Theology of Liberation'" (*Libertatis Nuntius*, 1984) promulgated by the Congregation for the Doctrine of the Faith (CDF), affirmed that the church is clearly committed to the poor and the oppressed, endorsing the "preferential option for the poor," while warning against those who might remain neutral or indifferent to the problems of human suffering and injustice. It also supported the efforts of those Christians motivated by faith who were actively involved in "the struggle for justice, freedom and human dignity because of their love for their disinherited, oppressed and persecuted brothers and sisters."[37] This

Vatican instruction acknowledged that many papal, council, and synod documents, as well as those created by national episcopal conferences, especially Medellín and Puebla, had actively proposed justice and solidarity with the poor and oppressed (sect. V, #1–8) and recognized that the documents of these conferences were the basis for and supported the development of liberation theology.

The main criticism of liberation theology was its alleged reliance on Marxist ideology. The instruction referred to the warning of Pope Paul VI that Marxism leads to a "totalitarian society" (*Octogesima Adveniens*, #34). It stated that "atheism and the denial of the human person, his liberty and his rights, are at the core of Marxist theory" (sect. VII, #7–9). Another criticism of Marxism was that it encouraged class struggle. Such a struggle, the CDF contended, was evident in the writings of various liberation theologians and could distort history and prevent charity by fracturing communities. The instruction was also critical of rereading Scripture from a political point of view.

The instruction, in Haight's view, used Marxist analysis in an objective sense, "as a closed system of understanding the whole of reality" based on the nineteenth-century theorist Karl Marx. The instruction positioned Marxism in opposition to Christian faith. Haight argues, however, that Marxist analysis could be understood in "a subjective and existential sense," meaning that "Marxist concepts, categories and distinctions" are used to analyze and describe a particular social situation.[38] The subjective sense means that one is open to other realities even as certain categories of Marxism are used in a limited way.

As with any new way of thinking, liberation theologians express a broad spectrum of views. When the instruction was issued, liberation theologians denied that they were reducing or politicizing the gospel. Rather, they insisted that the inspiration for their concern for the poor was both spiritual and biblical, as evidenced by the ecclesial base communities. Overall, while the first instruction both affirmed and challenged liberation theology, its greatest effect was to focus attention of many inside and outside the Catholic Church on liberation theologies, even as dialogue among theologians and church leaders continued and developed.

The Vatican followed the first instruction with publication of the "In-struction on Christian Freedom and Liberation" (*Libertatis Conscientia*, 1986).[39] This instruction addressed freedom and liberation from a Chris-tian perspective and was more positive than the first instruction when addressing liberation theology themes. Liberation in *Libertatis Conscien-tia* is viewed in terms of salvation and the freeing of men and women from the bondage of evil and sin. Freedom is considered the "freedom to do good," and truth and justice are identified as "the measure of true freedom" (#26). The second instruction pointed out that while a per-son's freedom is grounded in a relationship with God, this freedom is expressed through community involvement, and poverty is caused by individual sin as well as by structures that exploit and enslave, a situa-tion identified as "social sin" (#75).

The document clearly noted that consistent with the biblical sense of justice, the church is committed to "a love of preference" for those "oppressed by poverty," a love expressed in works of charity and in the church's efforts to "promote structural changes in society" (#68). It also affirmed that the church's social teaching emphasizes the dignity of each individual, created in God's image, a teaching that is summarized in the commandment of love of God and neighbor. The instruction singled out solidarity, the obligation to "contribute to the common good of society at all levels," and subsidiarity, which calls for individuals and communi-ties to be allowed to function freely by their own initiative, as the prin-ciples that ensure and protect the dignity of each person (#72–73). Base communities are recognized as "a source of great hope for the Church," provided they "live in unity with the local Church and the universal Church" (#69).

Throughout the second instruction there are numerous positive com-ments tempered by warnings about negative elements. Solidarity and subsidiarity are contrasted with the dangers of social and political in-dividualism and collectivism (#73). Human rights, basic to liberation, are contrasted with the "systematic recourse to violence" that the CDF condemned as "a destructive illusion" because it causes "new forms of servitude" (#76).

A year after the second Vatican instruction on liberation theology was issued, Pope John Paul II wrote about liberation themes in his encyclical, *Sollicitudo Rei Socialis* (1987). The pope was aware of both the value and the risks of theological reflection based on liberation. He noted that there is an "intimate connection" between liberation and development, since both of these aspire to free the individual and society from every kind of slavery. The pope identified sin and the structures produced by sin as the main obstacle preventing authentic liberation. Pope John Paul II also stated that solidarity, "the love and service of neighbor, especially of the poorest," unites all in the process of development and liberation (#46). He added that despite difficulties with liberation theology, the church has confidence in a *true liberation*, that is based on its awareness of God's promise that history is open to the activity of God, and on confidence in the human person created in the image of God, every one of whom is called to defend people's God-given dignity using peaceful means (#47).

Despite criticisms of its alleged use of Marxism, liberation theology has positive features that could assist North Americans in confronting poverty, a daily reality for millions of people in the United States. These positive factors include a love for the poor as expressed in the preferential option for the poor, a prophetic call to justice, reliance on Scripture as God's word, recognition of the dignity of each person, and the right to share the necessities of life and enjoy the blessings of culture. Christian base communities serve as a model for people of many races and nationalities to meet, pray, and work together for the common good. The theologies of liberation that have developed in many countries and cultures have much to offer in terms of learning how to live joyfully and work to achieve justice.

LETTY M. RUSSELL: A FEMINIST LIBERATION THEOLOGY

Liberation theology has profited from the efforts of women as they claimed their true worth in the world. The Rev. Dr. Letty M. Russell (1929–2007) is a sterling example of a feminist liberation theologian whose insights are helpful in considering the human condition beset by poverty, racism, and myriad other problems. After a brief introduction, I will turn to her writings to enlarge the discussion of liberation.

Letty M. Russell investigated human participation in God's mission of liberation. As Christian educator and then pastor at the Church of the Ascension, a Protestant parish in East Harlem in New York City, Russell devoted seventeen years to a ministry of liberation. Her professional career included teaching at Manhattan College in the Bronx, after which she joined the faculty of Yale Divinity School in 1974.[40] As professor of theology at Manhattan College (1969–1974) and on the faculty of Yale Divinity School (1974–2001), Russell combined disciplined scholarship with a collaborative approach to encourage her students to research deeply and ask insightful questions to uncover misconceptions. Retirement from Yale Divinity School in 2001 provided Russell with the freedom to read, research, write, and preach, and most important, to coordinate with Shannon Clarkson an International Feminist Doctorate of Ministry program sponsored by the San Francisco Theological Seminary. Courses have been conducted in Chile, Costa Rica, Korea, Japan, Ghana, Kenya, and Switzerland to accommodate students from third world countries. Her work for justice began in Harlem but has incorporated a worldwide perspective since the 1950s when she first worked with the World Council of Churches.

A white, middle-class, educated, professional American woman, Russell sought to identify with and share the lives of the oppressed. She painstakingly peeled away her layers of privilege in order to accompany her students and parishioners on a quest for liberation and freedom. Rosemary Radford Ruether, also a feminist theologian, observed that for white middle-class women to relate to the oppressed they must first be aware of the privileged state in which they were born. For Russell, "thinking theologically from the 'other end' is always complemented by thinking socially from the 'bottom,' by concrete listening and being taught by women and men of oppressed classes and races."[41]

Russell's quest for liberation was broadened after she completed her doctorate and married in 1970. At that time, she began to develop an intentionally feminist approach to theology. Then, when she left Harlem to teach at Yale Divinity School, she moved from "a ghetto created by poverty and racism to a largely white, middle-class academic ghetto." Her work to eliminate racism was broadened as she drew upon her developing feminist sensibilities and began to address issues of sexism.[42] Overall, Russell's life experience consistently informed her developing theological vision. Her theological reflections were formed as a result of experiencing firsthand the problems and possibilities of life both in the inner city and in a largely white, middle-class community. Perhaps this is why she has sought a way to speak with both the oppressed and the oppressors.

Feminist Theology and Liberation Theology. Russell defined feminist theology as "advocating the equality and partnership of women and men in church and society." Liberation theology, according to Russell, is "an attempt to reflect upon the experience of oppression and our actions for the new creation of a more humane society." Russell also identified the common features of feminist and liberation theologies; both emerge from an experience of oppression, both hope for salvation viewed as a journey toward freedom, both require working together, and both looked toward hope and inclusiveness as part of God's plan for human liberation.[43] Feminist and liberation theologies share a common experience and hope for the future, as well as a sense of solidarity whereby people collaborate to effect God's plan of liberation.

Aware of the disparities between the sexes, Russell wrote at length about women who are programmed by the context of their culture to be subservient to their father and husband. In her words, the oppression of women is the "most universal form of exploitation," one in which men claim the right to dominate women consistently, and persistently subject another "human being to a permanent status of inferiority because of sex." She noted that throughout history women have been, with few exceptions, invisible "in an androcentric or male-dominated church and culture." In addition, being born female most often equaled a lifetime of servitude. Russell has observed that in recent times feminist theologians have worked to bring to light what was largely hidden. They have interpreted Scripture from a feminist perspective and dedicated themselves to thorough scholarship to break down iconoclastic interpretations and introduce new insights. She argued that for the goal of freedom to be realized, human relations have to be examined so " the basic polarity of *authority-submission*"[44] can be challenged at its very root.

Russell appreciated the power of language and language patterns in forming our concepts of God, our relationships with the world, with other people, and ourselves. For instance, aware of the exegetical and hermeneutical problems in reading and interpreting the Bible, she was convinced that change in linguistic patterns as well as continued inter-pretation are needed so that "the gospel message becomes 'good news' in present society." Thinking of the barrier of language, Russell pointed to the *forgotten names of God*: God as servant or helper; God as Creator, Liberator, and Reconciler; God as mother or wife. She added that Chris-tians can look to Jesus who "embodies in his life, death, and resurrection what a truly human being (*anthropos*) might be like. One who would love and live and suffer for love of God and for others."[45]

Russell identified conscientization as essential for liberation. Paulo Freire, a twentieth-century Brazilian educator and activist, developed con-scientization as a process that goes beyond consciousness-raising about oppressive situations to an action-education process. Conscientization includes cultural action, that is, intentional action united with ongoing education about one's culture, and a continuing process of praxis, that is, action united with reflection that aims at transforming oppressive cul-ture. Drawing on Freire's theory, Russell has described conscientization in terms of stages of historical awareness and action whereby one moves from *doxa* (Greek for opinion and belief), a naïve state, to *logos*, when people develop a critical awareness of the world around them; to *praxis*, which is action to transform the world; and finally to *utopia*, which is a vision of the future as a good place.

Russell also cited Rosemary Ruether who wrote about liberation as a dialectical process where conscientization questions the myths and cul-ture that control people's lives. According to Ruether, oppressed peoples achieve liberation through a three-stage process: 1) the woman or op-pressed person begins as a *happy slave*, that is, someone who accepts her lot in life as fulfilling or someone who seeks fulfillment by *emulating the oppressor* as a way to get ahead; when women realize that they are en-slaved, they often react angrily against the culture of oppression; 2) the person seeks individual and group self-affirmation in her or his search for *cultural identity;* 3) *the person seeks a new awareness and an ability to act.*

Overall, according to Russell, the process of conscientization can be compared to conversion. Both of these processes lead to a new aware-ness and a transformation of one's life and the world. The change ef-fected by conscientization stresses human initiative, while conversion stresses God's action.[46] Both require a radical rootedness and an opening up to new hope and possibilities. The end product is similar, namely, new life and power. In this way conscientization and conversion can both lead to liberation.

Russell recognized that liberation theology could be applied to op-pressive structures within the church and could lead to seeking a greater openness within the church to overcome these structures of oppression. She saw that liberation theology requires opening the church to the world and proposed an open ecclesiology whereby the church would join with God and work for change. However, she emphasized that com-munion with God and others must always be seen as part of a dialogic process whereby "God speaks to us through the Holy Spirit. We respond to God and one another in shared words, emotions, and obedient ac-tions." She suggested the rainbow of all the diverse groups of God's people as the best metaphor to express the openness of the church (Gen 9:12–13). This shift in ecclesiology would result in a wider ecumenism, as proposed in *Lumen Gentium* (#13–16).[47]

Openness, as Russell stated, is the preparation for dialogue, which depends on people being united in solidarity when they experience suf-fering and alienation and are willing to work for change. It also requires a sense of humility, knowing where one stands and whence one has come, and trust in the persons and groups with whom one works. The obstacles to dialogue include distinctions based on ecclesiastical rank, sex, race, and class within the church, and on economic, political, na-tional, and racial tensions. And yet, Russell stated, "We share a common humanity and can learn to move from *identity* toward *mutuality.*" Russell also summarized three models of dialogue: 1) mutual interpellation:

when people think their way together into action; 2) dialogical action: when men and women act their way into action; and 3) shared world: when people experience the same environment together, which becomes a process of learning by living together.[48]

Partnership. As a result of her work with parishioners and students to effect liberation, Russell identified a new metaphor, partnership, to personify liberation. Her first discussion of this metaphor is found in *The Future of Partnership* (1979). She defined partnership as "a new focus of relationship in which there is continuing commitment and common struggle in interaction with a wider community context."[49] The three essential qualities of partnership as expressed in this definition are commitment, common struggle, and contextuality. Partnership, then, is a form of community that energizes people to remain committed to one another as they unite in a common struggle.

In answering the question of God's role in partnership, Russell considered God's actions from the beginning (creation) and from the end (eschatology). From both perspectives God chooses to give life and share power with both women and men. Moreover, God chooses to partner with creatures even when their actions go against God's directions. When people are in conflict, when humanity strays far from the initial relations of "equality, complementarity, and community,"[50] even then God is with and for the people. God is an active God, interested in being with people and saving them from destruction. Active in history, God's mission is to be with and to liberate humanity.

For Russell, God is the model of partnership. She wrote of God as both the Immanent Trinity and the Economic Trinity. As the Immanent Trinity, God communicates love among the persons of the Trinity. As the Economic Trinity, God communicates love to the world and invites human beings into partnership with God. The communication of love among the persons of the Trinity allows humanity to marvel at their mutual sharing and respect, and their sharing in "the work of salvation and the mission of the world." God's activity of "being partner in God's self and being partner with us" is the model for partnership among women and men. Sensitive to those oppressed by patriarchy and hierarchy, Russell also set before us feminine images of God, such as a mother who gives birth and shelters the people (Deut 32:11, 18; Mt 23:37; Ps 51:1; 131:2; Prov 1:20–33). She remarked that the Trinity can be identified as *Creator*, "the continuing source of life"; as *Liberator*, "who sets the captives [humans] free"; and as *Advocate*, "continually present with us as a witness." God is actively "for us, and not against us."[51] Such an understanding of God, Russell contended, can reinforce the belief that we are partners with a loving, active God.

Russell's experience in East Harlem helped her realize that those who have suffered oppression "look for a God who has known suffering and 'Godforsakenness' and has conquered the power of evil through suffering love." She commented that when the men and women of her congregation identified Jesus as Liberator, they often "learned to live out small signs of freedom in the midst of bad housing, addiction, and poverty."[52]

Russell's marriage to Hans Hoekendijk was a living reminder of the beauty and strength of partnership. Their mutual love gave their lives new meaning and enhanced their ability to share in work and ministry. Her experience demonstrated that rather than diminishing one's self, partnership allows one to grow. This is consistent with her thoughts about God's arithmetic. It defies normal mathematical formulae because "the relationships are not just quantitative, but are qualitative."[53]

Service. A recurring theme for Russell is service. Along with Rosemary Radford Ruether, she called for transforming the roles of men and women based on the reality of the church as a Christian community whose ministry depended on *diakonia* where "women are freed from exclusive identification with the service role and called to join the circle of disciples as equal members."[54] Russell contended that *diakonia* or service, as Jesus showed by his example, is accomplished in *koinonia*, Christian community. She also claimed that service can be based on recognition of the need for mutual sharing of each person's gifts and can lead to the experience of solidarity. Ideally, according to Russell, service in community can be "a partnership of discipleship modeled on servanthood and not on hierarchical structures of domination and subordination." She added, "*Diakonia* practiced in a context of partnership is a service of calculated inefficiency!" The most efficient way often excludes or ignores other people; *diakonia* requires placing ourselves at the disposal of others and exposes our vulnerability. Service based in partnership may appear to be "calculated inefficiency," but this is what "allows room for all partners to grow and participate fully." An example of how partnership as service functions is found in Russell's ministry among the oppressed.

> I experienced the function of partnership as service in seventeen years of shared ministry with oppressed people of an economic and racial ghetto in New York City. Those most oppressed, subordinated, and dehumanized by lack of employment, poverty, crime, and racism, those who were "nobodies," found that they were "somebodies" as part of a community that encouraged their ministry to others. In actions of service they came to know themselves as empowered to be human beings, able to care and to act for others and, therefore, for themselves.[55]

Russell's analysis shows how service can free people to be themselves as they work with and for others, and how empowerment and liberation can flow from freely giving and risking lives in the ministry of Jesus Christ.

Liberation Theologies. With the publication of *Growth in Partnership* (1981) Russell enlarged the discussion of liberation, focusing on the adoption of liberation theology by many different communities. Rather than discussing liberation theology (singular), she wrote of the "style of liberation theologies" (plural) which she identified as *collective*, that is, living faith in a community; *committed to justice*, because they shared God's bias and concern for the poor and marginalized; *contextual*, because they were rooted in particular experiences that shaped their understanding of God's call to freedom; and *critical reflection*, calling for action. Russell envisioned the phases of this process as "a dialectic of liberation in which persons become aware of freedom as a problem and a possibility in their lives."[56]

Russell also developed a theology of anticipation to emphasize how liberation implies partnership with God's liberating actions. Such a the-

ology involves thinking from the end of God's New Creation, and looking for and acting to achieve *small reversals* in the present that could lead
us more fully toward God's New Creation. She pointed out that when
least expected, life's suffering will often yield to moments of reversal. To
be open to such moments, we need to be able to expect the unexpected.
This requires openness to the future wherein "we are more likely to hear
the words of judgments we need to hear in the midst of comfort as well
as words of hope in situations beyond hope." The reversals may only be
small advances and the time may well go beyond our lifetime. In terms
of faith communities reflecting on the meaning of God's future and how
it affects their lives, Russell referred to Elisabeth Fiorenza who wrote that
"the New Testament interprets the end of history as *already present* in the
resurrection of Jesus Christ and also as *not yet present* until the return of
Christ and the fulfillment of the New Creation." Russell pointed out that
God's New Creation can break into the present and impel us "to live out
a new reality of partnership with others."[57]

While liberation directly addresses the concerns of those who are poor
and oppressed, can there also be liberation for those who bear the responsibility for causing poverty and imposing oppression? As part of her
concern for liberation, Russell developed a theology for oppressors. If
liberation flows from God's actions for mending creation, these actions
effect justice and shalom for the oppressed. Referring to Luke 4:16–30,
Russell acknowledged that Jesus began his ministry with a "prophetic
word of comfort for the oppressed." However, for the townspeople of
Nazareth these words could also be seen as judging them. She pointed
out that oppressors who desire solidarity with the oppressed must pay
a price in terms of "repentance and justice." Reconciliation for oppressors, namely, those who have built or benefited from the structures of
racism, sexism, and classism, demands reparations.[58] Only when they
make reparation will they begin to understand how Jesus was inspired
"to bring good news to the poor" (Lk 4:18). God's justice always favors
the poor. Like the townspeople of Nazareth, oppressors have much to
learn from this message.

Russell suggested that a theology for oppressors will analyze how "the
structures of racism, sexism, and capitalism perpetuate evil." In devel-

oping such a theology, she turned to an article by Jürgen Moltmann and Douglas Meeks, "The Liberation of Oppressors." Moltmann and Meeks contended that domination perpetuates "the inner evil of self-justification and pride through myths of inferiority, and the outer evil of aggression and subjugation of other persons." Russell also highlighted Moltmann's analysis of capital as resulting in large part from the labor of others and only in small part to one's own labor. That is, the accumulation of capital entails the use of power over people. Moreover, when such power is misused, "Every human being is doubly exploited, first by being identified as work power rather than as person, and second by being made slave to consumption in order to increase profit." Moltmann named "the root cause of these structures of aggression and self-justification" as "love that is distorted." Russell argued that self-love or the "hunger for power and will to subjugate" often displaced the love of God. Yet she suggested that change is possible and can occur through the transformation of people's relationships with God, other people, and creation. For oppressors, such transformation can come through faith when they seek a "new relationship of freedom in community with others," the cost of which is "refusing to conform to the status quo of this world."[59] Russell referred to Paul who wrote, "Do not conform yourselves to this age but be transformed by the renewal of your mind, so that you may judge what is God's will, what is good, pleasing and perfect" (Rom 12:2).

Hope is also a theme in *Growth in Partnership*. Russell argued that in the midst of suffering the task of liberation theologies is to reflect on God's presence and actions so as to articulate a vision of "hope against hope." On this journey through the wilderness toward the New Creation, "they speak from the perspective of the victim and, therefore, emphasize judgment for the victimizer and grace for the victim."[60] Liberation theologies call for accountability and witness to the bias of God's justice for the poor and marginalized. They are practical in that they search for the meaning of suffering and offer hope of liberation. Focusing on incarnated truth rather than abstract truth, they use an ongoing process of action/reflection through which people share stories and investigate and reinterpret biblical stories for their meaning for today.

In *Church in the Round: Feminist Interpretation of the Church* (1993) Russell discussed the growing diversity of liberation theologies.[61] She cited examples of the many churches and church leaders from different countries and continents that employ ideas based on liberation theologies. Once again she cited many examples of feminist theologies. Russell now envisioned the action/reflection model as a continuing spiral.[62] She reaffirmed her conviction that theology's vital issues are always examined through a particular lens (language, thought, action) indicative of the social and ecclesial context of people's experience and learning. She also called for experience to be subjected to critical analysis, connected to Christian faith traditions, and finally, to enter into collaborative efforts with others aimed at achieving greater fullness of life.

Moreover, Russell pointed out that common to all liberation and feminist theologies is the struggle for justice based on solidarity, and that these contextual theologies are

> shaped out of a commitment to act in solidarity with the poor and oppressed, making use of their situations of pain, and continuing the theological spiral with serious rereading of the Gospel and church tradition. They conclude with a call to themselves and the churches to confess their sins of worshiping the false gods of imperialism, money, and racism and to move to action in the struggle for justice.[63]

While acknowledging Dietrich Bonhoeffer's commitment to view history from below "from the perspective of those who suffer" and Gustavo Gutiérrez's "theology from the underside of history" in his concern for the nonperson,[64] Russell preferred to speak of *the margin*. As a feminist, she rejected the hierarchical stance of patriarchy with its emphasis on domination and subordination, and chose to work from the margin. She noted that there can be a constant movement from the margin to the center and back again. At the margin one identifies and stands in solidarity with the oppressed, and the goal is always to join the one at the center of life, Jesus Christ. Overall, she contrasted patriarchal styles of leadership (standing above, accumulating power) with feminist styles (standing with, sharing authority in community).

She suggested that the latter have the most potential for empowering those on the margins.

Shared Authority. In *Church in the Round*, Russell remarked that liberation structures are found in basic Christian communities and feminist Christian communities. These communities call for an end to domination, and advocate shared authority in community and partnership in church and society. They also have the potential, Russell contended, to see a unity in creation: salvation working to restore the wholeness of creation and uniting social and personal salvation to reflect the harmony of God's plan. Russell claimed that if people can begin to work together to mend creation, then more harmonious relations can be fostered between women and men so that women can claim their full humanity with men. Ultimately, she envisioned a spirituality of connection that can be fostered within "alternative, nonpatriarchal communities where partnership is lived," suggesting that in such communities a living faith will connect the members "to the struggles for justice in a discipleship of freely chosen service in the name of Jesus Christ."[65]

The Welcome Table. A *welcome table* is an apt metaphor for liberation theology. Russell explained that the welcome table purposely makes "very welcome those who feel least welcome." In the black church tradition the welcome table "symbolizes the communion table and every gathering at table." In Russell's words, "At God's welcome table those who have been denied access to the table of the rich white masters are welcomed and may welcome others as a foretaste of the final moment of full partnership with God." The welcome table can remind us of God calling us into being, welcoming us into existence. In Russell's thought, this table of hospitality reverses "the household codes or lists of cultural norms adopted as the duties of the Christian patriarchal household in the Pastoral Epistles" (see Eph 5:21—6:9; Col 3:18—4:1). The reversal occurs when persons "become part of God's reality of love and justice." The welcome table can also become a symbol and reminder of what it means to be followers of Jesus. In story and deeds Jesus welcomed the sick, the poor, and the outcast, offering words of life, actions of healing, and trust in a loving God. A community that gathers around the table needs to welcome others, following the example of Jesus who "welcomed the outsiders into God's household."

Finally, the welcome table can be a symbol and source of strength to continue the struggle for justice in our time. Russell reminded us that God's eschatological banquet reverses expectations. Just as "God in Christ has reached out to make us all partners in the celebration," so too are community members called to stand in solidarity with the poor and oppressed.[66] God helps people to overcome oppressive behaviors and attitudes so they can approach the table and learn to value not just themselves, but also the particular giftedness of their diverse neighbors. Together we can approach the welcome table to be strengthened to continue the struggle for justice in our time. We will rejoice in small victories as we journey toward wholeness and unity, knowing that God is with us in the struggle for liberation.

SUMMARY

In summary, this chapter presented the writings of the Latin American bishops' conferences at Medellín and Puebla, and the work of Gustavo Gutiérrez, the first articulations of liberation theology. The insights of Roger Haight were drawn upon to present liberation themes and methodologies from a North American perspective. Finally, Letty Russell expanded the understanding of liberation to include both a feminist perspective and the concerns of those on the margin—people of color and people from varied national backgrounds. Overall, liberation theologies offer North Americans an understanding of what it can mean to seek greater justice for the poor and oppressed. They also suggest that there is an essential connection between reflection on the realities of poverty, and action for greater justice in solidarity with the poor and oppressed.

In striving to understand and foster justice for the poor and the oppressed, we must now consider ways to educate for justice. Hence, in the next chapter I discuss a number of approaches and principles for educating for justice from a Christian faith perspective. These educational frameworks will suggest ways that Christians can be partners with God in God's work of justice. They will present ways in which Christians, as coworkers with God, can learn to welcome the poor to the table of social interaction and decision making.

QUESTIONS FOR REFLECTION AND DISCUSSION

1. Describe the effect the Second Vatican Council had on theology, especially the approach to doing theology in Latin America.

2. What was the historical situation when the Latin American bishops met at Medellín in 1968? Outline the main concepts of the documents on Peace, Poverty, and Catechesis, especially regarding poverty and justice. Explain how the bishops broke with "political and social traditions."

3. Christian base communities are identified as a means of catechizing the poor. What is meant by Christian base communities? How could these communities meet the needs of the poor? Russell noted that basic Christian communities and feminist Christian communities have similar aims; explain the similarities.

4. What did the Latin American bishops mean when they called for "a preferential option for the poor"?

5. Discuss the major contributions of the Latin American bishops' conferences at Medellín and Puebla regarding justice for the poor.

6. Gustavo Gutiérrez is a theologian who applied the thinking of Vatican Council II to the situation of Latin America. Explain his three senses of poverty. Defend this statement: Gutiérrez made the needs of the poor a major focus in his writings. What are the three meanings of liberation, according to Gutiérrez? How is liberation theology rooted in spirituality?

7. Roger Haight offers a North American perspective on liberation theology. Explain liberation theology using the themes he proposed. Which methodological themes does he present to under-

stand liberation theology? How is liberation theology related to social justice?

8. The Catholic Church has consistently criticized Marxism. How is Marxism connected to liberation theology? What is the Vatican's view of Marxism? How does Roger Haight distinguish the use of Marxism in liberation theology?

9. Letty M. Russell was a feminist liberation theologian. How did her experience working with the poor in East Harlem for seventeen years impact her theology? Explain how Russell viewed the connection between feminist theology and liberation theology. Describe the contribution of Paulo Freire to dialogic education by referring to his theory of conscientization.

10. How do the themes of partnership and service enlarge the view of liberation theology? Why are there different liberation theologies? What is the importance of "theology for oppressors"? How is hope related to liberation theologies? Explain why solidarity is essential for working with the poor. Why is "the welcome table" an apt metaphor for liberation theology?

SUGGESTED READINGS

Brown Robert, McAfee. *Liberation Theology: An Introductory Guide*. Louisville: Westminster/John Knox Press, 1993.

Cliford, Anne M. *Introducing Feminist Theology*. Maryknoll, NY: Orbis Books, 2001.

Couture, Pamela D. *Blessed Are the Poor?* Nashville: Abingdon Press, 1991.

Dorr, Donal. *Option for the Poor: A Hundred Years of Vatican Social Teaching*. Revised Edition. Maryknoll, NY: Orbis Books, 1992.

Faithful Citizenship: Civic Responsibility for a New Millennium. Washington, DC: United States Conference of Catholic Bishops, 2003.

Farley, Margaret A., and Serene Jones (eds.). *Liberating Eschatology: Essays in Honor of Letty M. Russell*. Louisville: Westminster/John Knox Press, 1999.

Forming Consciences for Faithful Citizenship: A Call to Political Responsibility. Washington, DC: United States Conference of Catholic Bishops, 2007.

Freire, Paulo. *Pedagogy of the Oppressed.* New York: Seabury Press, 1970.

Gebara, Ivone. *Out of the Depths: Women's Experience of Evil and Salvation.* Ann Patrick Ware, transl. Minneapolis: Fortress Press, 2002.

Gutiérrez, Gustavo. *A Theology of Liberation.* Translated and edited by Sr. Caridad Inda and John Eagleson. Maryknoll, NY: Orbis Books, 1973.

_____. *The Power of the Poor in History: Selected Writings.* Robert R. Barr, transl. Maryknoll, NY: Orbis Books, 1983.

_____. *The Truth Shall Make You Free: Confrontations.* Matthew J. O'Connell, transl. Maryknoll, NY: Orbis Books, 1990.

_____. *Essential Writings.* James B. Nickoloff, ed. Maryknoll, NY: Orbis Books, 1996.

_____. "The Task and Content of Liberation Theology," *The Cambridge Companion to Liberation Theology.* Christopher Rowland, ed. New York: Cambridge University Press, 1999.

Haight, S.J., Roger. *An Alternative Vision: An Interpretation of Liberation Theology.* New York: Paulist Press, 1985.

Hennelly, Alfred T. *Liberation Theologies: The Global Pursuit of Justice.* Mystic, CT: Twenty-Third Publications, 1995.

Herzog, Frederick. *Liberation Theology: Liberation in the Light of the Fourth Gospel.* New York: Seabury Press, 1972.

_____. *Justice Church: The New Function of the Church in North American Christianity.* Maryknoll, NY: Orbis Books, 1980.

_____. *Theology from the Belly of the Whale.* Joerg Rieger, ed. Harrisburg, PA: Trinity Press International, 1999.

Isasi-Díaz, Ada María. *La Lucha Continues: Mujerista Theology.* Maryknoll, NY: Orbis Books, 2004.

Jones, Serene. "Women's Experience between a Rock and a Hard Place: Feminist, Womanist, and Mujerista Theologies in North America," in *Horizons in Feminist Theology*, Rebecca Chopp and Sheila Greeve Davaney, eds. Minneapolis: Fortress Press, 1997.

_____. *Feminist Theory and Christian Theology: Cartographies of Grace*. Minneapolis: Fortress Press, 2000.

Kater, Jr., John L. "Whatever Happened to Liberation Theology? New Directions for Theological Reflection in Latin America," *Anglican Theological Review* 83.4 (Fall 2001).

Keely, Barbara Anne. *Faith of Our Foremothers: Women Changing Religious Education*. Louisville: Westminster/John Knox Press, 1997.

Lernoux, Penny. "The Long Path to Puebla," in John Eagleson and Philip Scharper, eds. *Puebla and Beyond: Documentation and Commentary*. Maryknoll, NY: Orbis Books, 1979.

Mich, Marvin L. Krier. *Catholic Social Teaching and Movements*. Mystic, CT: Twenty-Third Publications, 1998.

Puebla and Beyond: Documentation and Commentary. John Eagleson and Philip Scharper (eds.). Maryknoll, NY: Orbis Books, 1979.

Russell, Letty M. *The Future of Partnership*. Philadelphia: Westminster Press, 1979.

_____.*Growth in Partnership*. Philadelphia: Westminster Press, 1981.

_____. *Household of Freedom: Authority in Feminist Theology*. Philadelphia: Westminster Press, 1987.

_____. *Church in the Round: Feminist Interpretation of the Church*. Louisville, KY: Westminster/John Knox Press, 1993.

_____, and J. Shannon Clarkson, eds. *Dictionary of Feminist Theologies*. Louisville, KY: Westminster John Knox Press, 1996.

Schüssler Fiorenza, Elisabeth, ed. *The Power of Naming: A Concilium Reader in Feminist Liberation Theology*. Maryknoll, NY: Orbis Books, 1996.

Sigmund, Paul E. *Liberation Theology at the Crossroads: Democracy or Revolution?* New York: Oxford University Press, 1992.

NOTES

[1] Roberto Oliveros Maqueo, "Meeting of Theologians at Petropolis" (March 1964), in Alfred T. Hennelly, S.J. (ed.), *Liberation Theology: A Documentary History* (Maryknoll, NY: Orbis Books, 1990), 43-47.

[2] *Third World Bishops*, "A Letter to the People of the Third World" (August 15, 1967), in Hennelly, 48-57.

[3] Latin American Priests, "*Populorum Progressio* and Latin American Realities" (November 1967), #3, in Hennelly, 58-61.

[4] Gustavo Gutiérrez, "Toward a Theology of Liberation" (July 1968), in Hennelly, 75.

[5] Provincials of the Society of Jesus, "The Jesuits in Latin America" (May 1968), #3, in Hennelly, 78.

[6] Marvin L. Krier Mich, *Catholic Social Teaching and Movements* (Mystic, CT: Twenty-Third Publications, 2001), 241.

[7] The Church in the Present-Day Transformation of Latin America in the Light of the Council, II, Conclusions (Bogotá, Colombia: General Secretariat of CELAM, 1970), "Peace," #16.

[8] Penny Lernoux, "The Long Path to Puebla," in John Eagleson and Philip Scharper (eds.), *Puebla and Beyond: Documentation and Commentary* (Maryknoll, NY: Orbis Books, 1979), 11.

[9] Ibid., 19.

[10] Ibid., Penny Lernoux explains the unique qualities of Christian base communities: "They are born at the bottom, not imposed by some government agency at the top; their principal characteristic is solidarity…; and they have the institutional support of the Church, both locally and regionally."

[11] Mich, 245.

[12] Paul E. Sigmund, *Liberation Theology at the Crossroads: Democracy or Revolution?* (New York: Oxford University Press, 1990), 41.

[13] Ibid.

[14] Mich, 247.

[15] Curt Cadorette, M.M., "Puebla," in Judith A. Dwyer (ed.), *The New Dic-*

tionary of Catholic Social Thought (Collegeville, MN: Liturgical Press, 1994), 798.

[16] Gustavo Gutiérrez, *A Theology of Liberation* (Maryknoll, NY: Orbis Books, 1973), 15.

[17] Ibid., 289.

[18] Ibid., 295.

[19] Ibid., 290.

[20] Ibid., 298.

[21] Gustavo Gutiérrez, *The Truth Shall Make You Free: Confrontations* (Maryknoll, NY: Orbis Books, 1990), 8.

[22] Gustavo Gutiérrez, "The Task and Content of Liberation Theology," Christopher Rowland (ed.), *The Cambridge Companion to Liberation Theology* (New York: Cambridge University Press, 1999), 24.

[23] Ibid.

[24] Ibid., 25.

[25] Gutiérrez, *A Theology of Liberation*, 295.

[26] Gutiérrez, "The Task and Content of Liberation Theology," 29.

[27] Gutiérrez, *The Truth Shall Make You Free: Confrontations*, 13.

[28] Gutiérrez, "The Task and Content of Liberation Theology," 26.

[29] Gustavo Gutiérrez, "The Situation and Tasks of Liberation Theology Today," Joerg Rieger (ed.), *Opting for the Margins* (New York: Oxford University Press, 2003), 100.

[30] Ibid., 102.

[31] Gutiérrez, "The Task and Content of Liberation Theology," 35.

[32] Ibid., 37.

[33] Roger Haight, S.J., *An Alternative Vision: An Interpretation of Liberation Theology* (New York: Paulist Press, 1985), 15-24.

[34] Ibid., 44-47.

[35] Ibid., 79.

[36] Ibid., 234-39; 246-56.

[37] Introduction to "Instruction on Certain Aspects of the 'Theology of Liberation'" (Vatican City, 1984).

[38] Haight, 261.

[39] *Instruction on Christian Freedom and Liberation* (Vatican City, 1986).

[40] Barbara Anne Keely, "Educating for Partnership," *Faith of Our Foremothers: Women Changing Religious Education* (Louisville: Westminster/John Knox Press, 1997), 166-67.

[41] Rosemary Radford Ruether, "The Theological Vision of Letty Russell," Margaret A. Farley and Serene Jones (eds.), *Liberating Eschatology: Essays in Honor of Letty M. Russell,* (Louisville: Westminster/John Knox Press, 1999), 21.

[42] Letty M. Russell, "Bread Instead of Stone," *Christian Century* 97 (January-June 1980), 665.

[43] Ruether, 19-21.

[44] Ibid., 29, 85, 146.

[45] Ibid., 95-101, 34.

[46] Ibid., 115-24.

[47] Ibid., 156-61.

[48] Ibid., 164-66.

[49] Letty M. Russell, *The Future of Partnership* (Philadelphia: Westminster Press, 1979), 18.

[50] Ibid., 25.

[51] Ibid., 31, 33.

[52] Ibid., 28-30.

[53] Ibid., 41, 25.

[54] Ibid., 70. Quoted from Rosemary Radford Ruether, *New Woman, New Earth: Sexist Ideologies and Human Liberation* (Seabury Press, 1975), 66.

[55] Russell, *The Future of Partnership*, 70-76, 118, 76.

⁵⁶ Letty M. Russell, *Growth in Partnership* (Philadelphia: Westminster Press, 1981), 73, 76.

⁵⁷ Ibid., 91, 105.

⁵⁸ Ibid., 113, 117.

⁵⁹ Ibid., 121-22.

⁶⁰ Ibid., 148.

⁶¹ The diversity of liberation theologies is evident in the following sources: Alfred T. Hennelly, S.J., *Liberation Theologies: The Global Pursuit of Justice* (Mystic, CT: Twenty-Third Publications, 1995); Frederick Herzog, *Liberation Theology: Liberation in the Light of the Fourth Gospel* (New York: Seabury Press, 1972); Robert McAfee Brown, *Liberation Theology: An Introductory Guide* (Louisville: Westminster/John Knox Press, 1993); Ada María Isasi-Díaz, *La Lucha Continues: Mujerista Theology* (Maryknoll, NY: Orbis Books, 2004), and *En La Lucha—In the Struggle: Elaborating a Mujerista Theology* (Minneapolis: Fortress Press, 2004); Ivone Gebara, *Out of the Depths: Women's Experience of Evil and Salvation* (Minneapolis: Fortress Press, 2002).

⁶² Russell prefers *theological* spiral: "This style of theologizing in a continuing spiral of engagement and reflection begins with *commitment* to the task of raising up signs of God's new household with those who are struggling for justice and full humanity. It continues by *sharing experiences* of commitment and struggle...leads to a *critical analysis* of the context of the experiences... *questions about biblical and church tradition* that help us gain new insight into the meaning of the gospel as good news for the oppressed and marginalized. This new understanding of tradition flows from and leads to action, celebration, and further reflection in the continuing theological spiral." Letty M. Russell, *Church in the Round: Feminist Interpretation of the Church* (Louisville: Westminster/John Knox Press, 1993), 30-31.

⁶³ Ibid., 82-83.

⁶⁴ Ibid., 25.

⁶⁵ Ibid., 93, 199.

⁶⁶ Ibid., 149-50.

CHAPTER 5

Educating for Justice

The American Dream of "liberty and justice for all" has drawn people from many nations and many classes to the United States of America because it resonates with their deepest yearnings. Young and old are drawn to what the American Dream promises—a good life, and in some cases, a better life for people who believe that one can share in the wealth of this young nation. This young nation is blessed with many natural resources, not least of which are the people whose hearts beat with hope and whose minds grapple with mundane realities, as they put their faith in the myriad possibilities offered to those willing to sacrifice and struggle for a better life.

While the American Dream is a powerful promise, many millions of people in the United States are currently struggling just to survive. Poverty is a serious threat to their lives and to the lives of their children. When parents cannot feed their children, find affordable housing, live in a safe neighborhood, get adequate health care, or send their children to schools that could open the doors of opportunity, "equality of opportunity" is a myth. In other words, the high level of poverty in the United States threatens the American Dream. Social justice is far removed from the actual lives of the poor. Too often they are treated in socially unjust ways by being denied access to the benefits of living in a free society with the right to participate fully.

A commitment to educating for justice provides one way of addressing the gap between the American ideal of justice for all and the injustices of poverty. Moreover, in order to educate for justice we need to seek common ground between the American Dream of justice for all and the Christian ideal of social justice. On the one hand, Justicia, the statue portraying a woman holding the scales of justice, adorns our public buildings and represents the American ideal of justice as fairness. As the blindfolded judge of conflicting claims, Justicia is a powerful symbol of just judgment that is not prejudiced by factors such as class, race, or wealth. The image of Justicia is a reminder that all who present their claims to the tribunals of justice in the United States will be treated as equals and their claims will be judged solely on their merits. On the other hand, the Christian sense of justice is based on the inherent dignity of the human person, and seeks justice not only for the individual but also for the community. A Christian understanding of social justice has the potential to enlarge the discussion of justice in the public sphere by upholding the value of every person and advocating for everyone to insure their inclusion as valuable members of the community.

A critical need in educating for justice is an expanded sense of justice that has the power to overcome injustice by creating ever-widening bands of human concern based on a genuine sense of caring. More fully developed ideals of fairness that are integrated with a Christian sense of the intrinsic dignity of each person can inspire us to value ourselves so we will think positively and seek ways to reach out to others. Our world cries out for ways to unify and overcome the divisions among peoples. An expanded, positive sense of justice allows us to see that what unites us as members of the human community is far stronger than what divides us. Overall, life-affirming ideals have the power to strengthen the weak, convert the privileged, empower the marginalized, and overcome ingrown resistance and negativity. Solidarity with the oppressed can result in transformation of consciousness; then collective action for justice and freedom from oppression and injustice can lead to true liberation. Everyone stands to gain when we embrace a richer, fuller understanding of social justice.

This chapter, then, presents a concluding and integrating reflection on educating for justice from a Christian faith perspective in the United States today. As Christians, our efforts to educate for justice need to be based on fundamental principles, including a commitment to seeing God as the model of justice, a recognition of the call to be partners with God in working for justice; a belief in a realistic sense of the goodness of creation, and a need to know our rights as citizens of our nation and the world and as members of a faith community. If we are to educate for justice for the poor, we must have an empirically based understanding of poverty and its effects. At the same time we need to be able to draw from Christian Scripture, history, and traditions as we strive to develop comprehensive ways of approaching issues of justice and injustice. The conclusion reinforces the belief that we live in one world among many people, but ultimately our hope is to welcome all to the social table for conversation, nourishment, and decision making.

EDUCATING FOR JUSTICE FROM A CHRISTIAN PERSPECTIVE IN THE UNITED STATES TODAY

This section will explore seven fundamental principles and approaches for educating for justice from a Christian faith perspective. These principles are rooted in and develop from reflection on Scripture and tradition. This study will be enriched by the writings of contemporary religious educators, Letty M. Russell, Thomas H. Groome, and Gabriel Moran, who will serve as guides on the journey to educating for justice. Their approaches to educating for justice show how we might educate in ways that foster an expanded, richer sense of justice that draws from both the national ideals of the United States and Christian Scripture, history, and traditions.

FUNDAMENTAL PRINCIPLES

1. Appreciating the goodness of creation and the dignity of each person. The starting point for our considerations is the goodness of creation and the dignity of each person. This first principle undergirds and inspires all that we do in working for justice. It is vital to remember that in Scripture God's response to the varied acts of creation was the simple but profound refrain, "God saw that it was good" (Gen 1:3, 10, 12, 18, 21, 25). This sense of goodness conveys the reality that all of the creatures and aspects of the world are inherently beautiful. God creates humans "in the image of God" (Gen 1:27), bestowing a unique dignity on every man, woman, and child. First and foremost, God identified God's self intimately with each human. Humans in turn, as well as all living creatures, share the wonders of nature. It is this anthropology, or exploration of the origins of humanity, that Groome emphasizes and that Moran states as his first step in educating for justice, gratitude for God's gifts. The simple pleasures of earthly existence need to be remembered in times of calm as well as when life and stability are threatened. We are blessed to be part of such a wondrous creation.

2. Recognizing that we are partners with God and with one another. Flowing from the largesse of a loving God is the second principle, that we are partners with God and one another. Russell emphasizes that God's partnership with humanity leads us to work more carefully and caringly with other people. God invites us to join in God's mission of working to sustain and improve the world. This mission is first and foremost God's initiative and we are invited to be partners by celebrating the Lord's presence in the Eucharist and most especially among the poor (Mt 25:31–40). God invites all to share in this mission to reconcile and mend the world (Rom 8:20–25). We can rejoice in God's activity in the world, knowing that the reign of God is among us and that it will be fully accomplished in God's time, a fact that frees us to be active partners with a loving God.

3. Encouraging contemplation. The third principle arises from the necessity of being grounded in theological convictions that flow from the goodness of creation, the dignity of each person, and the fact that we are partners with God and one another. This principle of contemplation is portrayed in Andei Rublev's icon, "The Holy Trinity." As described in Chapter 1, this icon is an image of the Triune God. It encourages reflection, provides a place where one observes in silence and listens with the heart, and ultimately invites action. Henri Nouwen reflected on icons that engage the viewer, noting that when we prayerfully and thoughtfully contemplate this icon of the Triune God, "we come to see with our inner eyes that all engagements in this world can bear fruit only when they take place within this divine circle." He stated that our being involved in "struggles for justice and in actions for peace" as well as fulfilling family and community obligations can still be accomplished "without ever having to leave the house of love."[1] In a very real sense, being in God's presence inspires and energizes us to act justly.

The Trinity illustrates perfectly how women and men are to approach each other: with respect, attention, and love. The icon captures the essence of Christianity: the contemplative stance, being fully and lovingly aware, in a world of action. This concept is foremost in the writings of Moran who considered a contemplative attitude at the heart of those who educate for justice. Groome also identified contemplation as essential if one is to have a "passion for justice." Russell extolled a spirituality of liberation based on a "Christian mysticism of partnership" that flows from contemplation.

4. Acknowledging the realism of sin. The fourth principle underlies this discussion of justice. Realism means that we identify and become aware of sin, how some things are far removed from God's plan at this time and in this place. Stated simply, even as we affirm the goodness of the world, we need to acknowledge that there are serious problems. All too often we easily forget our relationship with God by placing our perceived needs and desires for comfort ahead of everything or everyone else's needs. When we place ourselves above and before even God, we can easily ignore our responsibilities to family and our neighbor. As a result of misguided love, we ourselves may be guilty of personal sin, and in severing the bonds of solidarity we may also be complicit in social sin. Blinded by ambition or by a desire for wealth or power, and involved in harmful relationships, we can easily fall into a pattern of evil by direct participation and by approval, as when we order, advise, praise, or approve what is harmful, as well as by protecting and not admitting when something or someone is evil.[2] Personal sin often leads to social sin when we are involved in "social situations and institutions that are contrary to divine goodness" (*Catechism of the Catholic Church*, #1869). We may stand to benefit from institutions that limit and make life difficult and even deadly for other people A realistic appraisal of life in the United States may well lead us to question whether society through its political, economic, and social structures effectively denies people their right to "life, liberty, and the pursuit of happiness." In the name of efficiency and over-reliance on the market model, many individuals and families are locked out and denied access to a decent life. In all honesty we can say that equality of opportunity has not led to equality of outcome, and for many in the United States, life is grim.

And yet, this principle of realism draws us back to the principles already mentioned. Specifically, because the world has problems, we are called to respond to God's invitation to affirm and build upon the inherent goodness of the world and to work as partners with God and one another to address the problems. When asked how she kept going in the struggle for justice, Letty Russell admitted, "I know the world is a mess," but she also stated, "I'm always excited about what God might be doing and what I could be doing." She expressed the strong conviction that "God will mend creation." She admitted, "We don't succeed every time" but she believed that "there is more to come." For Russell, "Work for justice may not necessarily succeed, but it is the right thing to do."[3]

5. Knowing our rights as citizens and as members of a faith community. What else do we need to know to educate and work for justice? In responding to this question I state my next summary principle: We need to know our rights as citizens of our nation and of the world community and as members of a faith community. We need to educate all people to know and appreciate their rights. Those of us who are Americans are likely to think of our rights in terms of the American Dream, namely, the right to "life, liberty, and the pursuit of happiness." We are also likely to think of justice as a kind of fairness, as demonstrated by a desire for all of us to live freely and to have equal opportunities to access the basic necessities for ourselves and our families, specifically, nourishing food, adequate housing in a safe neighborhood, a job that pays a living wage, good schools, and affordable health care. We have a right to protection from any threats against us or our neighbors that stem from crime, disease, or poverty. The reason is simple: People need a safe environment in order to live healthy, productive lives. The principle of realism challenges us to re-evaluate how and why so many people in the United States are far removed from satisfying their basic needs and those of their children. We have a right to information about these problems and we have a right to be involved in efforts to address them with the hope of working to change unjust systems.

In a spirit of realism and justice I will focus again on the problem of poverty in the United States. The first question to raise in addressing poverty is how serious a threat it is to the lives of people. As previously discussed, poverty has increased to such a degree that millions of men,

women, and children are struggling to get adequate food, find affordable housing, educate their children, and have access to quality health
care. As data from the U.S. Census Bureau reveal, in 2005 poverty was
a real threat to 37 million people, of whom 12.9 million were children
under the age of eighteen. Since the U.S. welfare system was reformed in
1996, there are fewer persons receiving cash assistance and many more
working at minimum wage jobs. Thus, there are the poor as noted in the
statistics and the nearly poor, those working full-time and often second
jobs who are one paycheck away from not being able to pay their rent
or meet mortgage payments. In effect, becoming homeless is a fear for
those who are poor as well as for many of the working poor.

Poverty is a greater problem for certain people in the United States
than for others. Those at the greatest risk of being poor are women, especially those who are divorced or single mothers, and their children.
Among ethnic and racial groups, blacks and Hispanics are more likely
to suffer the effects of poverty, as are those who are foreign-born and
non-citizens. Members of these groups are disproportionately poor. Of
concern for families is the fact that the measure of the depth of poverty,
known as the poverty gap, has risen since the mid-1970s. The reality is
that millions of people who are poor suffer great deprivation. Poverty
translates into not having sufficient income to meet basic needs, namely,
food, clothing, and shelter. For children, long bouts of poverty, especially severe poverty, adversely affect physical health, school achievement,
and emotional and behavioral outcomes.

**6. Educating all people to see poverty as a threat to the
common good.** One may question why are there so many who do
not know about the extent or nature of poverty? The U.S. Census Bureau
releases an annual report each fall for the previous year documenting
the number and percentage of the population who are living in poverty.
The media report briefly on the statistics and some editorials comment
on poverty. Overall the media give poverty little coverage, even though
they gravitate toward bad news all the time: violence, crimes, storms,
accidents, and celebrity trials. As the title of David K. Shipler's book indicates, "the working poor" are "invisible in America." Hence, as a basic

principle for addressing poverty, I suggest that educators need to become familiar with the studies that document the realities of poverty, and they need to discuss these realities among themselves and with their students. Information about poverty is available, but it requires that we reflect critically on the causes of poverty and the disparities between those who are ultra-rich and those struggling to survive daily while working at minimum-wage jobs. Critical reflection is meant to address not just individual, but more especially, structural causes. Poverty is not his or her problem; it is our problem.

Another important question is whether poverty is a threat to American society. As suggested, we hope to bring all people to the table of decision making. This could benefit those who are poor and on the margins of society, and, just as important, it rewards those who welcome all people to the table. To ignore such a large segment of our population overlooks the fact that great scientists, philosophers, writers, technicians, and teachers are among the poor. As Gustavo Gutiérrez wrote in "The Task and Content of Liberation Theology," the poor are "brimming over with capabilities and possibilities." In the United States this is a challenge because many of the poor are from other cultures, speak different languages, and live apart from those in the middle and upper classes. We have only to think of our families to realize how many of our own relatives came from other countries with the hope of making a better life in the United States. Sadly, there is a growing chasm between the really affluent and those who are poor. Just as the Great Depression of the early 1930s shattered the dreams of many Americans, so too poverty threatens the lives of millions of people in the twenty-first century. When dreams die, we all suffer. Hence, I offer another principle for educating for justice: We need to educate all people to see poverty as a threat to the common good, because it robs our nation of the creative energies and talents of millions of people.

7. Remembering our Christian past—Scripture, history, traditions—as a resource to seek justice for the poor. Familiarity with the alarming realities of poverty can push a person toward despair and a sense of hopelessness and helplessness. At such times we need to return to our fundamental principles and face the realties of poverty. At the same time we need to affirm our belief in the goodness of our world, and in the power and potential of human efforts to change and even transform the world. Most important, we need to confirm our belief in the empowering presence of God who mentors us in the ways of peace and justice. Then, as the seventh principle indicates, we need to draw from Christian Scripture, history, and traditions as we reflect theologically on the meanings of justice and poverty and how God is enabling and inviting us to respond to the poor as a matter of justice.

Justice in many biblical texts is defined in terms of right relationships and loving kindness between persons and with God. In Psalm 112 we read that the just person is "gracious and merciful and just"; one who "gives lavishly to the poor." God is presented in the Bible as a defender of the poor and a champion of those who are powerless because of economic and social deprivation, especially orphans, widows, and aliens. God expects God's people as a matter of justice to do the same, to reach out to and care for the poor. Moreover, Jesus embodied how God acts in the world with compassion and mercy. Jesus' relationship with God inspired him to welcome those in need of healing, forgiveness, and inclusion. Jesus taught that love of God and love of neighbor are the commandments by which we are to live. His followers continued to care for the poor. They often proposed the total sharing of material resources for the benefit of those in need. In the first Christian communities church leaders encouraged believers to respond willingly and generously to the poor. Generally, within the early church and then continuing to the present day, Christians have seen loving service to the poor as a way of nurturing a vital connection with God.

During the Middle Ages a number of factors, such as rivalry and the quest for power and wealth, considerably diminished Christian concern for the poor. Yet, over the centuries there have always been Christians who dedicated their lives and fortunes to caring for the poor. Throughout the history of Christianity there are countless stories of believers engaging in works of charity to assuage the suffering of orphans, widows, those who were sick or destitute, the powerless.

By the nineteenth century social, economic, and political changes led to the development of severe social problems, such as an increasing number of the destitute and the working poor and their families. Marxism, liberalism, and other social theories were developed to explore the immediate effects of poverty on the systems or structures that caused poverty or contributed to it. Against this background, Catholic social teaching emerged. The encyclicals of Pope Leo XIII (*Rerum Novarum*, 1891) and Pope Pius XI (*Quadragesimo Anno*, 1931) proposed two essential principles: social charity, which may be defined as direct service to the poor out of a sense of loving kindness, and social justice, which can be conceptualized in terms of the rights of all people to participate fully in society and to share in the benefits of society. Throughout the twentieth century and into the twenty-first century the popes as well as bishops through national conferences showed great sensitivity to those excluded and oppressed by economic, political, and social systems. Church leaders were critical of systems that favored the wealthy and powerful at the expense of those who suffered destitution and servitude. They consistently reminded the world of the inherent dignity of each person and of the rights of all people to the goods of the earth and of society.

The Second Vatican Council (1962–1965) called for a commitment to social justice and a concern for the poor as it scrutinized "the signs of the times," interpreting these in "the light of the gospel" (*Gaudium et Spes*, 1965, #4). In 1971, the Synod of Bishops summarized more than a half century of Catholic social teaching about justice with the statement, "Action on behalf of justice and participation in the transformation of the world fully appear to us as a constitutive dimension of the preaching of the Gospel" (*Justice in the World*, #6). The U.S. Catholic bishops further elaborated their concern for justice in a pastoral letter on the economy, *Economic Justice for All*, 1986 (#13–18). The letter presented basic moral principles:

1. Every economic decision and institution must be judged in light of whether it protects or undermines the dignity of the human person.

2. Human dignity can be realized and protected only in community.

3. All people have a right to participate in the economic life of society.

4. All members of a society have a special obligation to the poor and vulnerable.

5. Human rights are the minimum conditions for life in community.

6. Society as a whole, acting through public and private institutions, has the moral responsibility to enhance human dignity and protect human rights.

The bishops identified poverty as a condition deeper than lacking "financial resources." The deprivation resulting from poverty is "a denial of full participation in the economic, social, and political life of society and an inability to influence decisions that affect one's life." Poverty is "being powerless" and is in effect an assault on "one's fundamental human dignity" (#188).

Throughout the twentieth century, Catholic social teaching addressed justice for the poor by affirming the preferential option for the poor. The Latin American bishops' conferences at Medellín (1968) and at Puebla (1979) addressed the intense suffering of their people that resulted from poverty. In recognizing that the poor challenged the church to conversion, service, and solidarity, the bishops also stated unequivocally that the option for the poor requires changes in unjust political, economic, and social structures (Puebla Document, 1979, #1147, 1155). In *Sollicitudo Rei Socialis* (1987), Pope John Paul II explained the preference for the poor as "an option, or a special form of primacy in the exercise of Christian charity" that applied to each person's life, but "equally to our social responsibilities and hence to our manner of living, and to the logical decisions to be made concerning the ownership and use of goods" (#42). In 1986 the U.S. Catholic bishops stated emphatically that "the poor have the single most urgent economic claim on the conscience of the nation." They went on to say that Americans have an "obligation to evaluate social and economic activity from the viewpoint of the poor and powerless" (*Economic Justice for All*, #86–87).

This seventh principle of educating for justice challenges educators to draw deeply from the riches of the Scriptures, history, and faith traditions, especially Catholic social teaching. Educators must present these riches through methods appropriate to the age, background, and social location of those to whom they minister. Stated differently, one of the tasks of religious educators is to remember our Christian past and to help others effectively remember it as a resource that can inspire and sustain their efforts to seek justice for the poor.

Staying current about justice issues is vitally important. Educating for justice for the poor depends upon studying issues of justice and injustice in the world and then viewing these issues in the light of Christian Scripture, history, and traditions. While no one person can follow all issues, there are resources that analyze contemporary social issues in the light of the accumulated wisdom of Christian faith traditions and that offer balanced information to assist people of good will. There are many Web sites with information on justice and poverty. These include but are not limited to: the United States Conference of Catholic Bishops; Catholic Campaign for Human Development: Poverty USA; Catholic Charities USA; Catholic Relief Services; Center of Concern: Education for Justice; Network, A Catholic Social Justice Lobby; Call to Renewal; Pax Christi USA; and Sojourners.[4]

When we turn to Christian theology, special mention must be made of liberation theologies. Liberation theologies are major contributors to discussions of justice for the poor. Poverty is a primary concern and starting point for liberation theology as it developed in Latin America, and no other contemporary theology has done as much as the liberation theologies as a collective whole to heighten our awareness of impoverishment and marginalization as theological issues. Moreover, when we review the history of liberation theology, the example set by the Christian base communities (*comunidades eclesiales de base*), which contributed to the development of Latin American liberation theologies, is particularly inspiring. Christian base communities were the means through which individuals and families met and formed community; they read the Bible, reflected on biblical stories, and applied these to their own lives. The lessons of social science as well as theology were used to address the effects of poverty and to change oppressive structures. Additionally, as liberation theologies have become more sensitive to factors of gender, race, and culture, they have enabled many marginalized and oppressed people to have a voice and to seek liberation from social sin and injustice in the midst of personal and communal suffering. The all-encompassing understanding of liberation theologies was expressed well by Gustavo Gutiérrez when he stated, "Salvation...embraces all human reality, transforms it, and leads it to its fullness in Christ."[5]

Liberation theologies offer hope for the future. They enable us to imagine God's reign of justice and peace as a future event that informs the present and inspires us to work in the here and now to effect the reign of God. Liberation theologies stress freedom: from oppression for those who are subjugated and considered by some to be non-persons; from attachment to riches, power, and spiritual blindness for those whose hearts and minds have turned from God. Liberation theologies affirm community, a way to be together as the people of God sharing the journey of faith. Liberation theologies offer a Bible-based spirituality: a method of prayer, study, and reflection that breaks open the word of God and relates to the concerns of people.

In summary, liberation theologies provide an inclusive vision of humanity—women and men, children and adults, rich and poor, the learned and those open to learning, all nationalities and races—as the loam into which God can breathe new life to re-create humans grounded in love for God, their neighbor, and the earth. While liberation theologies recognize that social problems continue to persist despite the best efforts of many people of good will, they offer a hope-filled vision of God and God's people working together to realize the reign of God in small ways every day, praying that God's desire for peace and justice will be realized over time in spite of hardened hearts and seemingly infertile soil.

SPECIFIC APPROACHES FOR EDUCATING FOR JUSTICE

Letty M. Russell. Educators concerned about educating for justice can find guidance in the writings of prominent religious educators, especially Letty Russell, Thomas Groome, and Gabriel Moran. As pastor and Christian educator, Letty M. Russell incarnated God's quest for justice. She encouraged Christians to join in God's mission of fostering justice in the world, inviting them to work as partners with God and with one another to bring liberation and justice to all, and to welcome all, especially those on the margins of society, so that women, men, and children who are oppressed, deprived, or excluded may come to know the welcoming presence of a loving God in community. Russell often wrote that the faith community needed to be actively engaged in service. She pointed out that education takes place within the community, that "liturgy, action, and nurture" can be educational and aid believers or participants to grow in partnership,[6] and that the leaders of Christian communities can provide ideas, inspiration, and support for those they serve.[7]

Russell has identified Paulo Freire (1921–1997), a Brazilian social change theorist and activist, as the most important twentieth-century educator. His concept of *conscientization* names a process with the potential to change consciousness.[8] In a spirit of interdependence, Russell suggested, partners on the journey to freedom would begin where people are on their journey, and then they would seek a common agenda. Exposure to new information and different experiences would enable people to participate in a variety of social experiences and provide opportunities to assume different roles and encounter other perspectives, all of which could lead to cognitive conflict with the potential for growth.[9]

Education that nurtures a sense of Christian mission in the world and that encourages growth in partnership, in Russell's view, should include a focus on the Bible. Russell has been deeply committed to the Bible for its critical or liberating tradition embodied in its "'prophetic-messianic'" message. She noted that in her seventeen years of ministry in "a poor, racially mixed community of struggle and witness in the East Harlem Protestant Parish in New York City…the Bible continued to speak to us in worship and house Bible study groups, in ministries of education and action."[10] She also observed that the Bible "came alive" among people who knew poverty, injustice, and racism; its stories infused "hope in the midst of oppression." Furthermore, with hope and the confidence that the God who suffered was with them, the people were energized to look for answers to confront and change adverse social, political, and economic aspects of their lives.

Russell claimed that educating for justice also requires the practice of hospitality, which is essential if all persons are to be welcomed at the table of worship and of life and thereby to be members of the community of faith. In relating the mission of the church to hospitality, she observed that "hospitality creates a safe and welcoming space for persons to find their own sense of humanity and worth." Russell suggested that as a community welcomes people of other races and cultures, it encourages interaction among all the members, and that "unity without uniformity...makes hospitality and diversity possible."[11] In her view, the church needs to move from the center outward to the margins to share in the concerns and struggles of those who have been marginalized so that they truly feel welcome and can overcome any sense that they may have of being outside, looking in on the community. Welcoming the stranger, Russell noted, can open the community to a larger world and broader concerns; the resulting diversity has the potential to enrich the community, provided it is receptive to the giftedness of other people.

Thomas H. Groome. In exploring justice as a mandate of Christian faith, Thomas H. Groome proposed that "every teacher and every system of education are responsible to educate for justice in society."[12] He summarized concern for justice in a variety of areas: an anthropology based on valuing people and treating them with dignity and respect; a sacramentality that allows people to "'see' and respond to the poor and oppressed of society and to imagine how to change unjust social structures and oppressive cultural mores"; teaching civic responsibility based on "right relationship" and the common good; justice presented as part of the tradition with models and "ways to live justly"; using reason to encourage ethical thought based on wisdom that flows from truth and goodness; spirituality as a "call to 'right relationship'"; and caring for all humanity and respecting diversity.[13]

Groome maintained that those who educate for justice need a "personal passion for justice" that "requires a deep empathy for those who suffer injustice." To help educators sustain a passion for justice, he suggested a variety of spiritual resources: asking for God's help by bringing "the struggle for justice to prayer"; redefining "success" to include simple efforts based on the conviction that some day these simple efforts, such as teaching children how to care for our environment, may bear great fruit; remembering personal experiences of suffering and oppression; doing direct work with the poor and oppressed; listening with a compassionate heart to stories of oppression so that our conscious awareness of injustice is raised; assisting those who suffer the ill effects of poverty, injustice, or oppression; avoiding guilt by centering our efforts to work for justice in the realization that "faith that does justice is a lifetime conversion for everyone"; and realizing that personal or social guilt is healthy, since it leads to repentance and transformation.[14]

Groome has always seen justice education as prophetic, that is, education with a strong awareness of oppression and injustice and a dedication to creating both structural and cultural conditions with the express purpose of promoting right relationships. He envisioned justice education in terms of a dedication to "educating *for life for all.*" Of special value, Groome suggested, is direct service whereby children and adults have "direct experiences of real service with real people." Equally important, he added, is building in "the opportunity to reflect on it and to share their reflections."[15] For Groome, direct service with the poor combined with the opportunity for reflection and sharing one's thoughts and feelings is essential for learning to live justly.

Gabriel Moran. Gabriel Moran's approach to educating for justice invites us to become contemplatives who are engaged in action/practices for justice. A contemplative is a person with a receptive attitude, whose life is centered in peace even as he or she works to undo injustice. In Moran's words, "The greater the injustice, the greater is the need for prayerful quiet in the midst of passionate activity." Another quality that he identifies as essential for working for justice is a sense of humor. In the midst of terrible injustices, there is a need to sustain people who suffer greatly. The irony, and therefore the humor, "arises from combining a vision of the universe's immensities with our passionate but small efforts in the middle of it all."[16]

Moran acknowledges the paradox of attempting to educate about justice religiously: Religion leads us to God and in a sense, beyond the ordinary cares of this world, while education leads us to dialogue with others as we seek our place in this world. Nonetheless, he presents a four-step plan for educating religiously about justice: Educators need to begin with a sense of gratitude for the gifts of this earth, realize that life is finite, move beyond the ordinary to a vision of a world greater than any brokenness, and break out of illusion through language, imagery, and practices that allow us to "affirm a life together in justice and peace."[17]

Moran applies these four principles to the areas of work, family, food, and ecology. For instance, in addressing the issue of work he maintains that religious education encounters a tension between "our ordinary job and our calling to accomplish God's work in this world." Moran distinguishes between the drudgery of labor and the life-giving qualities of meaningful work. Both labor and work are necessary components of life, but there is a need to develop a greater appreciation of all human endeavors. To label activities as the exclusive "domain of women" is often a way of devaluing what is necessary for daily living. Tasks such as preparing food and caring for children and the infirm are essential for people's survival, but are often undervalued. When labor is examined, one notes how tasks involving hard labor are the responsibility of certain classes or groups of people, such as migrants. Moran comments, "God did not ordain one sex, one race, one class, or one nation to do 'servile work.'"[18] The role of education is to show how the creativity of human work can transcend the limits of physical work.

In our efforts to achieve community, we need to reduce suffering and servility. Compassion is an essential quality if we are to value necessary labor and share the burdens of daily life. Children need to learn from their earliest years how to develop their motor skills. As they mature and are able to do manual work, they will more readily value the efforts of those who work to beautify our gardens, provide our food, build highways and bridges, service our cars, transport our garbage. In short, those who make our daily lives more livable are often taken for granted.

METHODS FOR TRANSFORMING AN UNJUST SOCIETY INTO A REIGN OF JUSTICE

As I draw from the ideas of Russell, Groome, and Moran, I would like to offer five specific methods for transforming an unjust society through education for justice.

1. Promoting inclusive education for justice. Justice issues need to reach those who are active members of churches as well as the educational community. Every week the community gathers together to worship and pray at the Eucharist. At the Eucharist we are welcomed by a loving God and are united by the desire to reach out to others. At the liturgy we welcome families, single parents, visitors, and individuals— children, young adults, and older adults—to pray together around the table of the Lord. We offer the substance of our lives as we share the word of God, which can comfort, challenge, and instruct us. A homilist has a unique opportunity to use God's word to let justice shine forth as a lived reality and as a call to conversion. The many scriptural references in the liturgy to how God acts justly can be woven into homilies to inspire all participants to live a life of justice and foster social justice. Ministers of music could also use music based on Scripture with the aim of reinforcing justice themes. Beautiful music enhances the spoken word and encourages the community to reflect on the words that are sung. Musical settings enhance Scripture, provide time and motivation for meditation, and challenge listeners to act like God—with compassion and a sense of justice.

Millions of students are required by law to attend school and study many subject areas over many years. Teachers can intentionally relate their subject matter to issues of justice. This is a matter of assessing the curriculum for their subject area and then presenting stories, historical events, issues, as well as music and the arts from alternative viewpoints. In multicultural settings it would be natural to include events and celebrations that relate to the life experience of the students and to ethnic groups who are part of the fabric of American life. When historical events are studied, role-playing could be used to explore how various groups acted and to learn how they were affected positively and negatively by events and their outcomes. Insightful questions are a powerful way to raise awareness. An example of questions that move beyond dry facts is: Who benefits from this action? Who is hurt by this action or event? Who has the power? Who has little or no power? What could make this better for more people? Since news coverage has become homogenized, is constantly interrupted by commercial advertising, and may well be controlled by large conglomerates, students should be directed to more balanced sources of information to explore issues so they could report and analyze issues in-depth. Now that technology is readily available, an exploration of how best to use Internet resources in a critical, caring, informed manner would be essential to learning about current as well as past events and integrating the concept of social justice.

Service opportunities for student volunteers at a community site—feeding the hungry, tutoring children, building or repairing houses, visiting residents of a nursing home—followed by reflection on their experiences allows them to learn firsthand about issues of hunger, illiteracy, homelessness, and the concerns of senior citizens. Personal contact with people who face problems is invaluable for opening minds and hearts. Travel abroad or to poor areas in the United States allows the students to see how people can live contented lives without all the creature comforts that many Americans take for granted. For example, consider the students who volunteered generously to help people repair their homes after Hurricane Katrina. As they worked side by side to reconstruct homes, the volunteers experienced community and had the satisfaction of assisting people who could not afford or were unable to do the repairs. Thanks to the students' efforts, these people, often elderly and poor, could live again in their refurbished homes. In turn, many students found that some of their basic assumptions about what they thought they wanted and needed were challenged, and their outlook on life was transformed.

2. Exploring justice issues. Catholics, and indeed all Christians, should be more fully informed about how and when church leadership responds to issues such as welfare, health care, Social Security, proposed federal, state, and city budgets, immigration, hunger, and housing. Diocesan newspapers can be used to present Catholic social teaching in a readable format along with stories of social ministries in our faith communities. Church bulletins can include information about groups sponsoring actions for justice and provide inserts with quotations from Catholic social teaching. Meetings at the parish or diocesan level could include statements about how their deliberations will affect the poor. Parish adult education could focus on models of social justice and the modern saints who have spent and are currently spending their lives defending the rights of others, caring for those in need, and seeking ways to improve social, religious, political, and economic conditions for a more balanced and productive life. Web sites that provide access to church documents and actions for justice are an essential component for learning about social justice and having user-friendly ways of sharing this knowledge. Generally, to be inspired to work for greater justice in the world, Christians need to know what justice work is already being done and be invited to participate in or sponsor these activities.

Injustice affects all people. While those in positions of leadership may have greater access to information about current issues, the fact is that every person encounters issues of justice in the family, at work, and in society. It is vital for people to learn the principles of social justice so they have a basis for working to overcome injustices. They also need to examine what is wrong—unjust—and seek ways to address the issue. Questions need to be asked: Who is suffering? Who is left out? Who is benefiting? Is there a way that this issue could be addressed that would benefit more or all people?

Advocacy is a way of working to eradicate injustices. When persons of good will bring their intelligence and dedication to address an issue, they will be motivated to work individually and as a group. Technology makes involvement easier, but there is always a need for people to realize that they have a right to express their opinions and that they have the means to raise consciousness. When one good person is genuinely concerned about an injustice, he or she has the ability to generate concern among friends, neighbors, and in society at large. Speaking with those affected; attending community board meetings; taking part in community actions, such as demonstrations or marches; contacting elected officials by mail, e-mail, or directly when they are in their home district; writing letters to the editor; registering and voting in primaries and general elections—all of these are activities that are necessary to maintain our democratic society and to address issues of justice.

3. Educating for involvement. As we learn about poverty and the real life conditions of those living in poverty, as well as the principles of Catholic social teaching, another method of educating about justice emerges: educating for involvement. This begins with people coming to a realization of their giftedness. God shares with all people the gifts of life and love. Every person has unique qualities and abilities. Accepting one's talents and strengths can lead to a sense of wonder. Why has so much been freely bestowed? How can these gifts be shared with others? How can working with others enhance life? Will caring for those in need make this world a better place? Does charity renew our hearts and open our minds to other people and their concerns? As we know from Scripture, Jesus' story of the Last Judgment (Mt 25:31–46) reminds us that our final judgment by God is based on recognizing Jesus in the person of those in need, and once having seen the suffering of our neighbors, responding lovingly to their needs. The problems of the poor are to be shared by us as we work with God, with the community, and with the persons who are suffering.

4. Viewing social justice as a continuum. Encouraging involvement in addressing social justice concerns raises many complex issues. Parents and educators know how different people are in terms of their personalities and preferences, their learning styles, their motivation, and their talents and assets. If we picture social justice as a continuum, each person is at a distinct place along that spectrum—from those who are disinterested and uninformed, to someone who knows somewhat but is unwilling or unable to get involved, to another with limited knowledge but open to doing whatever is needed, to some who are very knowledgeable and totally committed. Just as Jesus looked on the rich young man with love (Mk 10:21), so too we need to look on each person in the same way. God can move hearts, so we need to place our trust in God; justice is God's work, and we are privileged to be invited to join in this venture. We are called to be creative in becoming personally involved through direct action or service as well as speaking words of comfort and encouragement, challenging unjust situations by working to realize social justice, celebrating small victories publicly, encouraging people to be involved and to make connections, and sharing a vision of God's reign of justice and peace.

Achieving the reign of God may at times seem to be a distant goal, so difficult to achieve that it exceeds our abilities and resources. How can we share a vision of the Promised Land with those who feel they are still wandering in the desert? When persons become involved in working for justice, we need to express appreciation for what each is willing and able to do. The ecology of poverty makes us realize that there are many problems crying for attention. Rather than losing heart, we need to view these as possibilities, even opportunities. The goal is to tap into the talents and assets of the willing so that a concerned community uses its very real social, political, and economic assets to heal the effects of poverty, and, more important, to eliminate its causes. Serious problems require deep thought, careful planning, and personal and corporate action by capable, dedicated people. Throughout this process, we need to remember especially the children who suffer the effects of poverty; we need to strive to reach them before their eagerness to learn and their openness to life are adversely affected by the harsh realities of impoverishment. It is for those who are poor that we dream, plan, and work indefatigably. Struggling for liberation is a lifelong personal, social, and spiritual endeavor that will lead in God's time to transformation and salvation.

As Americans, we need to involve ourselves in the political process. This means knowing our local situation and participating by making an effort to learn about issues through reading, speaking with neighbors, listening to radio and television interviews, visiting informative Web sites, and attending meetings (school board, community board, church groups). To prepare for elections, we need to know the issues and learn the candidates' positions. With all the emphasis on candidates' personalities and how much money they have raised, Christians need to make

decisions based on principles such as those presented in the pastoral letter of the American bishops, *Forming Consciences for Faithful Citizenship:
A Call to Political Responsibility* (2007). We need to be involved directly in
the electoral process: voting in primaries, and later in local and national
elections. After officials are elected, we need to hold them accountable by
learning their positions on issues and contacting them by mail, e-mail, or
in person. Another way to communicate our pro-justice views is to write
letters to the editor of local or national papers and connect with persons
with similar concerns through church groups, the Internet, and panels
that are sponsored by colleges and universities. Being involved politically
is an ongoing process. Elected officials rely on constituents not only for
their vote, but also for sharing their concerns and, in many cases, helping
to educate them. Issues may be viewed from many vantage points and
each person has a particular and unique point of view to share.

5. Fostering justice as a habit of heart and mind. Before justice can become a habit, a person first needs to see justice in action.
Justice is modeled early in life by parents and caregivers such as teachers,
coaches, and church leaders. One essential element is empathy. Humans
are wired to respond to others in pain or distress. Babies will cry when
they see another baby cry. Obviously empathy needs to be encouraged
and taught by word and example, a lifelong process. It is common to
hear children say "It's not fair" when they do not get what they want, but
their reactions may be based on truth because the world is not always a
place where justice and kindness prevail, virtues that need to be planted,
nurtured, and encouraged over a lifetime. When people hurt or see loved
ones suffer, they are apt to react with anger and want revenge. Only love
can overcome the injuries that are part of life with and among others.
Developing a sense of justice is a matter of prayer, growth, and willingness to connect with a loving God and a caring community.

When we witness a person who acts justly, his or her words and actions provide a pattern that shows us that justice is possible. This can
help us to notice people we might not ordinarily see, those normally
outside our circle of care. When someone is generous and kind to another, seeking justice in some form, it can benefit not just the person

being helped but also those observing it. Moreover, when someone acts justly, it is not only the action that speaks to us; it is the person's attitude and generosity that touch us deeply, helping us to realize that this is something we could also do. Additionally, when we sometimes feel that we have exhausted our energy and cannot go another mile, at such times someone else's example may unleash the wellsprings of our personal reserves so we can continue or, in some cases, begin to act justly.

Developing the virtue of justice requires motivation, concentration, and opportunity. We need to be inspired to respond to requests for our time, energy, and assets. By repeated actions for good, justice can become as natural as breathing. As mentioned before, our involvement in justice varies over time, but the important thing is to begin to be involved and to follow through with meaningful actions. One such action is to welcome others. Welcoming the poor into our minds so that we notice and show respect for them as persons can lead to welcoming them into the church or civic community. As a result of sharing food, stories, and laughter, guests relax and feel welcome, and then they enter into the inner circles of our lives. Such inclusion in a welcoming setting encourages us to welcome all people to the table of decision making where people's giftedness will enlarge conversations and make us mindful of the concerns of all people, not only our family and friends.

Justice calls us to conversion so that our hearts will become attuned to God's ways. Being open to other people and their needs opens our minds and hearts to God and God's supreme love for all people. Their concerns may well outweigh ours and move us to enlarge our agenda. When we defend and work with those who appear helpless or who are truly oppressed and exploited, then with God's help we can move toward advocating for change. Only when we are concerned about the legitimate needs of others can we discover that the rewards of solidarity far outweigh the burdens of rugged individualism.

Those working for justice must also take time to care for oneself as they reach out to build a community based on justice. In the journey toward justice, it is important to celebrate the small triumphs in life, which helps the community move forward. Working for justice is a lifetime endeavor that requires dedication, discipline, and enormous energy. There will be moments of exhilaration, but often people encounter and have to work around roadblocks. The constant struggle can leave dedicated people in a state of exhaustion. Learning when and how to replenish our spirit is an art. Renewing our spirit includes taking time for self and making time to be with others—sitting quietly, resting in the realization that God is with us, reading Scripture and other inspirational works, appreciating the ever-changing beauty of nature, going on retreat, pursuing a hobby, listening to or creating music, reading poetry and literature, attending plays, viewing films, visiting a museum, traveling, exercising or being part of a team sport, entertaining or being entertained, laughing and talking with friends, and sharing a meal with comrades, family, and friends. The art of replenishing one's spirit involves decisions that flow from one's interests, personality, preferences, energy, time, and resources. Experience teaches us that the quest for wholeness is also the path to holiness. Each person needs to find what forms of self-renewal are appropriate. When we are whole, we are able to see a broader picture where the negative aspects of life are acknowledged but not given power to control or disrupt our lives. Then we are open to all of life and ready to see and appreciate that all of creation is good.

A PLACE AT THE TABLE

Sharing the table with others may appear idealistic and unreal in an age when people are out to earn the most money, have the best life, and are so wrapped up in their individual endeavors that they forget about others, especially those who are poor. Examples of people helping people, of people welcoming the poor, and of the poor recognizing their power and claiming the right to come to the table will illustrate that the concept of inclusion is thriving among many groups. First, we will learn how Keith Wasserman helps the homeless through Good Works, Inc. Then, we will review a case study on Camden, New Jersey, from the Catholic Campaign for Human Development.

Keith Wasserman: Good Works, Inc. Keith Wasserman admits that he lived a self-centered life as a teenager, especially when he experimented with drugs and sold them. By junior year in high school, however, he converted to Christianity when he sensed that his efforts to enjoy life had led him down many self-destructive paths. As a result of his friend's insistence, Keith prayed and eventually turned his life over to Jesus. This conversion led to new life as he devoted his energies to service with and for others. In 1976 he entered Ohio University in Athens, Ohio. Keith proposed an unusual project for his senior year project: housing the homeless in the basement of his family home. Ohio University accepted and then supervised the project. In fact, this project developed into a lifelong endeavor to help the homeless of Appalachia when Keith Wasserman founded Good Works, Inc., a Christian non-profit ministry to the homeless. Timothy House (1985) and Hannah House (1994) were opened to provide transitional housing for homeless single women and men with the goal of moving them to independent living. As Keith had learned from direct experience when he went to live on the streets, homeless people are victims of fear. All too often the homeless saw other people with weapons who threatened them and stole their few possessions. Because they have too much time to think and little to show for their efforts, homeless people often have little hope. As they struggle to get a meal or find a safe place to rest, they can even lose their identity as persons. The staff of Good Works relates to and works with residents to overcome the problems they have internalized. It strives to build community among the homeless by developing their sense of trust, responsibility, and faith in themselves and God.

Friday Night Community Suppers. Each year Good Works provides a safe home for over two hundred people as well as some 16,000 meals for the poor and homeless. In 1992 they initiated the Friday Night Community Supper for the poor and homeless and those who have donated money and clothing to help them. These Friday Night Suppers are a way for the disenfranchised to connect with well-to-do community members. Local churches sponsor these suppers by purchasing and preparing the food. Volunteers, including many of the poor, help with cooking, setting up, serving, and cleaning up after the meal. In effect, these suppers are a community event. At the Friday Night Community

Supper there are tables for eight people, enabling the small group to sit and enjoy good food and relaxed conversation. Unlike soup kitchens where the guests line up for food, food is served family-style. Some 130 people attend these meals each week and over time relationships develop.[19] This allows the poor and the better-off to tell stories, ask questions, and share information that is vital to the life and concerns of those trying to live and work in society. It also opens hearts and minds so people can relate with those they do not normally meet. In this way they experience the humanity and giftedness of each other. The Good Works Friday Night Community Supper is an example of people being welcomed to and sharing the table of life.

The Catholic Campaign for Human Development. The Catholic Campaign for Human Development (CCHD) founded in 1969 by the then National (now United States) Conference of Catholic Bishops has two purposes: to raise funds to support the groups of those who are poor so they can claim their economic and political power, and to educate them about problems that people face in today's society. Their goal is to promote a sense of solidarity. Since its founding, CCHD has provided over 7800 grants to self-help projects at the grassroots level. These projects have had a great impact on the lives of many as they worked to empower the poor, develop economic projects, and provide educational programs, all with the aim of breaking the cycle of poverty. Each year Catholic parishes throughout the United States are asked to support the efforts of the Catholic Campaign for Human Development. This special collection is the mainstay of efforts to empower the poor and educate people about the reality of poverty.[20]

Camden, New Jersey. In John P. Hogan's case studies of some of the projects funded by CCHD, he gives an in-depth study of the city of Camden, New Jersey, and the Camden Churches Organized for People (CCOP). Camden is one of the poorest cities in the United States. Yet it is located in one of the richest states. A person driving to Philadelphia on Route 676 will encounter streets riddled with potholes, the odor of raw sewage, abandoned homes too numerous to count, and drugs being sold openly on the streets. As these sights assail one's senses, it is important to note that children under the age of eighteen make up more than 38 percent of the population of Camden; these children have inadequate health care, an educational system that graduates only 51 percent of students enrolled in high school, and are exposed to violence on a daily basis. In terms of housing, Camden has the unenviable honor of having the most abandoned or vacant houses in New Jersey.

Camden Churches Organized for People. CCOP was founded in 1985, in the midst of urban decay, to train congregations of all faiths to organize and empower low-income families. Leaders from each church would meet to establish a network to address common problems. Since its founding, CCOP has represented thirty faith-based communities and over 10,000 people. It soon became a beacon of hope as it encouraged people to stand up to those who were destroying their neighborhoods. An example of one such effort was CCOP's efforts to take back an abandoned building where drugs were routinely sold, rapes and assaults committed, and young boys trained to use guns. Monsignor Robert McDermott, the pastor of St. Joseph's Parish, led a procession that blessed the infamous corner and asked for God's forgiveness as well as the action of God's Spirit. Defying the drug lords took enormous courage, but this action energized the people and allowed them to see that God would prevail. This public Way of the Cross overcame the fear that had paralyzed good people. As a result they were able to organize, confront the drug dealers, and get the cooperation of the police so they would be actively involved. CCOP drew upon the expertise of St. Joseph's Carpenter Society, a non-profit housing agency located in the parish, to purchase and then rehabilitate the abandoned property. What was once a danger to young and old alike was transformed into a home where a hardworking, values-oriented family now lives. It was a community action that showed how life could overcome death.

In the city's urban blight, homeowners faced higher taxes than other New Jersey cities and towns, even though they had limited access to services that other municipalities took for granted.

Local officials had a bad reputation in Camden, being unresponsive to the needs of the people or known to take bribes. When local, county, and state agencies ignored the community's problems for many years, churches and faith-based organizations responded to the needs of the community and assumed leadership roles. The issue that first united the people was the county's decision to locate a regional sewage treatment plant in the most densely populated area in Camden. The stench was yet one more glaring and physically offensive example of the government's disregard for the people of Camden. A three-year struggle ensued during which people learned about the issue and then organized to show the impact of the sewage treatment plant on their community. The result was that Camden is paid $3.2 million dollars annually to compensate for the people of the city having to endure foul odors and the overall negative impact of the sewage treatment plant. At least the city had some much needed revenue to counter the effects of a plant it had not chosen.

By the mid-1990s abandoned houses became a huge problem. Camden had high property taxes; as a result, it was easier for owners who could not afford to pay the taxes to walk away and leave their homes. Abandoned houses attracted rats, were vandalized, or became outposts for drugs dealers and hookers. Eventually arsonists wreaked havoc by setting fire to abandoned houses, an action that endangered nearby homes and destroyed neighborhoods. The situation was so dire that even city officials had no idea how many abandoned houses there were. CCOP was able to organize over 1000 volunteers who worked with Rutgers University's Center for Social and Community Development and the Camden police and fire departments to create an accurate count and determine the location of abandoned homes. When the survey was complete, they presented the information at a city meeting. The number of abandoned homes shocked elected officials, but it was factual and allowed them to move forward on a problem that had largely been ignored. The ensuing publicity moved officials to take action. As a result, over 2000 buildings were boarded up and another 500 housing units were demolished. Active participation by many people resulted in action for the common good; they experienced solidarity as they worked together to address a problem that had threatened their safety.

By early 2000 the people of Camden were working through CCOP, the churches, and non-profit organizations, which meant in effect, that these groups were acting as a substitute government. By the time state officials acknowledged the corruption and ineptitude of local officials, the government of New Jersey was covering 70 percent of the city's budget, most of which went to pay police and firefighters.

At this time a larger problem began to reach a point of crisis. For more than twenty years the city had not invested in infrastructure, and as a result the city was in danger of collapse. The blight in Camden was also spreading to surrounding areas. Consequently the state was discussing how to address these problems. One possible solution was a state take-over of the city.

A Vision for Camden's Recovery. CCOP worked in partnership with Concerned Black Clergy (CBC) to explore alternatives to a state takeover. Despite the dishonesty and ineptitude of local officials, the churches had confidence that a better solution could be found. They explored the deep-seated causes of the poverty that was endemic in Camden. They also searched for a positive approach based on their faith and the principles of Catholic social teaching: participation, solidarity, and subsidarity. What emerged from the people's deep involvement was "A Vision for the Recovery of Camden," which was presented to state and local officials in the presence of over 1200 people on June 13, 2000, at St. Joseph's Pro-Cathedral. Their plan was based on a vision of justice in which people would be respected and families, especially children, could lead normal lives.

The vision emphasized two areas: the need for competent leaders to deliver needed services to the people, and an infusion of funds to make development by public and private investors a reality. The church groups had begun by analyzing the problems they had experienced firsthand and then moved to address these problems at the structural and institutional level. They were also flexible because they knew that as impressive as their vision was, they had to deal with the bureaucracy of politicians and government officials. While the state had already assumed the supervision of Camden's finances in May 2000, CCOP still advocated for participation by the city's residents. Yet, CCOP faced an uphill struggle. One obstacle occurred at the end of 2001 when a rescue plan based on the "Vision for Recovery" was introduced into the state senate, but was shelved for lack of funds. On March 7, 2002, Governor McGreevy met with 1500 people in the Antioch Baptist Church in Camden's poorest neighborhood and stated that New Jersey was facing a huge budget deficit. One by one individuals rose to address the governor and to testify to the reality of poverty for them and their children, such as the danger their children faced in going to and coming from school. They read a message from Camden's Catholic Bishop, Nicholas DeMarzio, in which he stated that their children lacked "adequate education, health care, nutrition, safety—and hope." The crisis demanded immediate attention, and the longer the problems went unaddressed the more it would cost. Despite the fact that officials had disappointed the people of Camden over and over again, they were still hoping that he, the governor, would act to help them. Governor McGreevy was very impressed by all that he heard. It was evident that the members of CCOP were witnessing to their faith, had done a thorough analysis of the issues, and that their leaders ably presented their religious, political, and economic concerns. Near the end of the meeting children carried in a dummy on life support which they placed in the sanctuary of the church. This dramatic action showed how life support was at best an emergency measure; what was essential was that there be a long-range plan for the city so it could move toward recovery with the hope of becoming self-sufficient.

The Camden Recovery Bill. On June 13, 2002, two years after CCOP had shared its vision, the governor returned to Antioch Baptist Church to present his plan for the recovery of the city. The aim was to restore Camden's neighborhoods and to revitalize its economy. With the governor's support, Senator Bryant introduced a bill that was then passed by the legislature and signed into law on July 22, 2002. The Camden Recovery Bill called for $175 million dollars to be used for the renewal of Camden. These funds were to be dedicated to demolish more than 1000 abandoned buildings, renovate hundreds of residential units, repair water and sewer systems, revitalize business and downtown development, collaborate with the state police to improve public safety and anti-drug efforts, develop work force training programs for Camden residents, increase funding for higher education institutions and hospitals, construct five new schools, repave city streets, and offer tax incentives to businesses to relocate in the city. A chief operating officer was to be appointed to coordinate the efforts of city agencies. The state was to have greater control over the school board and public school operations. There would be two oversight boards that would include people from the community.[21]

The Voice of the People. The influx of funds attracted investors interested in establishing and expanding businesses. As they competed to receive funds, projects that would improve the lives of residents were forgotten or ignored. A survey of residents three years into the plan revealed people's dissatisfaction because funds were directed to the downtown business sector at the expense of residents. Colleges, hospitals, and the city's waterfront had benefited, but ordinary people felt left out. Neighborhoods were suffering: housing was deteriorating, services had not improved, schools were still marginal, and law enforcement efforts were below par.[22] By September 2006, however, CCOP had secured $7.5 million in state aid to upgrade 300 city homes. The Camden Home Improvement Program would provide grants for neighborhood restoration. As people improved their homes, state and local officials also needed to commit funds for neighborhoods to remove abandoned cars, clean up vacant lots, and bulldoze vacant houses that posed a threat to the area.[23]

The ongoing struggle to reinvigorate Camden, New Jersey, is a testament to the faith of its citizens. With the able leadership of local churches and CCOP, the people prayed together as they searched for ways to emerge victorious from the suffering imposed on them. Prayer was the first step in a process that led them to explore the causes of their problems. The people of Camden are racially, ethnically, and religiously diverse. As they faced a common problem—the erosion of their community—they learned to work together for the common good. Learning about the root causes of poverty introduced them to structural causes: the political, economic, and social realities behind the problems they faced. Leaders emerged when the people were inspired to speak first among themselves and later at large meetings. Women and men who had suffered silently were able to share their lived experience and offer a vision of how life could be. As they offered their reflections that flowed from prayer and in-depth analysis, their powerful, credible witness moved public officials. The people of Camden are a remarkable example of those who come to the table and realize their power in speaking of their lived reality.

What is evident from this case study is that the struggle for wholeness is a long process and involves the efforts of leaders, ordinary people with great potential, and those in authority who have power to recognize the needs of the people and to work with them to address issues of concern. For many years people living in the inner city have borne the burdens of pollution from abandoned factories and failed businesses, suffered be-cause leaders betrayed their trust and misused public funds, struggled to gain access to a good education, health care, and safe living conditions, experienced the blight of abandoned houses and the violence of gangs and drug dealers. Now that people have learned to fight back, those who live in more affluent areas have an obligation to learn about the real is-sues and support efforts for reform. All people wish to come to the table of life. Only when people of all races, nationalities, and religions are welcome and seek the common good can justice for all become a reality and not remain a distant dream.

CONCLUSION

In summary, organized religions are inspired to respond to people in need. Christians have a history of caring for the poor, and throughout the years have reached out to those in need around the world. Justice in our time includes the duty to educate believers to recognize that the call to seek justice is a constitutive dimension of Christian faith. Since justice and injustice affect people—their relationships and their responsibili-ties—educating for justice will happen between and among individu-als: in the family, in a religious congregation, in the church community, in the places where society's myriad groups meet, that is, in schools, churches, neighborhoods, in towns and cities, around the country, and throughout the world. Justice education is for people; it happens between people, between people and God, and among the members of organizations who form the very fabric of life in the personal, civic, and religious realms. Social justice, then, will enable us in the United States to work together to limit poverty by bringing all people to the table of fellowship where we are equal before God. Those who were voiceless or invisible will share their stories so we can all learn from their life experiences as well as from our own. United by a common purpose, we will unite in service and solidarity with our neighbors to effect the reign of God on earth.

QUESTIONS FOR REFLECTION AND DISCUSSION

1. When did you first become aware of the goodness of creation? How does this relate to speaking of the dignity of each person?

2. Describe moments when you have had a sense of the sacred. What would you like to discuss with Henri Nouwen regarding the Trinity and contemplation?

3. Explain what is meant by personal sin and social sin. How does this relate to poverty in the United States?

4. Discuss how you exercise your rights as a citizen and as a member of a faith community.

5. Explain why poverty is a threat to the common good.

6. How does the memory of our Christian past serve as a resource for seeking justice for the poor?

7. Develop your own approaches and methods for educating for justice. Include references to the educators mentioned in this chapter.

8. Explain the meaning of "social justice as a continuum." Where are you on this continuum?

9. How does each of the case studies illustrate the concept of "a place at the table"?

SUGGESTED READINGS

Allen, JoBeth, ed. *Class Actions: Teaching for Social Justice in Elementary and Middle School.* New York: Teachers College Press, 1999.

Benson, Peter L. *All Kids Are Our Kids: What Communities Must Do to Raise Caring and Responsible Children and Adolescents.* San Francisco: Jossey-Bass, 1997.

Goodman, Diane J. *Promoting Diversity and Social Justice: Educating People from Privileged Groups.* Thousand Oaks, CA: Sage Publications, 2001.

Groome, Thomas H. *Christian Religious Education: Sharing Our Story and Vision.* San Francisco: Jossey-Bass, 1980.

_____. *Sharing Faith: A Comprehensive Approach to Religious Education and Pastoral Ministry.* San Francisco: Harper & Row, 1991.

_____. *Educating for Life: A Spiritual Vision for Every Teacher and Parent.* Allen, TX: Thomas More, 1998.

Hogan, John P. *Credible Signs of Christ Alive: Case Studies from the Catholic Campaign for Human Development.* New York: Rowman & Littlefield, 2003.

Moran, Gabriel. *Interplay: A Theory of Religion and Education.* Winona, MN: Saint Mary's Press, 1981.

_____. "Of a Kind and to a Degree," in Marlene Mayr, ed., *Does the Church Really Want Religious Education? An Ecumenical Inquiry* (Birmingham, AL: Religious Education Press, 1988.

Myers, Bryant L. *Walking with the Poor: Principles and Practices of Transformational Development.* Maryknoll, NY: Orbis Books, 1999.

Nouwen, Henri J. M. *Behold the Beauty of the Lord: Praying with Icons.* Notre Dame, IN: Ave Maria Press, 1987.

_____. *Creative Ministry.* New York: Doubleday, 1971.

Ruether, Rosemary Radford. *Liberation Theology: Human Hope Confronts Christian History and American Power.* New York: Paulist Press, 1972.

_____. *Integrating Ecofeminism, Globalization, and World Religions*. Atlanta: Scholars Press, 1995.

Russell, Letty M. *Christian Education in Mission*. Philadelphia: Westminster Press, 1967.

_____. *The Future of Partnership*. Philadelphia: Westminster Press, 1979.

_____. *Growth in Partnership*. Philadelphia: Westminster Press, 1981.

_____, ed. *Changing Contexts of Our Faith*. Philadelphia: Fortress Press, 1985.

_____, ed. *Feminist Interpretation of the Bible*. Philadelphia: Westminster Press, 1985.

_____. *Household of Freedom: Authority in Feminist Theology*. Philadelphia: Westminster Press, 1987.

_____, ed. *Inheriting Our Mothers' Gardens*. Louisville: Westminster Press, 1988.

_____. *Church in the Round: Feminist Interpretation of the Church*. Louisville: Westminster/John Knox Press, 1993.

_____, coedited with Mary John Mananzan, Mercy Oduyoye, Elsa Tamez, J. Shannon Clarkson, and Mary Grey. *Women Resisting Violence: Spirituality for Life*. Maryknoll, NY: Orbis Books, 1996.

Sider, Ronald J. *Just Generosity: A New Vision for Overcoming Poverty in America*. Grand Rapids, MI: Baker Books, 1999.

_____. *Rich Christians in an Age of Hunger: a Biblical Study*. Downers Grove, IL: Inter-Varsity Press, 1977.

NOTES

[1] Henri J. M. Nouwen, *Behold the Beauty of the Lord: Praying with Icons* (Notre Dame, IN: Ave Maria Press, 1987), 21.

[2] *Cathechism of the Catholic Church* (Washington, DC: United States Catholic Conference, 1997), #1868.

[3] Letty M. Russell in discussion with the author, February 3, 2005, Yale Divinity School, New Haven, CT.

[4] Web sites for issues related to justice and poverty: United States Conference of Catholic Bishops: www.usccb.org; Catholic Campaign for Human Development: Poverty USA: www.usccb.org/cchd; Catholic Charities USA: catholiccharitiesusa.org; Catholic Relief Services: crs.org; Center of Concern: Education for Justice: www.educationforjustice.org and www.coc.org; Network: www.networklobby.org; Call to Renewal: www.calltorenewal.com; Pax Christi USA: www.paxchristiusa.org; Sojourners: www.sojo.net

[5] Gustavo Gutiérrez, *A Theology of Liberation* (Maryknoll, NY: Orbis Books, 1973), 151.

[6] Letty M. Russell, *Growth in Partnership* (Philadelphia: Westminster Press, 1981), 59.

[7] Ibid., 126-27.

[8] Ibid., 75, 78.

[9] Ibid., 79, 54.

[10] Ibid., 95-96.

[11] Letty M. Russell, *Church in the Round: Feminist Interpretation of the Church* (Louisville: Westminster/John Knox Press, 1993), 173-74.

[12] Thomas H. Groome, *Educating for Life: A Spiritual Vision for Every Teacher and Parent* (Allen, TX: Thomas More, 1998), 379.

[13] Ibid., 380.

[14] Ibid., 381-84.

[15] Ibid., 390-91.

[16] Gabriel Moran, *Interplay: A Theory of Religion and Education* (Winona, MN: Saint Mary's Press, 1981), 144.

[17] Ibid., 145-47.

[18] Ibid., 147-48.

[19] Michael J. Papa, Arvind Singhal, and Wendy H. Papa, *Organizing for Social Change: A Dialectic Journey of Theory and Praxis* (Thousand Oaks, CA: Sage Publications), 2006, 207-12. "Homeless by Choice: It's Not Semi-

nary, But You Can Learn a Lot," 1-4. http://www.afajournal.org/2005/march/3.05wasserman.asp

[20] Catholic Campaign for Human Development: http://www.usccb.org/cchd/inbrief.shtml

[21] John P. Hogan, "Taking a City off the Cross: Camden Churches Organized for People," 45-63. *Credible Signs of Christ Alive: Case Studies from the Catholic Campaign for Human Development* (New York: Rowman & Littlefield, 2003).

[22] Dwight Ott, "Revitalization Effort Gets Failing Grade, Survey Says," *Philadelphia Inquirer*, July 19, 2005.

[23] Editorial, *Courier-Post*, September 8, 2006.

Index